The Future of Children
PRINCETON-BROOKINGS

VOLUME 20 NUMBER 2 FALL 2010

Fragile Families

www.futureofchildren.org

Introducing the Issue

Sara McLanahan, Irwin Garfinkel, Ronald B. Mincy, and Elisabeth Donahue

Nonmarital childbearing increased dramatically in the United States during the latter half of the twentieth century, changing the context in which American children are raised. The proportion of all children born to unmarried parents grew tenfold over a seventy-year period—from about 4 percent in 1940 to nearly 40 percent in 2007. The overall impact of these changes has been greatest for African Americans and Hispanics, with seven out of ten black babies and half of Hispanic babies now being born to unmarried parents.[1]

In the 1990s, the term "fragile families" was coined to describe the reality of these new family arrangements.[2] The word "family" signals that these partnerships are not simply casual encounters. As described below, most unmarried parents are in a romantic relationship at the time their child is born, with approximately 51 percent cohabiting and another 31 percent romantically involved but living apart. The word "fragile" signals that these partnerships face greater risks than more traditional families do in terms of their economic security and relationship stability.[3] To understand fully the complexity of fragile families, however, it is important first to understand the decades-long debate over this issue.

The Debate

Researchers have long disagreed about whether the increase in nonmarital childbearing in the United States should be a cause for concern. At one extreme, analysts argue that nonmarital births are a sign of progress, reflecting an expansion of individual freedom and the growing economic independence of women. For these analysts, unmarried parents are much like married parents, lacking only "the piece of paper." To support their claim, they point to similar childbirth trends throughout Western industrialized countries, particularly Scandinavia, where nonmarital childbearing is more common than it is in the United States and where most unmarried parents are in relatively stable unions. At the other end of the spectrum are scholars who argue that nonmarital births are the product of casual relationships with minimal commitment on the part of fathers who either will not or cannot support their children financially and emotionally. Occupying the middle ground are those who argue that although

Sara McLanahan is editor-in-chief of *The Future of Children*, as well as director of the Center for Research on Child Wellbeing and the William S. Tod Professor of Sociology and Public Affairs at Princeton University. Irwin Garfinkel is the Mitchell I. Ginsberg Professor of Contemporary Urban Problems at Columbia University and co-director of the Columbia Population Research Center. Ronald B. Mincy is the Maurice V. Russell Professor of Social Policy and Social Work Practice and director of the Center for Fathers, Children, and Family Well-being at Columbia University. Elisabeth Donahue is the executive director of *The Future of Children* and the assistant dean for public and external affairs at the Woodrow Wilson School of Public and International Affairs, Princeton University.

unmarried parents may be committed to each other and to their children, American fragile families, lacking the generous government support provided by other Westernized countries, experience high poverty rates and severe instability. This last perspective suggests that the increase in nonmarital childbearing in the United States may be contributing to the persistence of racial and class disparities in future generations.

Whatever their place on the spectrum, most analysts agree that for a sizable share of the U.S. population, the conventional sequence of events in the transition to adulthood—school, employment, marriage, and finally parenthood—has been turned upside down. Today's young adults often become parents before they have finished their education, gotten a stable job, and married. As a result, many American children are born into families headed by young, unmarried, and underemployed parents who often go on to have children with other partners.

The nation's debate over the causes and consequences of nonmarital childbearing began almost half a century ago. In his now famous 1965 report, *The Negro Family,*[4] Daniel Patrick Moynihan (then assistant secretary of labor under President Lyndon Johnson) argued that a "tangle of pathology," consisting of nonmarital childbearing, high male unemployment, and welfare dependency, was making it more difficult for African Americans to take advantage of the new opportunities created by the civil rights movement. Initially praised by black leaders for focusing national attention on a serious problem, the report soon became the target of harsh and widespread criticism from liberals (and eventually black leaders themselves). In the aftermath of the debate, social scientists generally avoided discussing the negative aspects of nonmarital childbearing until the 1980s, when the eminent sociologist William Julius Wilson reopened the debate.[5] During that same decade, the behaviors first noted by Moynihan in black families were being widely adopted by whites and Hispanics, making nonmarital childbearing an issue for disadvantaged families of all races today.[6]

Despite the importance of the topic and the intensity of the debate, empirical evidence on unmarried parents (including fathers) and their children was limited until recently.

The Research

Despite the importance of the topic and the intensity of the debate, empirical evidence on unmarried parents (including fathers) and their children was limited—and the discussion necessarily remained somewhat theoretical—until recently. To build a body of research about the causes and consequences of nonmarital childbearing based on sound evidence, a team of researchers at Columbia and Princeton Universities, which included three editors of this volume, designed and implemented a large national survey, the Fragile Families and Child Wellbeing Study.[7] Between the spring of 1998 and fall of 2000, the team interviewed parents of approximately 5,000 newborns in hospitals in large cities, with an oversampling of unmarried parents.[8] They conducted follow-up interviews when the children were approximately one, three, and five years old. The study data, which are nationally representative of births in large U.S. cities, form the underpinnings of the findings presented in this volume.

Because not all of the research described in this volume is based on the Fragile Families Study and because other data sets may complicate efforts by analysts to identify fragile families, it is important to be clear about definitions. A fragile family is one in which the parents are unwed at the time of their child's birth. These parents may be cohabiting or living apart. Because relationships change over time, some parents in fragile families may have been married before having a nonmarital birth while others may marry (each other or new partners) afterwards. Thus being a parent in a fragile family is not the same as being a never-married parent. Nor is it the same as being a single parent, which typically means raising a child without a partner. Many mothers who have a child outside marriage are cohabiting or co-parenting with the biological father, and many single mothers were married at the time their child was born (and subsequently divorced). The authors in this volume have attempted to clarify the populations they are examining when using data that do not allow them to identify fragile families precisely.

Finally, although a primary motivation for conducting the Fragile Families Study was to enable researchers to learn more about the fathers in these families, especially those living apart from their children, and although the study has provided new insights about these men, many important research and policy questions related to fathers remain unanswered. For example, the article in this volume on higher education is based almost entirely on studies of mothers in higher education, because few data sources or studies of higher education collect or analyze data on the college enrollment or performance of men by their parental or residential status. Similarly, despite the thirty-odd-year history of responsible-fatherhood programs and the growing interest of policy makers in fatherhood programs in the past two decades, these programs have rarely been rigorously evaluated.[9] Rather, most responsible-fatherhood programs are the result of grassroots efforts to address father absence in low-income, minority communities with little involvement from the research community. Thus the paper in this volume that examines marriage and fatherhood programs cannot tell us very much about the community-based programs.

The Findings

To resolve the debate about the causes, consequences, and policy implications of nonmarital childbearing, it is important to lay out the basic questions that this volume addresses.

First, who are these families? What are their capabilities? What is the nature of parental relationships and how do they change over time? Are children born outside of marriage connected to both parents, and do they remain connected? In other words, are fragile families in the United States made up of stable cohabiters as is typical of unmarried parents in Scandinavian countries, or do they look different, and if so, how?

Second, how do children in these families fare? Do their births into nontraditional families have positive, negative, or neutral effects on their well-being? What are the mechanisms and pathways that are responsible for these effects?

Finally, with the trend toward forming fragile families showing no sign of slowing, should researchers and policy makers be concerned? Does the ongoing trend pose problems, and if so, what is the role of government policy in providing solutions? How should current policies aimed at reducing child poverty and improving child well-being be modified if fathers in fragile families are in fact more involved than conventional wisdom acknowledges? Perhaps more controversially, is there an appropriate role for government in preventing the formation of fragile families in the first place?

To answer these questions, we commissioned a group of experts to write nine articles. The first four articles examine fragile families from various vantage points of the family: the couple, the mother, the father, and the child. The fifth looks at particular issues of race and ethnicity. The last four delve into policy issues that have special pertinence for fragile families: pregnancy prevention, incarceration, postsecondary education, and marriage and fatherhood programs. Next, we briefly highlight some of the papers' key findings.

Fragile Family Couples

In the first article, "Parental Relationships in Fragile Families," Sara McLanahan and Audrey Beck, both of Princeton University, focus on four aspects of the parental relationship: the stability of the living arrangement, the quality of the relationship itself, the nonresident father's involvement with his child, and the quality of the co-parenting relationship. Their analysis dispels conventional wisdom that nonmarital births are a result of casual encounters. At the time of the birth, most parents are romantically involved and have high hopes that they will get married; most, however, are not able to establish stable unions or long-term co-parenting relationships. Five years after birth, a third of fathers have virtually disappeared from their children's lives. New partnerships bringing new children are common, leading to high levels of instability and complexity in these families.

To understand why relationships among unmarried parents are so unstable, the authors look at the key determinants of parental relationships. Among the predictors of instability are low economic resources, government policies that contain marriage penalties, cultural norms that support single motherhood; demographic factors, such as shortages of marriageable men; and psychological factors that make it difficult for parents to maintain healthy relationships. No single factor appears to be dominant.

The authors also explore strategies for improving parental relationships in fragile families. They point out that although economic resources are a consistent predictor of positive outcomes, researchers and policy makers lack solid information on whether increasing fathers' employment and earnings will increase relationship quality and union stability. They note that analysts need to know more about whether relationship quality in fragile families can be improved directly and whether doing so will increase union stability, father involvement, and co-parenting quality. Although a recent interim evaluation of the Building Strong Families Project found no effects overall of programs designed to increase marriage and improve relationship quality among unmarried parents,[10] it did show positive effects for African American couples (combined across all cities), and in Oklahoma City it showed a number of positive effects on several outcomes for all racial groups combined, though not for marriage. The authors conclude that ongoing experiments to test the effectiveness of relationship programs, originally designed for married couples but now used for unmarried parents, are important for shaping future interventions.

Fragile Family Mothers

The second article, "Mothers' Economic Conditions and Sources of Support in Fragile Families," by Ariel Kalil of the University of Chicago and Rebecca Ryan of Georgetown University, examines the public and private resources that mothers contribute in fragile families. Data based on the Fragile Families Study show that very few unmarried mothers earn enough to support themselves and their children at more than twice the federal poverty level. Nor are mothers able to accumulate assets to tide them through inevitable financial difficulties.

Mothers in fragile families make ends meet in many ways. Although the authors show that various public programs, particularly those that provide in-kind assistance, do successfully lessen economic hardship in fragile families, many of the most effective programs, such as the earned income tax credit, hinge on mothers' employment. And because the nation's recovery from the Great Recession, which began in December 2007, has been painfully slow, there is reason for concern about the stability of the public safety net for mothers with little education and those who face other barriers to employment.

Because of limited safety net resources, mothers in fragile families may turn more often to private sources of support—friends, family, boyfriends—for cash and in-kind assistance. But though these private safety nets are essential to many mothers' economic survival, they cannot promote long-term economic mobility. Given that the fragile family is likely an enduring fixture in this country, the authors argue that it is essential to strengthen policies that both support these families' economic self-sufficiency and alleviate their hardship during inevitable times of economic distress. They advocate strengthening the public safety net—especially such in-kind benefits as Supplemental Nutrition Assistance Program (SNAP) benefits (formerly food stamps), Medicaid, housing, and child care—and bolstering community-based programs that can provide private financial support, such as emergency cash assistance, child care, and food aid when mothers cannot receive it from their own private networks.

Fragile Family Fathers

Robert Lerman, of American University and the Urban Institute, devotes much of the third article, "Capabilities and Contributions of Unwed Fathers," to examining how the capabilities and contributions of unwed fathers fall short of those of married fathers, and how those capabilities and contributions differ by the kind of relationship the fathers have with their children's mothers, a relationship that changes as infants grow into toddlers and kindergartners. He describes the striking heterogeneity in the earnings of unwed fathers, with the bottom quarter earning less than $10,000 per year.

Although most unwed fathers spend considerable time with their children in the years soon after birth, over time their involvement erodes. Men who lose touch with their children are likely to see their earnings stagnate, tend to provide less financial support, and often find themselves with new obligations when they father children with another partner. By contrast, the unwed fathers who marry or cohabit with their child's mother earn considerably higher wages and work substantially more than those who do not marry or cohabit. Although Lerman describes evidence indicating that much of the gap in earnings between unwed fathers who marry and fathers who remain single is attributable to marriage itself, this finding is controversial.[11] As he points out, marriage alone does not explain the significant differences in earnings that are associated with the lower age, education, and work experience of unmarried fathers. Many scholars including the editors go further and believe the evidence indicates that marriage can account for only a very small proportion of the gap in earnings between men who have children within marriage and men who do not, given the large disparities in the human capital between these two groups of men.

Lerman points out that several factors influence the extent to which unwed fathers stay involved with their children. Better-educated fathers, those who most identify with the father's role, and those with good relationships with their children's mothers, are most likely to sustain a relationship with their children. Some studies even find that strong child support enforcement increases father involvement, though for many low-income fathers, child support obligations represent such a large share of their incomes that they are discouraged from entering the formal job market, particularly when those benefits go to the state for reimbursement of welfare outlays rather than to their children.

Until recently, policies dealing with noncustodial unwed fathers focused almost entirely on increasing child support collections. Recognizing the limits of that approach and the need to raise the earnings capacity of unwed fathers generally, policy makers have begun considering new steps. One initiative includes programs to improve the relationship and communication skills of unwed fathers and mothers. As noted, the jury is still out as to whether these efforts, which are still in their early stages, offer the promise of increasing marriages, improving marital stability, and enhancing couple relationships—and thus perhaps of increasing the earnings of fathers. Adding employment components would likely enhance these marriage education initiatives. Another promising strategy is to raise earnings through targeted training, such as apprenticeships that allow unwed fathers to earn a salary while they learn skills.

Fragile Family Children

The fourth paper, "Fragile Families and Child Wellbeing," concludes that children who grow up in single-mother and cohabiting families fare worse than children born into married-couple households. Jane Waldfogel and Jeanne Brooks-Gunn, both of Columbia University, and Terry-Ann Craigie, of Princeton University, note that analysts have investigated five key pathways that underlie the links between family structure and child well-being: parental resources, parental mental health, parental relationship quality, parenting quality, and father involvement. Researchers have also looked into the likely role of selection—the presence of different types of men and women in different family types—as well as the roles of family stability and instability. But they remain uncertain about which pathways explain children's outcomes.

In addition to providing an overview of findings from other studies using the Fragile Families Study, Waldfogel, Craigie, and Brooks-Gunn also report their own estimates of the effect of a consistently defined set of family structure and stability categories on a set of child outcomes at age five in the Fragile Families Study. They find that being raised in a fragile family does not have uniform effects on child outcomes. Family instability, for example, seems to matter more than family structure for cognitive and health outcomes, whereas growing up with a single mother (regardless of stability) is more

Until recently, policies dealing with noncustodial unwed fathers focused almost entirely on increasing child support collections. Recognizing the limits of that approach, policy makers have begun considering new steps.

important for behavior problems. Overall, their findings are consistent with other evidence that being raised by stable single or cohabiting parents seems to entail less risk than being raised by single or cohabiting parents when these family types are unstable.

The authors conclude by pointing to three types of policy reforms that could improve outcomes for children. The first reform is to lower the share of children growing up in fragile families by reducing the rate of unwed births or promoting family stability among unwed parents. The second is to address the pathways that place such children at risk—for example, through boosting resources in single-parent homes or fostering father involvement in fragile families. The third is to address directly the risks these children face—for example, through high-quality early childhood education and home-visiting programs.

Race and Ethnicity

Robert Hummer, of the Univerty of Texas–Austin, and Erin Hamilton, of the University of California–Davis, note that the prevalence of fragile families varies substantially by race and ethnicity. African Americans and Hispanics have the highest prevalence; Asians, the lowest; and whites fall somewhere in the middle. The share of unmarried births is lower among most foreign-born mothers than among their U.S.-born ethnic counterparts. Immigrant-native differences are particularly large for Asians, whites, and blacks.

The authors also find racial and ethnic differences in the composition and stability of fragile families over time. Although most parents of all racial and ethnic groups are romantically involved at the time of their child's birth, African American women are less likely to be in a cohabiting relationship than are white and Hispanic mothers. Over time, these racial and ethnic differences become more pronounced, with African American mothers having the lowest rates of marriage and cohabitation and the highest breakup rates, and Mexican immigrant mothers having the highest rates of marriage and cohabitation and the lowest breakup rates.

Fragile families have far fewer socioeconomic resources than married families, though resources vary within fragile families by race and ethnicity. White mothers, in general, have more socioeconomic resources than black, Mexican American, and Mexican immigrant mothers; they are more likely to have incomes above the poverty limit, more likely to own a car, less likely to have children from a prior relationship, and more likely to report living in a safe neighborhood. Access to health care and child care follows a similar pattern. The exception is education; black and white unmarried mothers are equally likely to have finished high school, and Mexican immigrant and Mexican American mothers are less likely to have done so.

The authors argue that socioeconomic differences are by far the biggest driver of racial and ethnic differences in marriage and family stability, and they support reforms to strengthen parents' economic security. They also discuss how sex ratios and culture affect family formation and stability. In particular, they note that despite severe poverty, Mexican immigrant families have high rates of marriage and cohabitation—an advantage that erodes by the second generation with assimilation. To address the paradox that marriage in these families declines as socioeconomic status improves, they support policies that reinforce rather than undermine the family ties of Mexican immigrants.

Pregnancy Prevention

Isabel Sawhill, Adam Thomas, and Emily Monea, all of the Brookings Institution, believe that in view of the well-documented costs of nonmarital births to both children and parents in fragile families, as well as to society as a whole, policy makers' primary goal should be to reduce births to unmarried parents, especially since so many unmarried parents have their first children when they are teenagers.

The authors observe that the swiftly rising nonmarital birth rate has many explanations —a cultural shift toward acceptance of unwed childbearing, a lack of alternatives to motherhood among the disadvantaged, a sense of fatalism or ambivalence about pregnancy, a lack of marriageable men, limited access to effective contraception, inadequate knowledge about contraception, and the difficulty of using contraception consistently and correctly.

Noting that these explanations fall generally into three categories—motivation, knowledge, and access—the authors discuss policies designed to motivate individuals to avoid unintended pregnancies, to improve their knowledge about contraception, and to remove barriers to contraceptive access. Some motivational programs, such as media campaigns, have been effective in changing behavior. Some, but not all, sex education programs designed to reduce teen pregnancy have also been effective at reducing sexual activity or increasing contraceptive use, or both. Programs providing access to subsidized contraception have also been effective and would be even more so if they could increase the use not just of contraceptives, but of long-acting, reversible contraceptive methods such as intrauterine devices (IUDs) and injections.

Finally, the authors present simulations of the costs and effects of three policy initiatives—a mass media campaign that encourages men to use condoms, a teen pregnancy prevention program that discourages sexual activity and educates teen participants about proper contraceptive use, and an expansion in access to Medicaid-subsidized contraception. All three have benefit-cost ratios that are comfortably greater than one and are sound investments worthy of consideration by policy makers. The Medicaid expansion has the largest benefit-cost ratio, followed by the condom use campaign and then by the teen pregnancy program.

Incarceration

Rapidly rising rates of incarceration in the United States since the mid-1970s have proved damaging to the nation's poor and minority communities. The effects of this prison boom have been concentrated among those already on the periphery of society: black and (to a lesser degree) white men with little schooling—the same segments of society in which fragile families are most likely to be formed. Christopher Wildeman, of Yale University, and Bruce Western, of Harvard University, explain that the drastic increases in the American incarceration rate were driven by urban manufacturing decline, a booming drug trade that fostered addiction and careers in crime, and a punitive turn in criminal justice policy.

Imprisonment diminishes the earnings of adult men, compromises their health, reduces familial resources, contributes to family breakup, and adds to the deficits of poor children—increasing the likelihood that the effects of imprisonment on inequality are transferred across generations. Perversely, incarceration has its most corrosive effects on families whose fathers were involved in neither domestic violence nor violent crime before being imprisoned. Because having a parent go to prison is now so common for poor, minority children and affects them so negatively, the authors argue that mass imprisonment may exacerbate future racial and class inequality—and may even lead to more crime in the long term, thereby undoing any crime-reducing benefits of the prison boom.

Wildeman and Western advocate several policy reforms. The first is to limit prison time for drug offenders and for parolees who violate the technical conditions of their parole (as opposed to committing new crimes), relying instead on inexpensive and effective alternatives such as intensive community supervision, drug treatment, and graduated sanctions that allow parole and probation officers to respond to violations without immediately resorting to prison sentences. A second reform is to support men and women returning home from prison, thus diminishing recidivism rates and improving employment among ex-prisoners.

But Wildeman and Western argue that criminal justice reform alone will not solve the problems of school failure, joblessness, untreated addiction, and mental illness that pave the way to prison. In fact, focusing solely on criminal justice reforms would repeat the mistakes of the prison boom, during which the nation tried to solve social problems with criminal justice policies. Addressing those problems, they say, will require a greater commitment to education, public health, and the employment opportunities of low-skilled men and women.

Education

Noting that access to higher education has expanded dramatically in the past several decades, Sara Goldrick-Rab and Kia Sorensen, both of the University of Wisconsin–Madison, focus on how postsecondary education affects the lives of unmarried mothers in fragile families. Contrary to the widespread expectation that access to college always promotes family stability and economic security, the authors argue that because current postsecondary educational policy and practice is insufficiently supportive, college attendance may, ironically, have substantial downsides for many families headed by unmarried parents.

Although rates of college attendance have increased substantially among unmarried parents, college completion rates are low. Many unmarried mothers struggle to complete degree or certificate programs because of inadequate academic preparation. And severe financial constraints can cause them to interrupt their studies or increase their work hours, thus decreasing their chance to finish their studies. Despite having made it to college, they are squeezed for time and money in ways that create significant stress and compromise both the quality of their educational experiences and the outcomes for their children.

The authors point out that many public programs, such as Pell Grants, federal subsidized loans, and welfare, offer support to unmarried mothers attending college. But the programs are neither well coordinated nor easily accessed. Over the past three decades, loans have increasingly replaced grants as the most common form of federal and state support for students seeking to finance college. Confusion about what is available leads many low-income students to the two most "straightforward" sources of income—loans and work, both of which involve significant costs and can work at cross-purposes with public forms of support. The Pell Grant penalizes students for attending college a few classes at a time and is not available to anyone with a drug conviction while in college.

Some evidence shows that providing social, financial, and academic supports to community college students can improve achievement and attainment for vulnerable students. For example, students who participate in contextualized learning programs—hands-on courses that tie the lessons to the lives and experiences of the students—are more likely than nonparticipants to move on from basic skills to credit-bearing coursework and successfully complete credits, earn certificates, and make gains on basic skills tests. Another successful initiative provides special counseling services to low-income students with a history of academic difficulties and gives them a small stipend of $150 per semester when they use those services. Several states are also conducting experimental performance-based financial aid programs at community colleges to test their effectiveness.

Marriage and Fatherhood Programs

To improve the quality and stability of couple and father-child relationships in fragile families, researchers are beginning to consider how to tailor existing couple-relationship programs (which generally target married or middle-income couples) and father-involvement interventions to the specific needs of unwed couples in fragile families. The goal, explain authors Philip Cowan and Carolyn Cowan, of the University of California-Berkeley, and Virginia Knox, of MDRC, is to provide a more supportive developmental context for mothers, fathers, and, especially, the children in fragile families.

The authors present a conceptual model to explain why couple-relationship and father-involvement interventions that were developed for middle- and low-income married couples might be expected to provide benefits for children of unmarried parents. They summarize the extensive research on existing couple-relationship and father-involvement interventions, noting that only a few of the programs for couples and a handful of fatherhood programs have been systematically evaluated. Of those that have been evaluated, few have included unmarried couples as participants and none has investigated whether interventions may have different effects when unmarried fathers live with or apart from the child. Furthermore, although programs for couples or fathers tout the potential benefits for children, they rarely assess child outcomes systematically.

The authors consider whether effective interventions designed for working- and middle-class fathers or couples might be helpful to fragile families. They offer the example of one project in which an intervention for low-income parents included random assignment to a couples group or a fathers-only group that focused on key facets of family life including parenting and couple-relationship quality. The intervention was equally effective for married and unmarried parents. Because the evidence suggests that couple-oriented programs also had a positive effect on father involvement and on lowering parenting stress, the authors recommend integrating couple and fatherhood interventions to increase their power to reduce the risks and enhance the protective factors for children's development and well-being. This conclusion, however, is tempered by the recent findings in the Building Strong Families evaluation that found, on average, no effects of relationship programs on a host of outcomes, including father involvement in most families in the study. The authors emphasize the need for more research on program development to understand the most effective ways to strengthen co-parenting by couples who are the biological parents of a child but who have relatively tenuous, or already dissolved, relationships with one another.

Policy Implications

Taken as a whole, this volume makes it clear that fragile families are both a consequence and a cause of economic inequality. Compared with married couples, couples who have children outside marriage are highly disadvantaged—younger, less healthy, much less educated—at the time of their child's birth. Moreover, although a majority of unmarried parents have "high hopes" for a future together, a nontrivial proportion of these young men and women express distrust of the opposite sex and believe that a single mother can raise a child as well as a married mother can. Together, these characteristics support the claim that nonmarital childbearing is a consequence of disadvantage. They also suggest that both economic and cultural factors have contributed to the rise in fragile families.

The volume also shows that nonmarital childbearing exacerbates pre-existing disadvantage by reducing opportunities for children as they grow up, primarily through family instability and complexity. Unmarried couples are much more likely than married couples to end their relationships, and the ongoing search for new partners leads to high levels of instability, periods of single motherhood, and declining father involvement in these families. Moreover, because most unmarried parents in fragile families are in their peak childbearing years, new partnerships frequently lead to new children, and ultimately to complex households in which mothers are forced to negotiate with several different fathers over visitation and over child support requirements, which many fathers have a hard time meeting because they have financial obligations to children in other households. Instability and complexity reduce parents' economic resources and increase mental health problems that, in turn, reduce the quantity and quality of the parenting that children receive. Ultimately, inadequate resources and poor parenting undermine children's opportunities, thus reproducing inequality in the next generation.

So what can and should be done? Is there a role for social policy? Some might argue that couples who form fragile families make many individual decisions that are private and outside the realm of the government. Among those decisions are whether to marry, whether to have children, whether to stay together; whether to visit, support, or abandon nonresident children; whether to facilitate or block nonresident father involvement. And yet the government is hardly neutral when it comes to forming policy that affects how families are formed, how their finances and access to children are treated, and how such matters as custody, child support, and property division are handled if families break up. Given the negative outcomes for fragile families that this volume documents, we believe the government should step in.

Government programs already play a large role in the lives of fragile families. Some of these programs succeed in reducing poverty and economic insecurity, though often at a personal cost to the families. Some, for example, compromise a couple's relationship—by discouraging marriage through income tests that keep parents from taking advantage of economies of scale or by increasing conflict between parents who live apart through sometimes unforgiving child support regulations. Other policies, such as using child support payments to reimburse government spending on children, create barriers to nonresident father involvement. Efforts to improve the lives of children in fragile families should focus on increasing resources and capacities *and* improving relationships among unmarried parents.

Drawing from the policies recommended throughout the volume and our own understanding of the issues, we believe that implementing the following four steps would strengthen fragile families. The first step would be to decrease the number of nonmarital births by "going to scale" with programs designed to encourage more responsible sexual behavior and by expanding access to effective contraception among individuals who might not otherwise be able to afford it. The second step would be to increase union stability and father involvement in fragile families by building on marriage-education programs aimed at improving relationship skills and community-based programs aimed at raising nonresident fathers' earnings, child support payments, and parental involvement. In the case of the marriage programs, this would mean expanding services to include employment and training and mental health components. In the case of the fatherhood programs, it would mean conducting rigorous evaluations to determine what works. The third step would be to redesign tax and transfer programs, especially in-kind programs, so that children have access to high-quality early education and high-quality health care, and so that these benefits are not cut or reduced if parents marry or live together. Finally, we are intrigued by the two articles in this volume that document the role of postsecondary education and penal policy in the lives of fragile families, and we urge researchers and policy makers to develop and rigorously evaluate new demonstrations in these two areas, especially policies that provide alternatives to incarceration.

Of all the findings from the Fragile Families Study that are highlighted in this volume, the one with by far the most critical policy implications is the high level of commitment among unmarried new parents. More than 80 percent of unmarried parents are in a romantic relationship at the time of their child's birth, and most of these parents have high hopes for a future together. Further, even after parents have ended their romantic relationships, about half of the fathers remain involved with their child on a regular basis, although this proportion declines as parents form new relationships and have children with new partners. Based on these findings, we believe that the birth of the child should be viewed as a "magic moment" when both fathers and mothers may be highly motivated to work together to improve their relationship and co-parenting skills and to deal with other problems that may limit their ability to support their children. For this reason, services to parents in fragile families should be immediate, intense, and focused on the couple in their role as cooperative parents. Fashioned as a bumper sticker, our recommendation would be "Support the three T's: Treat early, Treat often, and Treat together."

Conclusion

The dramatic increase in nonmarital births in the United States cannot be written off as a simple "lifestyle choice" that has no implications for child well-being. Nor is it simply a result of a rise in casual sexual encounters. The vast majority of children born outside of marriage are born to parents in committed yet fragile relationships. Our challenge in this volume is to explore the ramifications of this new reality and to fashion policy recommendations that reduce the number of fragile families in the first place, and that ensure that children born into fragile families receive the support they need to grow into healthy, productive adults.

Endnotes

1. *National Vital Statistics Report* 57, no. 7 (January 7, 2009), table 18.

2. Specifically, the term was developed by Ronald B. Mincy, one of the editors of this volume, as part of the Ford Foundation's Strengthening Fragile Families Initiative.

3. The Fragile Families and Child Wellbeing Study: National Report, Revised March 2003, page 3; found at www.fragilefamilies.princeton.edu/documents/nationalreport.pdf.

4. *The Negro Family: The Case for National Action* (Office of Policy Planning and Research, U.S. Department of Labor, March 1965).

5. William J. Wilson, *The Truly Disadvantaged* (Harvard University Press, 1988).

6. *National Vital Statistics Report* (see note 1).

7. For information about the Fragile Families and Child Wellbeing Study, go to www.fragilefamilies.princeton.edu/index.asp.

8. The final sample contained nearly 5,000 births, including approximately 3,600 births to unmarried parents and approximately 1,200 births to married parents. When weighted, the data are nationally representative of births in U.S. cities with populations of 200,000 or more.

9. See Earl Johnson, Ann Levine, and Fred Doolittle, *Fathers' Fair Share: Helping Poor Fathers Manage Child Support and Fatherhood* (Russell Sage Foundation, 1999).

10. Robert Wood and others, "The Building Strong Families Project: Strengthening Unmarried Parents' Relationships: The Early Impacts of Building Strong Families" (Mathematica Policy Research, May 2010). In eight sites across the country, 5,000 couples were randomly assigned to a Building Strong Families program or a control group after volunteering to participate. Data on whether the couples were more likely to stay together, get married, improve relationship quality, improve co-parenting, or increase father involvement were collected after fifteen months. When the results were averaged, no effects were found on these outcomes, with two exceptions. The Oklahoma City site had positive effects on a number of outcomes, though not marriage; the Baltimore site had negative effects, including an increase in domestic violence. The program also showed positive effects for relationship quality for couples in which both were African American.

11. Ronald Mincy, Jennifer Hill, and Marilyn Sinkewicz, "Marriage: Cause or Mere Indicator of Future Earnings Growth?" *Journal of Policy Analysis and Management* 28, no. 3 (2009): 417–39.

Parental Relationships in Fragile Families

Sara McLanahan and Audrey N. Beck

Summary

As nonmarital childbearing escalated in the United States over the past half century, fragile families—defined as unmarried couples with children—drew increased interest from researchers and policy makers. Sara McLanahan and Audrey Beck discuss four aspects of parental relationships in these families: the quality of parents' intimate relationship, the stability of that relationship, the quality of the co-parenting relationship among parents who live apart, and nonresident fathers' involvement with their child.

At the time of their child's birth, half of the parents in fragile families are living together and another third are living apart but romantically involved. Despite high hopes at birth, five years later only a third of parents are still together, and new partners and new children are common, leading to high levels of instability and complexity in these families.

Drawing on findings from the Fragile Families and Child Wellbeing Study, McLanahan and Beck highlight a number of predictors of low relationship quality and stability in these families, including low economic resources, government policies that discourage marriage, gender distrust and acceptance of single motherhood, sex ratios that favor men, children from previous unions, and psychological factors that make it difficult for parents to maintain healthy relationships. No single factor appears to have a dominant effect.

The authors next discuss two types of experiments that attempt to establish causal effects on parental relationships: those aimed at altering economic resources and those aimed at improving relationships.

What can be done to strengthen parental relationships in fragile families? The authors note that although economic resources are a consistent predictor of stable relationships, researchers and policy makers lack good causal information on whether increasing fathers' employment and earnings will increase relationship quality and union stability. They also note that analysts need to know more about whether relationship quality in fragile families can be improved directly and whether doing so will increase union stability, father involvement, and co-parenting quality.

www.futureofchildren.org

Sara McLanahan is editor-in-chief of *The Future of Children*, as well as director of the Center for Research on Child Wellbeing and the William S. Tod Professor of Sociology and Public Affairs at Princeton University. Audrey N. Beck is a postdoctoral research associate at the Center for Research on Child Wellbeing at Princeton University.

Nonmarital childbearing increased dramatically in the United States during the latter half of the twentieth century, changing the context in which American children are raised and giving rise to a new family form—fragile families, defined as unmarried couples with children. Some analysts see these changes as a positive sign of greater individual freedom and women's economic independence; others argue that they contribute to poverty and income inequality.[1] Given the importance of families to children's health and development, researchers and policy makers have become increasingly interested in the nature of parental relationships in fragile families and their implications for children's future life chances, especially children's access to resources and the stability and quality of these resources. Parents living in cooperative, stable unions tend to pool their incomes and work together to raise their child. By contrast, those living apart in noncooperative relationships can jeopardize their child's resources, both financial and social.[2]

In this article we review research findings about parental relationships in fragile families. We focus on four aspects of the parental relationship: the quality of intimate relationships, relationship stability, nonresident fathers' involvement with their child, and the quality of the co-parenting relationship between parents who live apart. Each of these indicators tells us something important about the parental relationship, and viewing them all together provides a more complete picture than looking at only one or two. In the first section of this article, we describe parental relationships at the birth of the child and examine how they evolve during the first five years after birth. In the second, we describe what is known (from nonexperimental research) about the determinants of good relationships. In the third, we discuss experiments that identify causal effects on parental relationships, as well as the implications of these findings for policy makers and practitioners. The first two sections are based primarily on analyses using the Fragile Families and Child Wellbeing Study because these data provide the most extensive (and recent) information on the population of interest—unmarried parents. Although a broader literature examines cohabiting unions and transitions into and out of cohabiting unions, it is based mostly on samples that combine childless adults with parents or divorced mothers with never-married mothers.[3] When such studies are included, we note it.

Parental Relationships in Fragile Families

In the following discussion we describe what we have learned about parental relationships in fragile families, starting with a description of the parental relationship at the time of the child's birth and continuing up to five years after the birth.

Relationships at Birth

According to data from the Fragile Families study, most unmarried parents are in a romantic relationship at the time their child is born. (See figure 1.) Approximately 50 percent are cohabiting, and another 30 percent are romantically involved but living apart (visiting). The proportion of romantically involved parents is similar for whites, blacks, and Hispanics, although blacks are less likely to be cohabiting than other groups.[4]

At the time of the birth, most parents are optimistic about their future together and report relatively high levels of relationship quality. As shown in table 1, more than 91

Figure 1. Parental Relationships at Birth

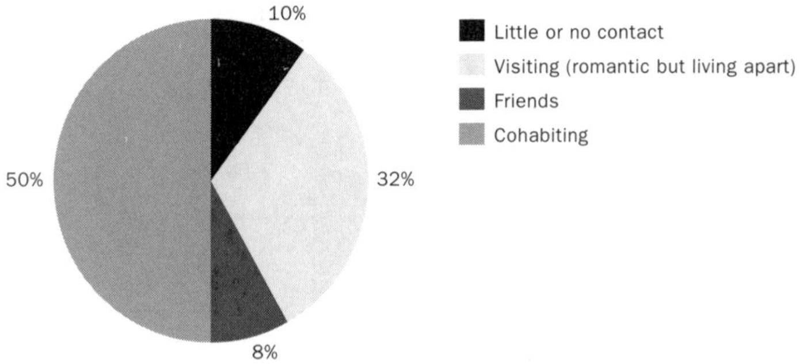

percent of cohabiting mothers and over half of single mothers say their chances of marrying the father are "fifty-fifty or better." Reports of relationship quality are measured on a supportiveness scale that notes how often the other parent is "fair and willing to compromise, loving and affectionate, critical or insulting, and encouraging." Such reports are quite positive among unmarried parents, with cohabiting parents reporting the same level of supportiveness as married parents. On a supportiveness scale from 1 (rarely) to 3 (very often), unmarried parents score 2.6 whereas married parents score 2.7. (These findings, it should be noted, are based on parents who are in a romantic relationship at birth and do not include parents who have ended the romantic relationship.) Unlike the largely positive reports of relationship quality, mothers' reports of domestic violence are nearly twice as high among unmarried mothers as among married mothers.[5]

Most unmarried parents also have very positive attitudes toward marriage. As shown in table 1, close to two-thirds of unmarried mothers and three-quarters of unmarried fathers agree with the statement that "it is better for children if their parents are married." At the same time, a high proportion of unmarried mothers—between 80 and 88 percent—also agree that "a mother living

Table 1. Marriage Attitudes and Relationship Quality at Time of Child's Birth

Percent unless otherwise specified	*Mothers*				*Fathers*			
	Married	**Cohabiting**	**Single**	**Total Unmarried**	**Married**	**Cohabiting**	**Single**	**Total Unmarried**
Chances of marriage are 50/50 or better	—	91.8	52.2	72.0	—	95.2	74.6	90.0
Marriage is better for kids*	83.4	68.1	61.2	64.6	90.5	78.8	77.4	78.3
Single mother can raise child alone*	59.5	80.4	88.2	84.3	33.8	48.8	56.7	51.9
Men/women cannot be trusted to be faithful*	10.4	18.1	33.1	25.7	4.5	12.7	20.6	15.8
Men/women are out to take advantage*	11.6	15.4	22.7	19.1	5.1	15.5	20.6	17.5
Supportiveness scale (1–3)	2.7	2.7	2.4	2.6	2.7	2.7	2.6	2.6
Any violence**	4.5	7.0	7.6	7.3	—	—	—	—

*Agree or agree strongly. **Uses questions from 1-year follow-up.

Table 2. Father's Involvement at Birth

Percent	Cohabiting	Visiting	Single
Gave money/bought things for child	96.5	84.0	27.9
Helped in another way	97.7	74.6	21.9
Visited baby's mother in hospital	96.5	71.4	29.2
Child will take father's surname	92.9	73.8	37.2
Father's name is on birth certificate	96.1	80.3	51.6
Mother says father wants to be involved	99.4	98.6	73.9
Mother wants father to be involved	99.3	98.5	70.7

alone can raise a child just as well as a married mother." These responses indicate that although most mothers believe that marriage is the ideal setting for raising children, they also think that a single mother can do the job alone. That mothers hold both beliefs at the same time is consistent with the view that marriage is an ideal but not a necessity. Andrew Cherlin, for example, argues that marriage has become a "capstone" rather than a normative life transition.[6] Similarly, Kathryn Edin and her colleagues argue that couples are reluctant to marry until they have reached an imaginary "marriage bar," which they associate with a middle-class lifestyle and view as essential for maintaining a stable marriage.[7]

Some researchers claim that gender distrust is an important obstacle to a successful marriage,[8] and indeed, these data indicate that a nontrivial share of unmarried mothers hold opinions of men that might discourage forming long-term stable unions. One-quarter of unmarried mothers believe that men cannot be trusted to be faithful, as compared with only 10 percent of married mothers. Unmarried mothers are also more likely to agree that "men are out to take advantage of women." Levels of gender distrust tend to be higher among unmarried couples than among married mothers, although cohabiting mothers are, on average, more trusting of men than mothers who are living alone.[9] These findings are supported by in-depth interviews with a subsample of mothers that indicate that most unmarried couples experience infidelity, most commonly by the father, and 73 percent report sexual jealousy.[10]

Unmarried fathers are highly involved with the mothers of their child during the pregnancy and around the time of the birth. As shown in table 2, virtually all cohabiting fathers provide financial support or other types of assistance during the pregnancy, come to the hospital to see the mother and baby, and say they want to help raise the child. Among nonresident fathers, fathers in visiting relationships with the mother are more likely to be involved than others, although involvement is high even among fathers who are not in a romantic relationship with the mother. Most important, perhaps, a high proportion of all unmarried fathers say that they want to be involved in raising their child, and the mothers say they want the father's involvement.

Racial and Ethnic Differences

As noted, white and Hispanic unmarried parents are more likely to be living together at the time of their child's birth than are black parents. There also are racial and ethnic differences in parents' expectations about marriage and views about marriage. In most instances, these differences are consistent with what one might expect. For example, minority parents are less likely than whites to say their chances of marriage are fifty-fifty or better and less likely to say that marriage is the best setting for raising children. Minority parents are also more likely than whites to say that a single mother can do as good a job of raising a child as a married mother. Finally, minority parents, especially Hispanic mothers, report more mistrust and more domestic violence than white parents. Whereas only 3 percent of white single mothers report that the father was violent in the past, the shares for black and Hispanic mothers are 8 and 12 percent, respectively. The gap among cohabiting mothers is even higher, with 32 percent of Hispanic mothers reporting violence as compared with 6 and 7 percent of white and African American mothers. One reason for the high rates of violence reported by Hispanic mothers in cohabiting unions is that such unions are more durable among Hispanics than among other groups, and thus mothers are at risk for violence longer.

Relationship Trajectories

Despite their high hopes, unmarried parents' bonds are fragile, with over 60 percent of nonmarital unions dissolving within five years of their child's birth. Couples that are cohabiting at birth are the most likely to remain in stable unions; 60 percent are still together in either a cohabiting or marital relationship five years after the birth. Couples that are visiting at birth are the most likely to dissolve their unions; only 20 percent are still together five years after the birth.[11]

Racial and ethnic differences in union dissolution are substantial. Black couples are more likely to end their relationships than white and Hispanic couples. Hispanic couples in cohabiting unions have a particularly low rate of dissolution, consistent with the view that cohabitation is a substitute for marriage in the Hispanic community. The gap in dissolution rates between married and cohabiting parents also differs by race and ethnicity, with whites having the greatest disparity and blacks having the least. Among blacks, the dissolution rates are 73 percent and 46 percent for cohabiting and married couples, respectively. Among whites, they are 65 percent and 17 percent.[12]

Growing Instability and Complexity

Not surprisingly, once the romantic relationship with the father ends, many unmarried mothers go on to form new partnerships.

As shown in table 3, 27 percent of mothers who were unmarried at birth either have had a new cohabiting or marital relationship or are currently living with a new partner (again, either a marital or nonmarital partner) five years after the birth. Not surprisingly, new partnerships are much more common among mothers who were not in a romantic relationship with their child's father at birth, because these mothers have had more time to search for a new partner. Interestingly, although black cohabiting mothers are more likely than whites to end their partnerships early, the prevalence of new cohabiting unions is similar for the two groups of mothers. This finding highlights the fact that cohabiting unions are much less common among black mothers than among whites. This difference, noted at birth, is repeated in the formation of new partnerships. Finally, many unmarried mothers have children with their new partners. According to table 3, a third of single mothers (20 percent of all unmarried mothers) have had a child by a new partner by year five.

Table 3. Unmarried-at-Birth Mothers' New Romantic Relationships and New Children by Year Five, by Race and Ethnicity and by Baseline Status

Percent	All	White	Black	Hispanic
New co-residential partners*				
All unmarried mothers	26.7	30.3	28.2	21.6
Cohabiting	19.7	25.1	21.6	14.7
Visiting	27.1	24.7	28.0	23.2
Single	45.0	51.7	43.8	43.7
Children with new partners				
All unmarried mothers	20.8	17.6	23.6	16.9
Cohabiting	14.9	15.8	17.6	11.3
Visiting	23.0	18.4	24.2	20.8
Single	32.6	22.8	35.4	32.1

*Includes cohabiting and marital relationships

The search for new partners results in high levels of instability for children, both in co-residential partnerships and in dating relationships, defined as relationships lasting at least two months. (Changes in mothers' dating relationships may affect children directly if the new partner is involved with the child, or they may operate indirectly by affecting the quantity and quality of mothers' parenting.) The average number of residential (cohabiting or married) partnership changes is three times higher among children of unmarried mothers than among children of married mothers, 1.09 compared with 0.32.[13] Even more striking, the average number of changes in dating relationships lasting two months or more is nearly four times as high for unmarried mothers as for married mothers, 1.46 compared with 0.35. The latter finding underscores the importance of taking dating relationships into account when describing children's exposure to family instability—a point that is especially important for children living with single mothers. Asking what share of unmarried mothers who were single at birth never cohabited with a man during the five-year period yields an answer of 30 percent. In contrast, asking what share of single mothers never changed partners during the five-year period, the answer is 3 percent. In short, stability is rare among single-mother families.

Father Involvement and Co-Parenting Relationships

Even after parental romantic relationships are over, a substantial majority of nonresident fathers continue to maintain a high level of contact with their child, although contact declines over time. One year after their child's birth, about 63 percent of nonresident fathers report seeing their child on a regular basis (at least once in the past month and twelve days on average). The share declines as the child gets older, to 55 percent at age three and to 51 percent at age five.[14] Nonresident fathers also continue to make financial contributions to their children, including both formal child support and informal support. Five years after the birth, 27 percent of fathers are providing formal support to their child, 33 percent are providing informal cash support, and 45 percent are providing in-kind contributions such as buying toys.[15] Father involvement continues to be high even among men with new partners and new children. For example, 71 percent of fathers without new partners or children report having contact with their child in the previous year as compared with 63 percent of fathers with new partners and children.[16]

Finally, many unmarried parents are able to maintain a positive co-parenting relationship even after their romantic relationship ends. Co-parenting quality is measured by questions that ask mothers whether the father: "acts like the father you want for your child, can be trusted to take good care of the child, respects your schedules and rules, supports you in the way you want to raise the child, talks with you about problems that come up with raising the child, and can be counted on to help when you need someone to look after the child for a few hours." On a scale from 1 (rarely true) to 3 (always true), mothers who are living apart from the father report a score of 2.12 as compared to 2.77 for mothers who are living with the father.[17] These scores, it should be noted, are based on the two-thirds of fathers who have some contact with their child. Hispanic mothers report somewhat higher levels of cooperation; otherwise, there are no racial differences.

Summary

In sum, at the time their child is born, unmarried parents have high hopes for a future together. About half of these parents are living together, and another 30 percent are romantically involved. Relationship quality and father involvement are high. Underlying this optimism, however, are signs of problems, including distrust of the opposite sex and a belief that a single mother can raise a child as well as a married mother. Five years later, the picture is more mixed. On the positive side, about a third of parents are living together, about half of noncohabiting fathers see their child on a regular basis, and co-parenting relationships are positive. On the negative side, a third of fathers have virtually disappeared from their children's lives, and new partnerships and new children are common, leading to high instability and growing complexity in these families.

Identifying Key Predictors of Parental Relationships

What explains the fragility of relationships among unmarried parents? We examine this question by looking at the key determinants of parental relationships, as reported by studies using data from the Fragile Families study. We focus on the same four aspects of parental relationships as in the previous section: co-residence and the stability of cohabiting unions, the quality of parents' intimate relationships, nonresident father involvement, and the quality of the co-parenting relationship among parents who live apart.

Figure 2 depicts how these four aspects of parental relationships are related to one another. As the diagram shows, the quality of the intimate relationship between parents predicts the stability of the union and also predicts nonresident father involvement and the quality of the nonresident co-parenting. Among these parents, cooperative co-parenting increases father involvement, and greater father involvement increases cooperative co-parenting, in part because mothers serve as gatekeepers to the child and discourage the involvement of fathers with whom they do not get along. The diagram assumes that most of the romantic relationships are limited to parents who live together. Although a substantial proportion of romantically involved parents are living apart at the time their child is born, these so called "visiting" relationships are very unstable, with most couples either moving in together or ending their relationship soon after the child's birth. The

Figure 2. Determinants of Parental Relationships

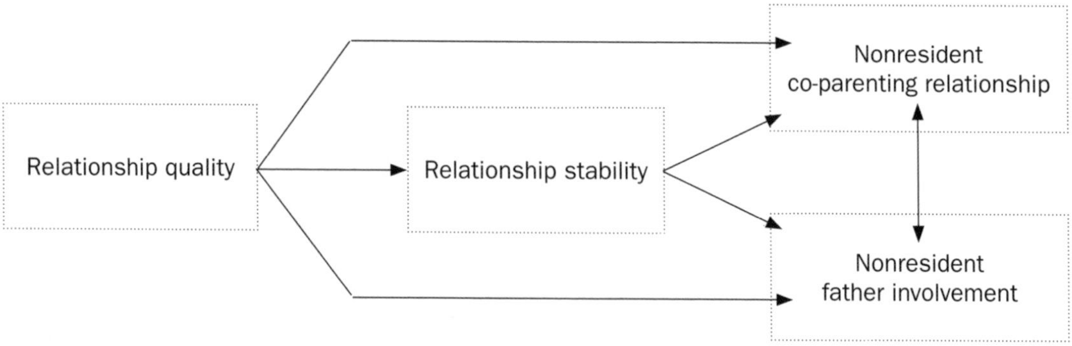

quantity of empirical evidence available for each of these four outcomes varies widely. Many studies examine union stability after a nonmarital birth, and a substantial number examine father involvement. Fewer look at relationship quality and co-parenting quality.

We focus on predictors in four categories—economic, cultural, demographic, and personal—that correspond roughly to different social science theories about the causes of family formation and parental relationships. According to economic theory, for example, couples with more economic resources will be more likely to form and maintain stable unions because they have more to share with one another than couples with fewer resources. Economic theory also predicts that couples will be responsive to economic incentives created by government policies such as Temporary Assistance to Needy Families (TANF) and child support. Sociological theory emphasizes the importance of social norms and values in shaping family behavior. The male breadwinner role, for example, has long been viewed as essential for sustaining a successful marriage. Couples with traditional views of marriage and gender roles will be more likely to form stable unions than couples with nontraditional views, and religious institutions are believed to reinforce such views. Demographers, by contrast, emphasize the importance of age, race and ethnicity, sex ratios, and prior family characteristics in shaping future relationships. And, finally, psychological theory sees relationship skills and the characteristics associated with such skills—for example, mental health and the ability to manage conflict—as important determinants of relationship quality and union stability.

Economic Resources

With respect to economic resources, some studies look at total family income; others, at a parent's individual earnings, employment, and educational attainment. A few studies attempt to measure parents' relative economic contributions, and at least one study examines the ratio of the father's to the mother's earnings. A diversity of economic predictors is found in studies of government policies, culture, demographic characteristics, and personal characteristics.

Comparing the findings of different studies can be difficult because studies often use different models. For example, in looking at the effects of economic resources on union stability, some researchers include measures of parental attitudes, such as whether or not they believe marriage is important, and relationship quality in their models, and others do not. If fathers' earnings have a causal effect on attitudes or relationship quality, including the latter two measures in the model will attenuate the benefits of fathers' earnings and may even make them insignificant. The same problem exists for studies that examine the effects of culture on parental relationships.

With that caveat in mind, we conclude that the empirical studies provide strong support for a link between parents' economic resources and relationship stability and quality. The strongest link is between fathers' economic resources and family behavior.[18] Paternal employment and earnings are positively associated with relationship quality and union stability. Among nonresident couples, employed fathers are more likely than unemployed fathers to have regular contact with their child and to be engaged with their child (for example, spend more days of the week engaged in shared activities).[19] The father's educational attainment is typically unrelated to relationship outcomes, presumably because earnings do a better job than education of capturing a father's economic resources.[20]

For mothers, the story is somewhat different. Education, rather than earnings and employment, is the strongest predictor of union stability, with more education being associated with more stability.[21] Although one study finds some evidence that mothers' earnings are associated with cohabitation, the link holds only for the contrast between mothers with low earnings (less than $10,000 a year) and mothers with no earning.[22] Earnings and employment are thought to be weaker measures of mothers' true economic resources because childbearing and rearing often result in spells of nonemployment or part-time employment for mothers. Many of the same difficulties in interpretation exist for research on broader samples of women. In some cases where maternal economic indicators appear unimportant, models either include many indicators of the same concept or include variables that mediate the impact on marriage.[23] Similar to the findings on unmarried parents, women's economic indicators tend to be inconsistent predictors of marriage among women more generally.[24]

The few studies that examine mothers' and fathers' relative economic contributions to family income find no evidence that mothers' relative employment or earnings reduce union stability or relationship quality, as suggested by some theories of marriage.[25] Indeed, there is some evidence that gender role specialization is associated with higher union dissolution among cohabiting couples.[26] Finally, two studies, using different samples and focusing on different stages of childhood, look at the link between family income and union stability and find mixed results.[27]

Government Policies

Many unmarried parents are eligible for government benefits such as TANF, food stamps, and public housing. These benefits, in turn, affect union formation behavior by creating incentives for couples to live apart in order to receive the benefit. To date, most research on the link between government programs and parental relationships in fragile families has focused exclusively on welfare generosity or other in-kind benefits such as housing subsidies. Studies using state-level measures of welfare generosity typically find a negative association between welfare and marriage, although one paper finds that higher welfare benefits deter the breakup of visiting unions.[28] Of particular interest, Jean Knab and her colleagues report estimates of "welfare effects" that are much larger than those reported by other studies, which typically include population groups, such as married mothers, that are much less likely to be affected by welfare. According to Knab's estimates, an 18 percent increase in generosity ($100) decreases marriage by 2 percent, while changing regimes from a permissive or moderately permissive environment to a strict one results in a 4 percent decrease. (The strictness of the welfare environment is measured by whether states enforce work requirements and time limits on recipients.) There is also evidence that the availability of housing subsidies acts as a disincentive to marriage and cohabitation.[29] Both public housing and section 8 housing are income-tested and may have other rules that favor single-mother families. Marah Curtis finds that an increase in section 8 housing significantly decreases the odds of marriage (relative to living alone).[30] In sum, the evidence indicates that income-tested cash and housing subsidies affect the family formation decisions of unmarried parents.

The empirical evidence shows a strong link between cultural factors and parental relationships.

Child support policies also affect incentives to marry or break up by altering the costs and benefits of cohabitation. For mothers, stronger child support enforcement reduces the costs of living apart from the father, whereas it increases the costs for fathers. Child support enforcement may also affect the co-parenting relationship between parents who live apart. The empirical evidence suggests that stronger enforcement lessens the chances that a couple will marry.[31] Nearly all of the effect of child support enforcement on marriage is concentrated among mothers whose partners have a child with a previous partner, suggesting that stronger enforcement deters marriage by reducing the income that fathers bring to the household.[32] The only study that has looked at the link between child support enforcement and domestic violence suggests that stronger enforcement reduces violence among cohabiting couples and increases violence among some groups of single mothers.[33]

Cultural Factors

As with economic resources, the empirical evidence shows a strong link between cultural factors and parental relationships. Measures of culture include attitudes toward marriage and single motherhood, distrust of the opposite sex, and religious denomination and church attendance. Studies show that mothers and fathers who view marriage favorably are more likely to marry.[34] The association between pro-marriage attitudes and cohabitation is weaker, and there is no association between pro-marriage attitudes and union dissolution.[35] There is also evidence that parents' distrust of the opposite sex decreases the chances of marriage and cohabitation[36] and increases the likelihood of breaking up.[37] No studies examine the link between pro-marriage attitudes and relationship quality or father involvement. Finally, religiosity is consistently related to both relationship stability and quality. The mother's and father's religiosity are both important in predicting entrance into marriage.[38] One study finds that fathers' religiosity is associated with lower rates of cohabitation (as compared with being single), perhaps because most religious fathers have already married and those who have chosen to be single may be different in a special way. In terms of relationship quality, the father's religiosity is more important than mother's religiosity in determining overall quality and supportiveness, both for unmarried couples generally and for particular subgroups of the population, such as Latino couples.[39] One study finds that consistent church attendance is a stronger predictor of union quality than a recent increase in attendance, suggesting that the benefits of religiosity take time to accrue and require consistency of church attendance.[40] The only paper that examines the link between religiosity on the one hand and father involvement and co-parenting on the other hand finds no association between nonresident fathers' religiosity and involvement or co-parenting.[41] Finally, religious denomination is unrelated to relationship quality or stability among unmarried couples, and no study to our knowledge has examined its association with nonresident father involvement or co-parenting.

Demographic Factors

Researchers have identified a number of demographic factors that are associated with parents' relationship quality and stability. Mate availability, as measured by the ratio of men to women in a community, is positively linked with both relationship quality and marriage.[42] Mate availability is strongly associated with mothers' reports that fathers are "fair and willing to compromise"; lack of availability is associated with domestic violence. Research also finds that divergent sex ratios of men to women can explain a good deal of the racial disparity in marriage. Race and ethnicity are also consistently associated with union instability. Black couples are less likely to marry and more likely to break up,[43] although black nonresident fathers are more involved with their children than other fathers and tend to have higher-quality co-parenting relationships.[44] Immigrant mothers report better-quality relationships, but their reports about transitioning into marriage are mixed,[45] perhaps because long-term cohabitation is normative among Hispanics (for a more detailed discussion see the article by Robert Hummer and Erin Hamilton in this volume), who make up the majority of the Fragile Families immigrant sample.

Parents' partnership and fertility histories are also important predictors of parental relationships and father involvement. Of particular interest is multipartnered fertility (having a child with another partner), which varies over time and by gender. For parents who are in a romantic relationship at birth, fathers' (but not mothers') children from a previous partnership have a negative effect on the quality and stability of the couple relationship.[46] Once the romantic relationship ends, however, if either parent has a new child with yet another partner, the quality of the co-parenting relationship deteriorates. More generally, contact between the nonresident father and child is very sensitive to the presence of new partners, especially mothers' new partners. When mothers form a new partnership, nonresident fathers' involvement declines; when the new partnerships end, father involvement increases.[47] This pattern of contact is similar when fathers have a new partner, although the association tends to be weaker.[48]

Personal Characteristics and Behaviors

Although it is not necessarily the major focus of their work, many researchers include information on parents' personal characteristics and behaviors, such as the father's incarceration history, drinking and drug use, and physical and mental health, in their studies of parental relationships. A growing literature examines the link between the father's prior incarceration and parents' relationship stability and quality, father involvement, and co-parenting, with all the evidence showing a negative association between incarceration and these outcomes.[49] Fathers' drinking and drug use show a similar association with union quality and nonresident father contact, but less so with union stability or co-parenting quality.[50] Finally, neither the father's nor mother's physical health is related to union stability, father involvement, or co-parenting,[51] although one study finds that mothers' poor or fair health is associated with greater conflict in relationships.[52] In contrast, some evidence shows that mothers' poor mental health reduces the chances of marriage, whereas fathers' mental health risk (measured by a family history of mental health problems) decreases co-parenting quality.[53] The occasional absence of a significant link between personal characteristics and union stability is explained by the inclusion of relationship quality itself in the model.

Relationship Quality

Thus far, we have treated relationship quality as an outcome variable. A number of studies, however, treat it as a predictor of union stability and father involvement. In this literature, researchers examine both positive and negative dimensions of relationship quality. Positive quality is measured as supportiveness; negative quality, as conflict and violence. As one would expect, the former is strongly linked with union stability and father involvement,[54] whereas violence and conflict reduce marriage and union stability.[55] Mothers' reports of father violence or conflict are generally unrelated to days of contact or father engagement, likely because violence and involvement have reciprocal relationships with one another that work in opposite directions.[56] On the one hand, father contact increases the opportunity for violence; on the other, violence reduces further contact with the father.[57]

What Do Social Experiments Show?

In the previous section, we examined the predictors of parental relationships based on studies using survey data. Next, we review experimental evidence—that is, evidence from social science experiments in which participants are randomly assigned to treatment groups and control groups so that the effects of the treatment can be evaluated accurately and independently of the characteristics of the treatment group. We look first at experiments that assess how economic resources affect union stability and father involvement and then at experiments aimed at improving relationship quality. There is little experimental evidence on the other predictors discussed in the previous section—personal, cultural, and demographic.

Economic Determinants and Government Programs

Several evaluations of welfare-to-work experiments during the 1990s provide information on the effects of economic interventions on marriage and union stability. The Minnesota Family Investment Program, for example, included a 38 percent earnings disregard for mothers in the treatment group. An evaluation found increases in marriage among all single mothers (although these effects dissipated over time for all but a few subgroups of mothers)[58] and also found declines in union dissolution rates, as well as in domestic violence, among couples who had received welfare before the program. Similarly, Vermont's Welfare Restructuring Project, which allowed individuals to accumulate assets without losing their benefits, found small increases in marriage among single mothers. (Although the employment of participants in the Vermont program increased, their family income did not increase, which means that family income was not the cause of the increases in marriage.)[59] In contrast, Florida's Family Transition Program, which increased neither income nor assets, showed no increase in marriage.[60]

Two other social experiments provide evidence on the causal effects of income on family stability. The Canadian Self-Sufficiency Project, which provided income subsidies to single mothers on welfare, found a positive effect on marriage in New Brunswick but not in British Columbia.[61] Similarly, the New Hope Anti-Poverty Program, which provided income subsidies to families in two communities in Milwaukee, found large increases in marriage among never-married mothers in the treatment group.[62]

In addition to income programs described above, several large-scale demonstrations designed to increase the human capital of disadvantaged youth have reported mixed evidence on marriage. Whereas early programs, such as Job Corps and JOBSTART, found no effects on marriage, career academies, which are career-oriented academic programs with employer partnerships, found substantial effects among young men.[63]

Another set of experiments provides some information on the effects of economic resources on father involvement, although again, it is unclear whether the improvements came from gains in fathers' economic circumstances or some other facet of the program. For example, the Parent's Fair Share Demonstration (see the article by Philip Cowan, Carolyn Cowan, and Virginia Knox in this volume), which targeted low-income noncustodial fathers whose children were receiving welfare, increased involvement among the least-involved fathers. There is also some evidence that the program led to an increase in couple disagreements, largely about childrearing.

Relationship Quality

Another area that offers a good deal of experimental evidence is relationship quality. Although our discussion of studies using survey data focused primarily on determinants of relationship quality such as income, employment, and religion, most experiments on relationship quality are conducted by psychologists who focus on teachable skills relevant to interpersonal interaction—for example, communication, problem solving, and conflict management—as well as expectations and attitudes. Psychologists have also honed in on specific transitions, such as marriage, parenthood, and divorce, as critical points of intervention. Over the past few decades, their experiments in relationship quality have evolved toward a therapy-centered approach facilitated by professionals. Most recently, those experiments have begun to address the multifaceted needs of low-income populations.

One of the most widely studied programs, representative of an early wave of relationship quality experiments, the Prevention and Relationship Enhancement Program (PREP), focused on improving communication skills among engaged couples as they negotiated the transition to marriage. Evaluations of the PREP program found that couples in the treatment groups had better marital quality and were less likely to divorce than those in the control group.[64]

The Becoming a Family Program represented two important departures from the early experiments. It used skilled clinicians, and it focused on a transition (parenthood) wherein couples might be more amenable to relationship intervention. The program showed positive effects on marital quality at both the five- and ten-year follow-up, but, surprisingly, no effect on marital stability.[65] Findings from a related program, Bringing Baby Home, also showed higher marital quality at the one-year follow-up.[66]

These studies have a number of limitations for our purposes. First, early experiments were conducted on samples of largely middle-income couples, rather than fragile-family couples. It is unclear whether programs that succeed with more advantaged groups will be sufficient for this latter population, which faces multiple problems. A few pilot experiments, however, have focused on low-income couples. The Supporting Father Involvement Program,[67] for example, found that parenting counseling for fathers or relationship counseling for couples increased father involvement and improved the co-parenting relationship among cohabiting couples.

Second, experiments sometimes have a selection bias: people who are offered the program but do not enroll, or who later drop out of the program (attrite), often have different characteristics than those who remain in the treatment sample, potentially biasing the results. For example, PREP's positive results may be subject to selection bias as 50 percent of potential participants declined the offer—and were more likely to break up before marrying than participants were.[68] A third limitation of some relationship quality programs is that they have only short-term effects, dissipating within a few years; in some cases, long-term effects are never assessed. Finally, many of these programs do not examine whether improving marital quality affects union stability, co-parenting quality, or father involvement.

Two recent healthy marriage initiatives with experimental designs, launched by the Administration for Children and Families, capitalize on the strengths and lessons learned from previous studies to address relationship quality among more disadvantaged families. The Building Strong Families Project (BSF) focuses on strengthening unmarried-couple relationships, whereas the Supporting Healthy Marriage Project (SHM) focuses on economically disadvantaged married couples. Building Strong Families was prompted by the finding of the Fragile Families and Child Wellbeing Study that many unwed mothers were in cohabiting relationships at the time of the child's birth. Supporting Healthy Marriage aimed to address the high divorce rates among low-income couples. Both include group sessions with trained facilitators focused on healthy marriage skills, such as communication and anger management, as well as additional support services. Additionally, BSF includes a service coordinator, whereas SHM includes extracurricular activities designed to enhance the couple's relationship. Evidence from these programs will become available in the next few years.

Conclusions

In examining the trajectories of parental relationships in fragile families, we find that despite high hopes at the time of their child's birth, most unmarried parents are not able to establish stable unions or long-term co-parenting relationships. Among the predictors of instability in these families are low economic resources; government policies that contain marriage penalties; cultural norms that support single motherhood; demographic factors, such as sex ratios that favor men and children from prior unions; and, finally, psychological factors that make it difficult for parents to maintain healthy relationships. Although each appears to play a role in shaping parental relationship and union stability, no single factor appears to have a dominant effect.

What, then, can be done to improve the quality and stability of relationships in fragile families? Economic resources are a consistent predictor of positive outcomes, but the evidence is mixed with respect to whether the effect is causal. There is also some discrepancy between the lessons learned from survey data and the findings from the social experiments. Whereas the former show that fathers' earnings are the most important economic factor in predicting union stability and parental relationship quality, the social experiments do not really test this hypothesis. Instead, they typically target single mothers and focus on increasing mothers' income or earnings. Thus good information is lacking on the potential effect of increasing fathers' employment and earnings. That said, it is notable that the two experiments that had the largest impact on marriage—the New Hope Anti-Poverty Program and the Minnesota Family Investment Program—also provided the largest income gains to two-parent families.

Attitudes and religion are consistent predictors of parental relationships, although, again, evidence is lacking that these associations are causal. Demographic characteristics, such as race and sex ratios, are also important, but most are not amenable to intervention. An important exception is multiple-partner fertility, which is a product of instability and which is associated with all four domains of parental relationships, including the quality and stability of parents' romantic relationship, nonresident father involvement, and co-parenting quality. Although no experimental evidence is available on multiple-partner fertility, statistical models offer reasonably good evidence that it has a causal effect on parental relationships.[69]

Finally, strong evidence shows that relationship quality has a causal effect on union stability, father involvement, and co-parenting quality, although most of the experimental evidence available to date is based on samples of married couples with stable incomes and no serious behavior problems. Whether these programs will be able to substantially improve parental relationships in fragile families and how large the effect will be is unclear at this time, although better answers will be available soon once the evaluations of the marriage programs (Building Strong Families Project, Community Healthy Marriage Initiative, and Supporting Healthy Marriage Project) are complete.

Endnotes

1. Sara McLanahan and Christine Percheski, "Family Structure and the Reproduction of Inequalities," *Annual Review of Sociology* 34 (2008): 257–76.

2. Maria Carlson and Robin Högnäs, "Coparenting in Fragile Families," Working Paper 09-13-FF (Princeton: Center for Research on Child Wellbeing, September 2009).

3. Daniel T. Lichter, Zhenchao Qian, and Leanna M. Mellott, "Marriage or Dissolution? Union Transitions among Poor Cohabiting Women," *Demography* 43, no. 2 (2006): 223–40; Valerie Kincade Oppenheimer, "Cohabiting and Marriage during Young Men's Career-Development Process," *Demography* 40, no. 1 (2003): 127–49; Sharon Sassler and James McNally, "Cohabiting Couples' Economic Circumstances and Union Transitions: A Re-Examination using Multiple Imputation Techniques," *Social Science Research* 32, no. 4 (2003): 553–78; Pamela J. Smock, Wendy D. Manning, and Meredith Porter, "'Everything's There Except Money': How Money Shapes Decisions to Marry among Cohabitors," *Journal of Marriage and the Family* 67, no. 3 (2005): 680–96; Zheng Wu and Michael Pollard, "Economic Circumstances and the Stability of Nonmarital Cohabitation," *Journal of Family Issues* 21, no. 3 (2000): 303–28.

4. Unless otherwise indicated, the numbers presented in this section are taken from Sara McLanahan, "Children in Fragile Families," in *Changing Families in an Unequal Society,* edited by Marcia Carlson and Paula England (Stanford University Press, forthcoming).

5. These estimates are consistent with other estimates of violence for this population of mothers. Sandra Danziger, Mary Corcoran, and Sheldon Danziger, "Barriers to the Employment of Welfare Recipients," in *Prosperity for All? The Economic Boom and African Americans,* edited by Robert Cherry and William Rodgers (New York: Russell Sage, 2000), pp. 245–78.

6. Andrew J. Cherlin, *The Marriage-Go-Round* (New York: Alfred A. Knopf, 2009).

7. Kathryn Edin and Maria Kefalas, *Promises I Can Keep: Why Low-Income Women Put Motherhood before Marriage* (University of California Press, 2005); C. Gibson-Davis, Kathryn Edin, and Sara McLanahan, "High Hopes but Even Higher Expectations: The Retreat from Marriage among Low-Income Couples," *Journal of Marriage and the Family* 67, no. 5 (2005): 1301–12.

8. Orlando Patterson, *Rituals of Blood: The Consequences of Slavery in Two American Centuries* (New York: Basic Civitas, 1998).

9. Marcia Carlson, Sara McLanahan, and Paula England, "Union Formation in Fragile Families," *Demography* 41, no. 2 (2004): 237–61; Kathryn Edin, Paula England, and Kathryn Linnenberg, "Love and Distrust among Unmarried Parents," paper presented at the National Poverty Center Annual Poverty Conference, Washington, September 2003.

10. Heather D. Hill, "Steppin' Out: Infidelity and Sexual Jealousy among Unmarried Parents," in *Unmarried Couples with Children,* edited by Kathryn Edin and Paula England (New York: Russell Sage, 2007), pp. 104–23, uses the Time, Love, and Cash among Couples with Children Project (TLC-3), an embedded qualitative component of the Fragile Families and Child Wellbeing Study.

11. McLanahan, "Children in Fragile Families" (see note 4).

12. Authors' own calculations.

13. Audrey Beck and others, "Partnership Transitions and Maternal Parenting," *Journal of Marriage and Family* 72, no. 2 (2010): 219–33.

14. Marcia Carlson, Sara S. McLanahan, and Jeanne Brooks-Gunn, "Coparenting and Nonresident Fathers' Involvement with Young Children after a Nonmarital Birth," *Demography* 45, no. 2 (2008): 461–88.

15. Lenna Nepomnyaschy and Irwin Garfinkel, "Child Support, Fatherhood, and Marriage: Findings from the First 5 Years of the Fragile Families and Child Wellbeing Study," *Asian Social Work and Policy Review* 1, no. 1 (2007): 1–20.

16. Laura Tach, Ronald Mincy, and Kathryn Edin, "Parenting as a Package Deal: Relationships, Fertility, and Nonresident Father Involvement among Unmarried Parents," *Demography* 47, no. 1 (2010): 181–204.

17. Carlson and Högnäs, "Coparenting in Fragile Families" (see note 2).

18. For example, Marah Curtis, "Subsidized Housing, Housing Prices, and the Living Arrangements of Unmarried Mothers," *Housing Policy Debate* 18, no. 1 (2007): 145–70; Kristen Harknett, "Mate Availability and Unmarried Parent Relationships," *Demography* 45, no. 3 (2008): 555–71; Robin S. Högnäs and Marcia Carlson, "Intergenerational Relationships and Union Stability in Fragile Families," Working Paper 09-08-FF (Princeton: Center for Research on Child Wellbeing, March 2010).

19. Carlson, McLanahan, and Brooks-Gunn, "Coparenting and Nonresident Fathers' Involvement with Young Children after a Nonmarital Birth" (see note 14); Karen Guzzo, "Maternal Relationships and Nonresidential Father Visitation of Children Born outside of Marriage," *Journal of Marriage and Family* 71, no. 3 (2009): 632–49; Tach, Mincy, and Edin, "Parenting as a Package Deal: Relationships, Fertility, and Nonresident Father Involvement among Unmarried Parents" (see note 16); but see Lenna Nepomnyaschy, "Child Support and Father-Child Contact: Testing Reciprocal Pathways," *Demography* 44, no. 1 (2007): 93–112.

20. For example, Carlson and Högnäs, "Coparenting in Fragile Families" (see note 2); Carlson, McLanahan, and Brooks-Gunn, "Coparenting and Nonresident Fathers' Involvement with Young Children after a Nonmarital Birth" (see note 14).

21. For example, Curtis, "Subsidized Housing, Housing Prices, and the Living Arrangements of Unmarried Mothers" (see note 18); Harknett, "Mate Availability and Unmarried Parent Relationships" (see note 18); Margaret L. Usdansky, Andrew S. London, and Janet M. Wilmoth, "Veteran Status, Race-Ethnicity, and Marriage among Fragile Families," *Journal of Marriage and Family* 71, no. 3 (2009): 768–86; but see Carlson and Högnäs, "Coparenting in Fragile Families" (see note 2); Cynthia Osborne, "Marriage Following the Birth of a Child among Cohabiting and Visiting Parents," *Journal of Marriage and Family* 67, no. 1 (2005): 14–26.

22. Carlson, McLanahan, and England, "Union Formation in Fragile Families" (see note 9).

23. Lichter, Qian, and Mellott, "Marriage or Dissolution? Union Transitions among Poor Cohabiting Women" (see note 3).

24. Arnstein Aassve, "The Impact of Economic Resources on Premarital Childbearing and Subsequent Marriage among Young American Women," *Demography* 40, no. 1 (2003): 105–26; Megan Sweeney, "Two Decades of Family Change: The Shifting Economic Foundations of Marriage," *American Sociological Review* 67, no. 1 (2002): 132–47.

25. Harknett, "Mate Availability and Unmarried Parent Relationships" (see note 18); Bryndl Hohmann-Marriott, "Father Involvement Ideals and the Union Transitions of Unmarried Parents," *Journal of Family Issues* 30, no. 7 (2009): 898–920; Laura Tach, "Economic Contributions, Relationship Quality, and Union Dissolution among Married and Unmarried Parents," unpublished manuscript (2009).

26. Hohmann-Marriott, "Father Involvement Ideals and the Union Transitions of Unmarried Parents" (see note 25); Tach, "Economic Contributions, Relationship Quality, and Union Dissolution among Married and Unmarried Parents" (see note 25).

27. Christina Gibson-Davis, "Money, Marriage, and Children: Testing the Financial Expectations and Family Formation Theory," *Journal of Marriage and Family* 71, no. 1 (2009): 146–60; Tach, "Economic Contributions, Relationship Quality, and Union Dissolution among Married and Unmarried Parents" (see note 25).

28. Marcia Carlson and others, "The Effects of Welfare and Child Support Policies on Union Formation," *Population Research and Policy Review* 23, no. 5-6 (2004): 513–42.

29. Curtis, "Subsidized Housing, Housing Prices, and the Living Arrangements of Unmarried Mothers" (see note 18); Mark Turner, "Cohabitation of Unwed Parents in Federally Subsidized Housing: Effects of Income and Housing Prices" (Washington: Urban Institute, 2003); Jean Knab and others, "The Effects of Welfare and Child Support Policies on the Incidence of Marriage Following a Nonmarital Birth," in *Welfare Reform and Its Long-Term Consequences for America's Poor,* edited by James Ziliak (Cambridge University Press, 2009), pp. 290–307.

30. Curtis, "Subsidized Housing, Housing Prices, and the Living Arrangements of Unmarried Mothers" (see note 18).

31. Carlson and others, "The Effects of Welfare and Child Support Policies on Union Formation" (see note 28); Knab and others, "The Effects of Welfare and Child Support Policies on the Incidence of Marriage Following a Nonmarital Birth" (see note 29).

32. Knab and others, "The Effects of Welfare and Child Support Policies on the Incidence of Marriage Following a Nonmarital Birth" (see note 29).

33. Angela Fertig and others, "The Effect of Child Support Enforcement on Bargaining Power among Married and Cohabiting Couples," Working Paper 05-08-FF (Princeton: Center for Research on Child Wellbeing, March 2005).

34. For example, Carlson and others, "The Effects of Welfare and Child Support Policies on Union Formation" (see note 28); Kristen Harknett and Sara McLanahan, "Racial and Ethnic Differences in Marriage after the Birth of a Child," *American Sociological Review* 69, no. 6 (2004): 790–811.

35. Carlson, McLanahan, and England, "Union Formation in Fragile Families" (see note 9); Carlson and others, "The Effects of Welfare and Child Support Policies on Union Formation" (see note 28); Osborne, "Marriage Following the Birth of a Child among Cohabiting and Visiting Parents" (see note 21).

36. Carlson, McLanahan, and England, "Union Formation in Fragile Families" (see note 9); Carlson and others, "The Effects of Welfare and Child Support Policies on Union Formation" (see note 28); Harknett and McLanahan, "Racial and Ethnic Differences in Marriage after the Birth of a Child" (see note 34);

Maureen R. Waller and Sara McLanahan, "'His' and 'Her' Marriage Expectations: Determinants and Consequences," *Journal of Marriage and Family* 67, no. 1 (2005): 53–67.

37. Carlson and others, "The Effects of Welfare and Child Support Policies on Union Formation" (see note 28); Waller and McLanahan, "'His' and 'Her' Marriage Expectations" (see note 36).

38. For example, Julien Teitler and others, "Effects of Welfare Participation on Marriage," *Journal of Marriage and Family* 71, no. 4 (2009): 878–91; Maureen R. Waller and H. Elizabeth Peters, "The Risk of Divorce as a Barrier to Marriage among Parents of Young Children," *Social Science Research* 37, no. 4 (2008): 1188–99; W. Bradford Wilcox and Nicholas H. Wolfinger, "Then Comes Marriage? Religion, Race, and Marriage in Urban America," *Social Science Research* 36, no. 2 (2007): 569–89.

39. W. Bradford Wilcox and Edwin I. Hernandez, "*Bendito Amor:* Religion and Relationships among Married and Unmarried Latinos in Urban America," Working Paper 07-06-FF (Princeton: Center for Research on Child Wellbeing, March 2007); W. Bradford Wilcox and Nicholas H. Wolfinger, "Living and Loving 'Decent': Religion and Relationship Quality among Urban Parents," *Social Science Research* 37, no. 3 (2008): 828–43.

40. Wilcox and Wolfinger, "Living and Loving 'Decent': Religion and Relationship Quality among Urban Parents" (see note 39).

41. Carlson and Högnäs, "Coparenting in Fragile Families" (see note 2); Carlson, McLanahan, and Brooks-Gunn, "Coparenting and Nonresident Fathers' Involvement with Young Children after a Nonmarital Birth" (see note 14).

42. Harknett, "Mate Availability and Unmarried Parent Relationships" (see note 18).

43. For example, Carlson and others, "The Effects of Welfare and Child Support Policies on Union Formation" (see note 28); Harknett, "Mate Availability and Unmarried Parent Relationships" (see note 18).

44. Carlson and Högnäs, "Coparenting in Fragile Families" (see note 2); Carlson, McLanahan, and Brooks-Gunn, "Coparenting and Nonresident Fathers' Involvement with Young Children after a Nonmarital Birth" (see note 14); Tach, Mincy, and Edin, "Parenting as a Package Deal" (see note 16).

45. Harknett, "Mate Availability and Unmarried Parent Relationships" (see note 18).

46. Marcia J. Carlson and Frank F. Furstenberg Jr., "The Consequences of Multi-Partnered Fertility for Parental Involvement and Relationships," Working Paper 06-28-FF (Princeton: Center for Research on Child Wellbeing, May 2007); Carlson and Högnäs, "Coparenting in Fragile Families" (see note 2); Carlson, McLanahan, and Brooks-Gunn, "Coparenting and Nonresident Fathers' Involvement with Young Children after a Nonmarital Birth" (see note 14); Carlson, McLanahan, and England, "Union Formation in Fragile Families" (see note 9); Carlson and others, "The Effects of Welfare and Child Support Policies on Union Formation" (see note 28); Harknett, "Mate Availability and Unmarried Parent Relationships" (see note 18); Harknett and McLanahan, "Racial and Ethnic Differences in Marriage after the Birth of a Child" (see note 34); Nepomnyaschy, "Child Support and Father-Child Contact" (see note 19); Tach, Mincy, and Edin, "Parenting as a Package Deal" (see note 16); Wilcox and Wolfinger, "Then Comes Marriage? Religion, Race, and Marriage in Urban America" (see note 38).

47. Carlson, McLanahan, and Brooks-Gunn, "Coparenting and Nonresident Fathers' Involvement with Young Children after a Nonmarital Birth" (see note 14); Guzzo, "Maternal Relationships and Nonresidential Father Visitation of Children Born outside of Marriage" (see note 19); Tach, Mincy, and Edin, "Parenting

as a Package Deal: Relationships, Fertility, and Nonresident Father Involvement among Unmarried Parents" (see note 16).

48. Guzzo, "Maternal Relationships and Nonresidential Father Visitation of Children Born outside of Marriage" (see note 19); Tach, Mincy, and Edin, "Parenting as a Package Deal" (see note 16).

49. For example, Carlson and Högnäs, "Coparenting in Fragile Families" (see note 2); Raymond Swisher and Maureen Waller, "Confining Fatherhood: Incarceration and Paternal Involvement among Unmarried White, African American, and Latino Fathers," *Journal of Family Issues* 29, no. 8 (2008): 1067–88; Julien O. Teitler and Nancy E. Reichman, "Mental Illness as a Barrier to Marriage among Unmarried Mothers," *Journal of Marriage and Family* 70, no. 3 (2008): 772–82; Maureen R. Waller and Raymond R. Swisher, "Fathers' Risk Factors in Fragile Families: Implications for 'Healthy' Relationships and Father Involvement," *Social Problems* 53, no. 3 (2006): 392–420.

50. For example, Carlson and Högnäs, "Coparenting in Fragile Families" (see note 2); Carlson, McLanahan, and Brooks-Gunn, "Coparenting and Nonresident Fathers' Involvement with Young Children after a Nonmarital Birth" (see note 14); Waller and Swisher, "Fathers' Risk Factors in Fragile Families" (see note 49); Wilcox and Wolfinger, "Living and Loving 'Decent': Religion and Relationship Quality among Urban Parents" (see note 39).

51. For example, Carlson and Högnäs, "Coparenting in Fragile Families" (see note 2); Carlson and others, "The Effects of Welfare and Child Support Policies on Union Formation" (see note 28); Harknett, "Mate Availability and Unmarried Parent Relationships" (see note 18); Tach, Mincy, and Edin, "Parenting as a Package Deal" (see note 16).

52. Harknett, "Mate Availability and Unmarried Parent Relationships" (see note 18).

53. Carlson and Högnäs, "Coparenting in Fragile Families" (see note 2); Teitler and Reichman, "Mental Illness as a Barrier to Marriage among Unmarried Mothers" (see note 49).

54. Marcia Carlson, "Involvement by Young Unmarried Fathers before and after Their Baby's Birth," *The Prevention Researcher* 11, no. 4 (2004): 14–17; Carlson and others, "The Effects of Welfare and Child Support Policies on Union Formation" (see note 28); Bryndl E. Hohmann-Marriott, "Emotional Supportiveness and the Union Transitions of Married and Unmarried Parents," *Marriage and Family Review* 45, no. 1 (2009): 4–25.

55. For example, Carlson and others, "The Effects of Welfare and Child Support Policies on Union Formation" (see note 28); Harknett, "Mate Availability and Unmarried Parent Relationships" (see note 18); Hohmann-Marriott, "Emotional Supportiveness and the Union Transitions of Married and Unmarried Parents" (see note 54); but see Carlson, McLanahan, and England, "Union Formation in Fragile Families" (see note 9), and Usdansky, London, and Wilmoth, "Veteran Status, Race-Ethnicity, and Marriage among Fragile Families" (see note 21), who find no relationship between violence and cohabitation or marriage.

56. Marcia Carlson and Sara McLanahan, "Fathers in Fragile Families," Working Paper 09-14-FF (Princeton: Center for Research on Child Wellbeing, 2009); Carlson, McLanahan, and Brooks-Gunn, "Coparenting and Nonresident Fathers' Involvement with Young Children after a Nonmarital Birth" (see note 14); Waller and Swisher, "Fathers' Risk Factors in Fragile Families" (see note 49).

57. Waller and Swisher, "Fathers' Risk Factors in Fragile Families" (see note 49).

58. Lisa A. Gennetian, Cynthia Miller, and Jared Smith, "Turning Welfare into a Work Support: Six-Year Impacts on Parents and Children from the Minnesota Family Investment Program" (New York: MDRC, July 2005); Robert Lerman, Gregory Acs, and Anupa Bir, "An Economic Framework and Selected Proposals for Demonstrations Aimed at Strengthening Marriage, Employment, and Family Functioning Outcomes" (Washington: Urban Institute, December 2007).

59. Lisa A. Gennetian and Virginia Knox, "Staying Single: The Effects of Welfare Reform Policies on Marriage and Cohabitation," Working Paper 13 (New York: MDRC, 2005); Susan Scrivener and others, "WRP: Final Report on Vermont's Welfare Restructuring Program" (New York: MDRC, September 2002).

60. Dan Bloom and others, "The Family Transition Program: Final Report on Florida's Initial Time-Limited Welfare Program" (New York: MDRC, December 2000).

61. Kristen Harknett and Lisa Gennetian, "How an Earnings Supplement Can Affect Union Formation among Low-Income Single Mothers," *Demography* 40, no. 3 (2003): 451–78.

62. Anna Gassman-Pines and Hirokazu Yoshikawa, "Five-Year Effects of an Anti-Poverty Program on Marriage among Never-Married Mothers," *Policy Analysis & Management* 25, no. 1 (2006): 11–31.

63. James J. Kemple and Cynthia J. Willner, *Technical Resources for Career Academies: Long-Term Impacts on Labor Market Outcomes, Educational Attainment, and Transitions to Adulthood* (New York: MDRC, July 2008); Lerman, Acs, and Bir, "An Economic Framework and Selected Proposals for Demonstrations Aimed at Strengthening Marriage, Employment, and Family Functioning Outcomes" (see note 58).

64. M. Robin Dion, "Healthy Marriage Programs: Learning What Works," *Future of Children* 15, no. 2 (2005): 139–56; Mari Jo Renick, Susan L. Blumberg, and Howard J. Markman, "The Prevention and Relationship Enhancement Program (PREP): An Empirically Based Preventive Intervention Program for Couples," *Family Relations* 41, no. 2 (1992): 141–7.

65. Carolyn Pape Cowan and Philip A. Cowan, *When Partners Become Parents: The Big Life Change for Couples* (New York: HarperCollins, 1992); Philip A. Cowan and Carolyn Pape Cowan, "Developmental Psychopathology from Family Systems and Family Risk Factors Perspectives: Implications for Family Research, Practice, and Policy," in *Developmental Psychopathology*, edited by Dante Cicchetti and Donald J. Cohen (New York: Wiley, 2006), pp. 530–87.

66. Alyson F. Shapiro and John M. Gottman, "Effects on Marriage of a Psycho-Communicative-Educational Intervention with Couples Undergoing the Transition to Parenthood, Evaluation at 1-Year Post Intervention," *Journal of Family Communication* 5, no. 1 (2005): 1–24.

67. Philip A. Cowan and others, "Promoting Fathers' Engagement with Children: Preventive Interventions for Low-Income Families," *Journal of Marriage and the Family* 71, no. 3 (2009): 663–79.

68. Howard Markman and others, "Preventing Marital Distress through Communication and Conflict Management Training: A 4- and 5-Year Follow-Up," *Journal of Consulting and Clinical Psychology* 61, no. 1 (1993): 70–77.

69. Tach, Mincy, and Edin, "Parenting as a Package Deal" (see note 16).

Mothers' Economic Conditions and Sources of Support in Fragile Families

Ariel Kalil and Rebecca M. Ryan

Summary

Rising rates of nonmarital childbirth in the United States have resulted in a new family type, the fragile family. Such families, which include cohabiting couples as well as single mothers, experience significantly higher rates of poverty and material hardship than their married counterparts. Ariel Kalil and Rebecca Ryan summarize the economic challenges facing mothers in fragile families and describe the resources, both public and private, that help them meet these challenges.

The authors explain that the economic fragility of these families stems from both mothers' and fathers' low earnings, which result from low education levels, as well as from physical, emotional, and mental health problems.

Mothers in fragile families make ends meet in many ways. The authors show that various public programs, particularly those that provide in-kind assistance, do successfully lessen economic hardship in fragile families. Single mothers also turn to private sources of support—friends, family, boyfriends—for cash and in-kind assistance. But though these private safety nets are essential to many mothers' economic survival, according to the authors, private safety nets are not always consistent and dependable. Thus, assistance from private sources may not fundamentally improve mothers' economic circumstances.

Policy makers, say Kalil and Ryan, must recognize that with rates of nonmarital childbirth at their current level, and potentially rising still, the fragile family is likely an enduring fixture in this country. It is thus essential to strengthen policies that both support these families' economic self-sufficiency and alleviate their hardship during inevitable times of economic distress.

The most important first step, they say, is to strengthen the public safety net, especially such in-kind benefits as food stamps, Medicaid, housing, and child care. A next step would be to bolster community-based programs that can provide private financial support, such as emergency cash assistance, child care, and food aid, when mothers cannot receive it from their own private networks.

www.futureofchildren.org

Ariel Kalil is a professor in the Harris School of Public Policy at the University of Chicago. Rebecca M. Ryan is an assistant professor of psychology at Georgetown University.

As rates of nonmarital childbirth have increased in the United States in the past half-century, a new family type, the fragile family, has emerged. Fragile families, which are formed as the result of a nonmarital birth, include cohabiting couples as well as noncohabiting, or single, mothers. Such families evoke public concern in part because they are more impoverished and endure more material hardship than married-parent families and have fewer sources of economic support. Father absence and family instability are also cause for concern. The economic fragility of these families stems largely from mothers' and fathers' relatively low skills and training, which often pose barriers to higher-wage work. Fragile families also have almost no financial assets. In this article, we describe the economic challenges facing mothers in fragile families and the resources they call upon to meet these challenges.

We begin by summarizing economic conditions in fragile families using the most recent data available. Next, we suggest reasons why mothers in fragile families face so much poverty and material hardship, focusing especially on their living arrangements, employment capacities, and assets. We go on to explain how, given their economic conditions and capacities, mothers in fragile families make ends meet in their households. Specifically, we describe the sources of public and private support available to them and the role each plays in mothers' economic survival.

Economic Conditions in Fragile Families

As Sara McLanahan has observed, until recently it was unclear where along the spectrum of economic conditions and capabilities the nation's fragile families were to be found.[1] Were these unwed U.S. parents similar to married parents in terms of their capabilities, thus resembling unwed parents in Scandinavia, whose capabilities are generally high? Or were they low-skilled individuals living in what might be described as a "poor man's marriage"? Extensive research from the Fragile Families and Child Wellbeing Study (FFCWS), the ongoing study of 5,000 children in large U.S. cities, three-quarters of whom were born to unwed parents, has shown that U.S. unwed-couple families fall closer to the disadvantaged end of the spectrum.

The economic well-being of fragile families varies somewhat by living arrangement (that is, whether couples live together or apart), but living arrangements do not necessarily cause differences in economic well-being; indeed they are equally likely to result from them. Unwed mothers and fathers with the highest education and earnings potential are more likely to choose to cohabit with one another than to choose to live apart. Consequently, they have somewhat higher levels of economic well-being than their counterparts who have chosen to live apart or who must, out of economic necessity, double-up with other adults. Nevertheless, even cohabiting unwed couples experience serious economic hardship.

Poverty in Fragile Families

Table 1 describes the economic and demographic characteristics of the three different types of mothers in the FFCWS. About a quarter are married. The unmarried mothers are divided into two groups: those in a cohabiting relationship with their child's father and those who are single, that is, not cohabiting with the father. Because about half the mothers in fragile families are cohabiting at their child's birth and half are not, the average

Table 1. Demographic and Economic Characteristics of Married, Cohabiting, and Single Mothers in the Fragile Families Study

Percent unless otherwise indicated	Relationship status		
Demographic and economic characteristics	**Married**	**Cohabiting**	**Single**
Demographic characteristics			
Mean age (years)	29.3	24.7	22.6
Teen parent	3.7	17.7	34.3
Child with other partner	11.7	38.8	34.5
Human capital and economic characteristics			
Education			
Less than high school	17.8	41.0	48.8
High school or equivalent	25.5	39.2	34.2
Some college	21.1	17.3	14.3
College or higher	35.7	2.4	2.4
Mean earnings	$25,618.86	$11,433.78	$10,764.05
Worked last year	79.3	83.4	79.40
Poverty status	14.0	32.5	53.1
Household income	$55,057.05	$26,548.43	$18,662.04
Health and behavior			
Poor/fair health	10.4	14.4	17.1
Depression	13.2	16.2	15.7
Heavy drinking	2.0	8.0	7.7
Illegal drugs	0.3	1.7	3.1
Child's father incarcerated	8.0	32.6	45.2

Source: Fragile Families and Child Wellbeing Study statistics, courtesy of Sara McLanahan.

for all unmarried mothers is about halfway between figures for each of those two groups.

As the table indicates, a defining feature of fragile families is their high poverty rates. At the inception of the FFCWS, 33 percent of mothers cohabiting with the child's father and 53 percent of single mothers in the sample were poor, compared with only 14 percent of married mothers. Not surprisingly, fragile families' average household incomes are low. The annual household income of cohabiting mothers in fragile families was $26,548, and that of single mothers in the sample was $18,662. By contrast, married mothers' annual household income was $55,057.

Material Hardship in Fragile Families

Researchers have long argued that official poverty statistics fail to capture the depth of economic hardship faced by unwed mothers.[2] Consequently, many researchers also examine how fragile families fare along such dimensions as food sufficiency, ability to pay bills, and hardships such as having heat or electricity disconnected. Julien Teitler and several colleagues examined data from the FFCWS during the years 1999–2001 and found that many unwed mothers experienced some material hardships.[3] Common concerns were not having enough income to pay bills (32 percent), not being able to pay utility bills (25 percent), and having phone service disconnected (17 percent). Roughly 5 percent of the unwed mothers reported more extreme financial difficulties such as hunger, eviction, utility shut-offs, homelessness, or insufficient medical care. Most important, more than half of the unwed mothers in the sample reported at least one type of hardship.

Why Are Fragile Families Economically Disadvantaged?

Three primary factors shape the rates of poverty and material hardship facing mothers in fragile families: their earnings capacity, their asset levels, and their living arrangements.

Mothers' Earnings Capacity

Mothers in fragile families typically earn low wages. As table 1 indicates, in the first year of the FFCWS, both cohabiting and single mothers earned approximately $11,000, far less than the $26,000 married mothers earned. These differences emerge even though most mothers in fragile families work extensively. Indeed, fully 80 percent of cohabiting, single, and married mothers in the study reported having worked in the previous year. Melissa Radey's more recent analysis of mothers in the FFCWS showed that more than half of the unmarried mothers were employed full time three years after a nonmarital birth and 64 percent were employed at least part time.[4] Thus, although it is the norm for mothers in fragile families to work, they still suffer economically because their earnings are typically low.

Demographic Characteristics That Limit Earnings Capacity

Unwed mothers face many barriers to higher-wage employment, but the primary obstacle is poor education. As table 1 shows, about 41 percent of cohabiting mothers and about 49 percent of single mothers in the FFCWS lack a high school diploma (compared with only 18 percent of married mothers) and only 2.4 percent of the unwed mothers have a college degree (compared with 36 percent of the married mothers). Importantly, Carol Ann MacGregor documented that between 40 and 47 percent of unwed mothers in the FFCWS reported being in school during at least one interview period during the first five years of the study and that about 40 percent of this population completed an educational or training program of some type during that time.[5] It has not yet been established, however, whether the returns to education and program completion among the mothers in the FFCWS sample have translated into higher earnings and economic security.

It is clear that many mothers in fragile families will experience one or more significant barriers to higher-wage employment. Even when they can secure sustained, full-time work, mothers in fragile families have low earnings capacity.

A second barrier to higher-wage employment typically faced by mothers in fragile families is that they are disproportionately young and more likely to be in their teens at the time of their first birth. As shown in table 1, 18 percent of the cohabiting mothers in the sample and 34 percent of single mothers were teen parents, compared with only about 4 percent of the married mothers. Because having a child at a young age can disrupt educational attainment, it is not surprising that such parents would have less success in the labor market and experience greater economic difficulties as a result. Moreover, despite being relatively young, it is not uncommon for unwed mothers in FFCWS to have children with multiple partners. Table 1 shows that among mothers in fragile families with more than one child, 39 percent of cohabiting mothers and 35 percent of single mothers had a child by another father, compared with only 12 percent of married mothers. Though it is not yet clear what the implications of having children with multiple partners are for unwed families' economic conditions, multipartner fertility is associated in the FFCWS with lower levels of economic support from family, friends, and former partners, a dynamic we discuss further in the next section.[6]

Psychosocial Characteristics That Limit Earnings Capacity

That unmarried parents in the FFCWS report higher rates of poor overall health, emotional problems, and drug use than married parents points to another explanation for their lower earnings capacity.[7] For instance, as shown in table 1, 14 percent of cohabiting mothers are in poor or fair health, compared with 17 percent of single mothers and 10 percent of married mothers. Similarly, about 16 percent of unwed mothers (cohabiting and single) suffer from depression, compared with 13 percent of their married counterparts. Unwed mothers are most distinct from their married counterparts in the FFCWS in terms of heavy drinking and use of illegal drugs. About 8 percent of unwed mothers (cohabiting and single) report heavy drinking, compared with 2 percent of married mothers, and between 2 and 3 percent of unwed mothers (cohabiting and single) report using illegal drugs, compared with 0.3 percent of married mothers.

Research by Aurora Jackson, Marta Tienda, and Chien-Chung Huang, based on a subset of families in the FFCWS, revealed more specific information about the employability and earnings capacity of mothers given their capabilities in a variety of areas that are necessary for getting and keeping higher-wage jobs.[8] A summary index of conditions likely to limit earnings capacity included poor health, substance abuse, experiencing domestic violence, youth, lacking a high school diploma, having no work experience, and having three or more children. Notably this study found that the presence of these conditions differed by mothers' relationship status. Like Wendy Sigle-Rushton and Sara McLanahan,[9] they found that single mothers in fragile families are more likely to encounter multiple such conditions than are cohabiting mothers: 40.8 percent of cohabiting unwed mothers reported none of these conditions compared with 35.2 percent of noncohabiting unwed mothers. In fact, Jackson and her colleagues concluded that "single mothers who are neither romantically involved with their newborn child's father nor cohabiting with them have especially precarious economic circumstances and constitute the most fragile of all families."

In summary, it is clear that many mothers in fragile families will experience one or more significant barriers to higher-wage employment. These barriers may also make it hard to sustain a full-time year-round job. But even when they can secure sustained, full-time work, mothers in fragile families have low earnings capacity. Indeed, Jackson and colleagues' analysis suggests that most unwed mothers in the FFCWS would be poor even if they worked 1,500 hours a year, and near-poor if they worked full-time, year-round (2,000 hours). Sigle-Rushton and McLanahan report more specifically that only 5 percent of unmarried mothers in the FFCWS could support themselves and their children at more than twice the federal poverty level, given their average earnings.

Asset Levels

One way for households to weather economically difficult times is to tap assets. A home is the primary asset in American families, but mothers with low earnings are unlikely either to be able to accumulate assets or to purchase a home. In the FFCWS, about 50 percent of married-couple households live in a home that is owned, compared with only about 11 percent of cohabiting couples and less than 6 percent of single-mother families.[10] As Rebecca Blank and Michael Barr report, low-income households' access to financial institutions is also limited.[11]

All of these factors pose a problem for mothers and children in fragile families, particularly because without savings or credit, it is difficult to maintain income in challenging economic times. With unwed mothers depending heavily on their own earnings, their incomes will cycle more closely with the economy. As the economy dips, their hours of work may fall, job losses may increase, and earnings may drop, creating greater income shocks. Having no financial cushion also makes unwed mothers more vulnerable to ordinary problems such as needing to repair a malfunctioning car. If a mother cannot repair the car, she may lose her ability to get to work and consequently lose her job. A job loss, with its attendant earnings losses, could set in motion a cascade of other problems that will make it all the more difficult for her to escape poverty. According to Blank and Barr, policies aimed at increasing the saving rate of low-income households could be particularly beneficial, for access to liquid savings may be more important in situations like these than access to illiquid assets.[12]

Living Arrangements

By definition, mothers in fragile families are not married at the time of their child's birth. Though a large share of these mothers are cohabiting with the child's biological father when the child is born, many such unions eventually dissolve. This single status contributes to high rates of poverty because if a union dissolves (or is never formed in the first place), mothers lose the economies of scale that two-parent households can enjoy (although, as noted, most two-parent unwed households nevertheless experience serious economic hardship). Moreover, mothers who end their cohabiting relationships often lose some or all of the fathers' earnings as a source of income.

But even if all mothers in fragile families could count on receiving a certain share of fathers' earnings, it is not clear that these contributions would lift them out of poverty. Both mothers and fathers who have children outside of marriage are relatively economically disadvantaged. Indeed, fully 25 percent of unmarried fathers in the FFCWS were not working at a steady job around the time of the child's birth. These unmarried fathers are also highly likely to have been incarcerated at some point in their lives (see table 1), a characteristic that is often linked with poor employment prospects. Because fathers in fragile families are more likely to have low and unreliable incomes, they find it hard to support their families, leaving mothers to shoulder much of the breadwinning burden.[13] The article by Robert Lerman in this volume elaborates on the conditions and capabilities of unwed fathers in fragile families.

Living Arrangements at Birth

One of the key (and largely unexpected) findings from the FFCWS was that many unmarried parents were in committed or quasi-committed relationships at the time their child was born. Sigle-Rushton and McLanahan were the first to examine the living arrangements of unmarried mothers in the FFCWS as well as the correlates of these arrangements.[14] They found unwed mothers living in one of four arrangements: cohabiting in a traditional "nuclear structure"—in which only a mother, father, and children live together; cohabiting in a "partner-plus" structure—in which the parents live with at least one of the baby's grandparents or some other adult; noncohabiting and living alone; and noncohabiting but living with other adults. Sigle-Rushton and McLanahan found that just under half of the unmarried mothers in the FFCWS were cohabiting with their babies' fathers at the time of birth, and that about one-third of all unmarried mothers were living in "nuclear family arrangements." Although the nuclear arrangement was the most common for cohabiting couples, a substantial minority lived in more complex arrangements. Nearly 30 percent of the cohabiting couples (15 percent of the full sample) were living with some other adults in the "partner-plus" category. Only 17 percent of the mothers were living alone at the time of birth, and just over one-third were living outside a cohabiting union but with other adults. In short, a relatively small share of unwed mothers in the FFCWS sample fit the stereotypical description of a single mother raising her children alone.

Most surprising was the proportion of mothers in romantic relationships with the father despite being unwed and often living apart. Indeed, more than 80 percent of unmarried parents were romantically involved (including those who were and were not cohabiting at the time of the child's birth), and an additional 8 percent characterized themselves as "just friends." Less than 10 percent of mothers said they had "little or no contact" with their child's father. These very high rates of involvement with the child's father might lead one to question why the mothers suffer from such high rates of economic hardship. One reason, as noted, is that these fathers have relatively few resources with which to augment mothers' economic circumstances. Another reason, which is explored in the articles by Robert Lerman and by Sara McLanahan and Audrey Beck in this volume, is that these initial high rates of contact and involvement with the child's father tend to drop off over time.

Sigle-Rushton and McLanahan found mothers' socioeconomic characteristics varied among these living arrangements.[15] First, women living in less independent arrangements (that is, "partner-plus" or "other-adult") were the most likely to be experiencing a first birth and were on average younger (as were the fathers of their children). Given their more limited resources, it is not surprising that younger mothers are less likely to be living independently than older mothers. Conversely, women who lived alone and women who lived in nuclear households were older, which may reflect people's tendency to move to more independent living arrangements as they age.[16] Women who were living with their babies' fathers and some other adult (that is, "partner-plus" arrangements) were the youngest and had the least education, most likely reflecting selection into different living arrangements based on economic need.

Based on these patterns, Sigle-Rushton and McLanahan concluded that older and more educated women are more likely to cohabit as a nuclear family at the time of birth and are the least likely to live with other adults. Similarly, women whose partners are older and more educated are also more likely to be cohabiting as a nuclear family at the time of birth. Though it would be tempting to conclude, based on this evidence, that cohabitation in a nuclear arrangement confers economic benefits on mothers in fragile families, it is most likely the case that unwed mothers and fathers with a higher earnings capacity choose this type of living arrangement (as opposed to living with other adults or living alone) because of their own and their partners' human capital and earnings capacities. Thus, policy makers aiming to target assistance to fragile families with the highest rates of economic hardship might wish to focus on those who are either "doubling up" with older adults or living on their own with their children.

Living Arrangements over Time

Another key finding from the FFCWS is that despite professed "high hopes" for marriage, most unmarried parents were unable to maintain a stable union over time.[17] Only 15 percent of the initially unmarried couples were married at the time of the five-year interview, and only 36 percent were still romantically involved—a large decline from the 80 percent who were romantically involved at the child's birth. Among couples who were already cohabiting at birth, 26 percent eventually married and another 26 percent maintained their unwed cohabiting arrangement. Almost half of couples who were cohabiting at birth, then, had ended their romantic relationship by the five-year survey. Other analysis of the FFCWS sample has revealed that these families also experience high degrees of instability in living arrangements over time.[18] The article by McLanahan and Beck in this volume elaborates on these phenomena.

These relatively low rates of movement into marriage, high rates of relationship dissolution, and high rates of change in living arrangements likely play a role in the economic trajectories of mothers in fragile families, although the specific linkages and the causal direction of these linkages are not yet fully understood and likely depend on the type of relationship that forms and dissolves.[19]

Summary

A defining feature of the families of the unwed mothers who make up an ever-increasing share of the U.S. population is poverty and material hardship. Although large numbers of mothers in fragile families work, employment does not enable them to escape poverty. Most have very low earnings because they are poorly educated and have health and emotional problems, all of which can make it difficult to find or keep a well-remunerated full-time job. Mothers in fragile families also have very few assets to help cushion the financial blow of a job loss or an unexpected health problem. Consequently, such hardships are more likely to drive their families into a downward spiral of even more difficult economic circumstances.

The living arrangements of mothers in fragile families may account for some of their low household incomes but are clearly not the predominant factor given the similarity in household incomes between cohabiting and single mothers. High rates of relationship dissolution and frequent changes in living arrangements may also play a role in the economic conditions of mothers in fragile families, but their relative importance has not yet been established. The major contributor to the economic challenges facing mothers in fragile families is their low earnings capacity. In the next section, we describe how these mothers manage to make ends meet amid these economic challenges.

Figure 1. Fragile Families' Income Distribution

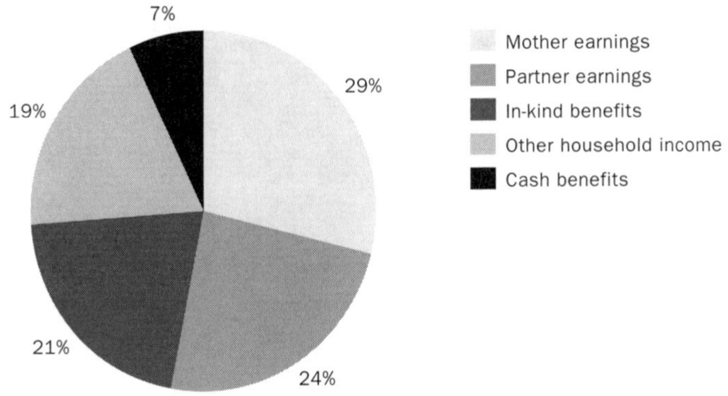

Source: Qin Gao and Irwin Garfinkel, "Income Packaging among Unwed Fragile Families: Variation across 20 Large U.S. Cities," Working Paper (School of Social Work, Columbia University, 2004).

Making Ends Meet: Mothers' Sources of Support in Fragile Families

In their 1997 study of low-income single mothers, Kathryn Edin and Laura Lein provided an answer to the question posed above: how do mothers in fragile families make ends meet? They found that unwed mothers seldom survived on income from paid work or welfare benefits alone.[20] Rather, the vast majority relied on a range of economic supports, including cash and in-kind benefits from public programs and help from relatives and friends. Despite substantial economic and policy changes since that time, Edin and Lein's findings still describe reality for many mothers in fragile families. Although most unwed mothers are employed, most also rely on public programs like welfare, food stamps, and public housing even as the numbers receiving cash assistance have declined. Moreover, as mothers in fragile families support children increasingly outside the welfare system, many are turning to private sources of support to ease their economic strain. In this section, we summarize the role that each income source and safety net plays in mothers' lives and what is known about how, together, they form fragile families' complex income packages.

Employment

With rising employment and declining welfare participation over the past fifteen years, unwed mothers' income packages have hinged increasingly on their own earnings. Thus, although mothers' earnings are relatively low, they nevertheless represent a significant share of mothers' total household income. In ongoing work with FFCWS data, Qin Gao and Irwin Garfinkel have parsed the proportion of mothers' total income package that comes from various sources, including own earnings, others' earnings, and cash and in-kind public benefits (see figure 1).[21] Among these sources, unwed mothers' own earnings account for nearly a third of the average household income package. Although exact estimates vary by subgroup of unwed mothers and income calculations, it is clear that mothers' own earnings make up an increasingly important part of fragile families' income.

Most mothers in fragile families also depend on other household members to make ends meet, which is one reason why cohabiting

Table 2. Sources of Support for Unwed Mothers in Fragile Families

Percent

Source of support	Cohabiting	Other relationship	No relationship	All unwed
Earnings from regular work	70	73	73	71
Public support				
WIC	83	84	84	83
Medicaid	66	73	73	70
Food stamps	42	53	51	48
TANF	24	41	40	33
Housing	22	30	30	26
Child care	14	18	19	16
Private support				
Father contributions*	100	89	53	86
From family or friends	57	70	72	64

Source: Julien O. Teitler, Nancy E. Reichman, and Lenna Nepomnyaschy, "Sources of Support, Child Care, and Hardship among Unwed Mothers, 1999–2001," *Social Service Review* 78, no. 1 (2004): 125–48. The survey included 1,299 cohabiting mothers, 928 mothers in other relationships, and 612 mothers in no relationship, totaling 2,839.
*Because of data limitations, it was assumed that all cohabiting mothers received father contributions.

and doubling up is so prevalent. Data from the FFCWS suggest that on average, income from cohabiting partners constitutes a quarter of the total household income package. That may be why cohabiting mothers in fragile families report slightly higher household incomes and somewhat lower levels of economic hardship than single mothers (although cohabiting mothers also earn more money than single mothers because of their higher levels of education).[22] Moreover, most unwed mothers in fragile families who are not cohabiting with romantic partners live with other adults who contribute earnings to the household income, as noted. The similarity of rates of employment across living arrangements suggests that most unwed fathers cannot support their families independently or that cohabiting men (and other adults) do not contribute enough of their income to reduce mothers' economic burden.[23] However, mothers' reliance on others' earnings also indicates that most do not shoulder the breadwinning responsibilities alone.

Public Programs

Most mothers in fragile families also depend on some type of cash or in-kind public benefit to make ends meet. Using data from the FFCWS, Julien Teitler, Nancy Reichman, and Lenna Nepomnyaschy found that one year after a nonmarital birth, 94 percent of the mothers were receiving some form of public support (see table 2 for unwed mothers' rates of receipt across public programs). According to the Survey of Income and Program Participation (SIPP), a national survey that provides information about the income and public program participation of individuals and households in the United States, 44 percent of all unwed mothers, who include never-married and divorced mothers, and 67 percent of never-married mothers participated in at least one government program in 2004.[24] Mothers' participation varies by specific program and by family composition, as does the role each plays in families' overall income packages. In this section we review these patterns, dividing public benefits into cash and in-kind benefits.

Cash Assistance Programs

The most direct source of cash assistance for low-income families is Temporary Assistance for Needy Families (TANF), which, as part of welfare reform in 1996, replaced a federal entitlement to cash benefits with time-limited, work-based assistance. Although welfare rolls have declined overall, TANF still serves an important economic function for many mothers in fragile families. According to data from the FFCWS, nearly one-third of unwed mothers received TANF benefits during the year following a nonmarital birth.[25] Rates of TANF participation were higher among mothers not cohabiting with the child's father than among cohabiting mothers, a pattern also found in an analysis of data from the 2001 Current Population Survey.[26] Still, according to both data sources, rates of TANF participation for cohabiting mothers resembled those of noncohabiting unwed mothers more than those of married mothers, suggesting that TANF plays an important role in the economic lives of fragile families regardless of family structure.

Despite fragile families' relatively high TANF participation rates, cash payments account for a small portion of their average income. Gao and Garfinkel estimate that among all unwed mothers in the FFCWS sample, income from TANF accounted for less than 5 percent of mothers' total income package, with in-kind benefits providing the lion's share after mothers' own earnings.[27] Among unwed mothers in the sample who received TANF or food stamps (most participants who receive TANF also receive food stamps), employed mothers received on average $2,500 and unemployed mothers received approximately $3,500 from TANF in the year after their child was born.[28] Lower TANF participation rates and the low value of TANF benefits may explain in part why unwed mothers are increasingly dependent on other forms of cash and in-kind public benefits.

As TANF caseloads plummeted after the mid-1990s, the numbers of low-income families, and unwed mothers in particular, receiving the earned income tax credit (EITC) substantially increased. The EITC, a refundable tax credit for low-income workers, disproportionately benefits families and single mothers. Its average value has increased substantially, from $601 in 1990 to $1,974 in 2007.[29] Because the credit is refundable, an unwed mother whose credit exceeds her taxes receives the difference in cash. Because it is a tax credit, payments increase with income up to a point, encouraging low-income unwed mothers to work even at very low-wage jobs. Janet Currie characterizes the EITC as a crucial part of unwed mothers' "invisible safety net" because it makes work pay, or at least pay more than it otherwise would.[30]

Because of the substantial value of the EITC for low-income families and its widespread use, the EITC likely constitutes a significant portion of working mothers' overall income package. According to estimates from the 2001 March Current Population Survey, the EITC represented 12 percent of net income for those in the lowest income quintile of unwed mothers.[31] According to Gao and Garfinkel's estimates, the EITC accounted for nearly one-third of unwed mothers' average cash benefits in the FFCWS, a significant proportion even if cash benefits overall accounted for a relatively small share of the total income package.[32] This finding underscores the importance of stable work for mothers in fragile families: losing employment today means losing not only one's income, but also a significant tax credit.

In-Kind Assistance Programs

In her 2006 book, *The Invisible Safety Net*, Janet Currie concludes that in-kind benefits such as food stamps and Medicaid constitute the most essential, though largely invisible, part of the public welfare system. She argues that in-kind benefits often make up the difference between low-income families' household earnings and what it costs to buy family essentials like food, shelter, medical care, and child care. For mothers in fragile families, in-kind benefits are the most commonly used public programs and represent the largest share of household income from public sources, contributing as much to mothers' income packages as their earnings. In Currie's words, these programs form "a broad-reaching and comprehensive net that especially protects young children in low-income families."[33]

The largest provider of food assistance to low-income families is the food stamp program, now called the Supplemental Nutrition Assistance Program (SNAP). The value of food stamps depends on household size and income, but the allotment is typically substantial enough to deflect a family's spending away from food to other essentials in a meaningful way. Thus food assistance serves a particularly important purpose in unwed mothers' economic support systems.

Changes in food stamp participation rates over the past ten years indicate the program has become a more important source of support for fragile families—and increasingly so since the economy entered into recession in 2007.[34] In the FFCWS, nearly half of unwed mothers received food stamps one year after a nonmarital birth, with higher participation rates among noncohabiting mothers.[35] Indeed, Teitler and colleagues estimated that unwed mothers in the FFCWS who received food stamps and were employed received about $2,000 on average in yearly benefits, and those who were unemployed received about $2,500. The same mothers received on average $2,500 and $3,500, respectively, in TANF benefits, suggesting that for mothers who receive either type of benefit, food stamps represent a substantial portion of mothers' total in-kind benefits—less than Medicaid and housing assistance but as much as other sources of food assistance and more than child care assistance.[36]

Food stamps may help mothers in fragile families by helping to keep household consumption consistent during times of relationship instability. According to a study by Daphne Hernandez and Kathleen Ziol-Guest, unwed mothers in the FFCWS were more likely to enroll in the food stamp program after exiting a cohabiting union and more likely to leave the program after entering a cohabiting union.[37] If food stamps help most when they offset income lost after a union dissolution, mothers in fragile families may depend on them more than other unwed mothers owing to their higher levels of relationship turbulence.

The U.S. Department of Agriculture's Women, Infants, and Children (WIC) program serves fewer families overall and has a lower dollar value than food stamps, but it may play a more important economic role for mothers in fragile families because it helps families with young children secure foods with high nutritional value.[38] Perhaps for this reason, more than 80 percent of unwed mothers in the FFCWS reported receiving WIC one year after the focal child's birth,[39] compared with about half who reported food stamp participation and 66 percent who reported receiving Medicaid. According to Gao and Garfinkel, WIC benefits made

For mothers in fragile families, in-kind benefits are the most commonly used public programs and represent the largest share of household income from public sources, contributing as much to mothers' income packages as their earnings.

up a sizable portion of fragile families' total in-kind benefits, similar in proportion to housing and food stamps. Together, WIC and food stamps made up a larger portion of fragile families' in-kind benefits than housing assistance.[40]

Janet Currie hails the expansion of publicly funded health care coverage for low-income children over the past fifteen years, largely through Medicaid and the State Child Health Insurance Program (SCHIP), as "a tremendous success story." Of all in-kind assistance programs, public health insurance is by far the most widely used among unwed mothers, with 28 percent participating in either Medicaid, Medicare, or other public insurance in 2008.[41] As with other public programs, mothers in fragile families are more likely to receive Medicaid than are unwed mothers overall. In the year following a nonmarital birth, 70 percent of all unwed mothers in the FFCWS received Medicaid.[42] Again, as with other programs, mothers in cohabiting relationships were less likely to receive Medicaid than those in noncohabiting relationships or those with no relationship with the child's father.

Because public health insurance covers expenses that are by definition irregular, it is not as clear how Medicaid affects unwed mothers' economic support systems. However, a few points are clear. First, because a mother in a fragile family no longer needs to receive welfare to have her child covered by Medicaid, the current public health insurance system does not discourage work—or the income that comes with it—the way it did before welfare reform. Second, patterns of cycling on and off Medicaid or SCHIP coverage, often called "churning," suggest that many mothers apply for Medicaid when their child needs specific medical services, ones she could not afford without insurance. In this way, public health insurance allows, and thus encourages, families to keep their incomes above the poverty line, and can in many cases defray very high medical costs for families living at the economic margins. Assuming average annual Medicaid payments for each eligible household child, Gao and Garfinkel estimated that Medicaid payments constituted the largest single share of unwed mothers' in-kind benefits.

The goal of public housing assistance is to reduce housing costs and improve housing quality for low-income families. Because housing often makes up a substantial portion of the typical family's budget, housing assistance by definition should represent an essential part of single mothers' economic support system. It also ensures that recipients' living conditions have at least a minimum standard of quality, despite public concern over the health and safety conditions in housing projects. Housing assistance, however, is not an entitlement, and many poor and low-income families who want and need housing assistance cannot get it, making it a system that works well for those who win assistance, but that leaves many out entirely.

Among mothers in fragile families, housing assistance plays a role similar to TANF benefits. More than a quarter of all unwed mothers in the FFCWS received some type of housing assistance in the year after a nonmarital birth, compared with about one-third receiving TANF, and many who received one form of assistance also received the other.[43] Thus, although most mothers in fragile families do not receive housing assistance or welfare, for those who do, housing assistance constitutes a significant proportion of their in-kind benefits. Not surprisingly, cohabiting mothers are less likely to receive housing assistance than mothers who live alone, or with family, presumably because cohabiting mothers' higher household incomes enable more of them to afford housing or because more of these households are ineligible for assistance. Thus, housing assistance, like TANF benefits, is a particularly important source of income for mothers who live without romantic partners or other adults.

Of all forms of in-kind assistance, however, child care may be the most crucial to fragile families' economic well-being even if its cash value is not always as high as that of housing or food assistance. With the new work requirements and time limits for cash assistance under TANF, nearly all low-income mothers must work. Child care is expensive, particularly for young children. Although poor families pay less for child care than wealthier families, they spend a larger share of their income on it than other families (25 percent compared with 7 percent), at least among those who pay out-of-pocket for care.[44] Without public assistance to help pay for child care, full-time employment would be untenable for many mothers in fragile families.

Acknowledging this dilemma, the federal government has substantially expanded funding for subsidized child care since putting welfare reform into place. Much of the funding flows through the Child Care and Development Fund (CCDF), a consolidation of various child care subsidy programs for low-income families and now the federal government's largest child care program.[45] Mothers can use the subsidy to pay for either center- or home-based care, including, in many states, care provided by relatives. The federal government also funds Early Head Start and Head Start, center-based interventions for poor and low-income children from birth to age five. Finally, states such as Oklahoma, Georgia, and New York now provide universal prekindergarten (UPK) programs to all children regardless of economic status. In 2002, an estimated 13 percent of poor families with preschoolers received some kind of government help to pay for preschool, and this percentage may undercount children in publicly funded preschool programs like UPK.[46]

Government-funded child care helps mothers in fragile families in two key ways. First, it reduces their out-of-pocket costs for care—costs that the vast majority could not likely afford. Using data from the FFCWS and a sample of mothers on a wait list for child care subsidies, Nicole Forry found that subsidy receipt reduced mothers' monthly child care costs by more than $250 and reduced the share of household income spent on child care by 10 to 14 percentage points.[47] In a study of nine experimental evaluations of twenty-one welfare and employment programs, Lisa Gennetian and her colleagues found that programs offering enhanced child care assistance prevented mothers' child care costs from rising even though their work hours increased, unlike programs that did not offer enhanced child care assistance, and reduced child care expenses for mothers of preschoolers.[48] For families at the economic margins, these cost savings may make other child-related needs, such as enriching children's home learning environments, far more affordable.

Second, and perhaps more important, subsidized child care allows mothers to work when they might not otherwise be able to do so. Using data from the 1999 National Survey of American Families, David Blau and Erdal Tekin found that child care subsidies increased employment among unwed mothers by as much as 33 percentage points and reduced unemployment by 20 percentage points.[49] Subsidies not only increase the likelihood mothers will work but they increase the hours worked and employment duration, both because assistance makes care more affordable and also because it can decrease child care instability.[50] For instance, a substantial proportion of mothers in the FFCWS report having their child care "fall through" so that it disrupted their work schedules.[51] But, using the same data, Nicole Forry and Sandra Hofferth found that child care–related work disruptions were far less likely among child care subsidy recipients.[52] For lowering costs of care and promoting stable employment, subsidized child care plays an essential role in many mothers' economic support systems.

Despite its potential benefits, not all eligible mothers receive child care assistance. Child care subsidies are a block grant rather than an entitlement, and many states can cover only a fraction of those mothers who are eligible.[53] Moreover, research suggests that many eligible mothers do not apply for subsidies because they are either unaware of the program or unable to navigate its administrative complexities.[54] These dynamics produce the seemingly incongruous result of long waiting lists and low take-up rates for child care subsidies in many states. Head Start is not a reliable alternative for many of these mothers because it has never been funded adequately to allow all eligible children to participate. Universal prekindergarten programs offer an attractive and dependable option but serve only preschool-aged children and are available in only a handful of states. Consequently, mothers often turn to private sources of child care among their friends and family. These arrangements, often called kith and kin care, no doubt help mothers economically and emotionally if the arrangement is free or low-cost and if they trust the provider to keep their child safe. However, quality in these arrangements is typically lower than in center-based programs.[55] As a result, with or without government-funded child care assistance, many mothers in fragile families are often left with few affordable, high-quality child care options.

Private Support

Edin and Lein's study of low-income single mothers described how the costs of working often outweighed the benefits.[56] Although most mothers they interviewed could get jobs (83 percent had some formal work experience), many had a hard time making ends meet because costs of child care, medical care, transportation, housing, and clothing for work increased when they left welfare. Overwhelmingly, those working mothers whom Edin and Lein identified as "wage-reliant" turned to cohabiting relatives or boyfriends and other relatives and friends to provide extra cash, essentials like diapers and food, free child care, and access to transportation. Edin and Lein see these forms of private economic support as the "private safety net" that mothers often need in addition to earnings and the public safety net of welfare, food assistance, and housing assistance.

Although the expansion of work supportive programs like the EITC and child care assistance has improved the trade-off between work and welfare for unwed mothers, private safety nets still play a crucial role in fragile families' economic survival. According to research from the FFCWS, the vast majority of unwed mothers received financial or instrumental help from partners, relatives, or friends in the years following an unwed birth. For example, Teitler and colleagues report that 96 percent of unwed mothers received cash or in-kind support from private sources, with 86 percent receiving help from the children's fathers and 64 percent from family or friends (see table 2).[57] Employed mothers were just as likely to receive help from private sources as were unemployed mothers, and most mothers in both groups received both public and private support of some kind. For all unwed mothers in fragile families, private support was the most common form of economic help received next to own earnings and WIC food assistance, suggesting that private safety nets are essential regardless of employment status.

Although the vast majority of mothers in fragile families receive private economic support, the source and availability of support vary by mothers' relationship status.

Although the vast majority of mothers in fragile families receive private economic support, the source and availability of support vary by mothers' relationship status. For instance, data from the FFCWS suggest that cohabiting mothers relied more often on their partners for cash assistance, in-kind gifts, and instrumental help with child care and transportation than on other family members, whereas single, or noncohabiting, mothers relied more often on family and friends, particularly when they had no relationship with the father.[58] Mothers' fertility patterns also affect the overall availability of private support. Kristin Harknett found that unwed mothers in the FFCWS with children by more than one man reported significantly less available support than those with children by one man.[59] She concluded from these patterns that smaller, denser kin networks offer stronger private safety nets than broader, weaker ties of the kind multipartnered fertility might bring. Thus, assuming sources of support are relatively interchangeable, multipartnered fertility puts mothers in fragile families at greater risk for low levels of private support than does nonmarital childbirth itself.

Cash Assistance

Cash assistance from private networks is a small but important part of many single mothers' economic support systems. Edin and Lein found that among the 165 wage-reliant mothers they interviewed, nearly half received some cash from private networks in a typical month, excluding nonresident fathers, with an average of $140 from family and friends and $226 from boyfriends among those who received any help.[60] More recently, Melissa Radey and Yolanda Padilla estimated that nearly 30 percent of unwed mothers in the FFCWS received cash from family or friends, excluding fathers, three years after a nonmarital birth, with the average being $1,172 a year or about $100 a month.[61] Typically, this cash is used to make up the difference in a given month between earned income, cash assistance, and the money needed to buy food, pay rent and utilities, or cover emergency expenses like car repairs. Other studies suggest that although many unwed mothers rely on cash assistance from social networks periodically, the size of private cash loans is typically small, accounting for no more than 5 percent of mothers' income.[62] In this way, cash assistance from private sources may help mothers cope during stressful times but does not fundamentally change their economic circumstances.

In-Kind Assistance

A more common form of private support from family and friends than cash loans is in-kind assistance like presents for children and household items. Mothers in Edin and Lein's study reported regularly receiving household essentials like diapers and groceries as well as coveted clothes and toys for children from family members, boyfriends, and nonresident fathers.[63] Recently, in a qualitative study of mothers participating in the New Hope Project, a work support program for low-income families in Milwaukee, Eboni Howard found that material assistance was the most prevalent—and perceived to be the most helpful—type of informal support mothers received.[64] In the FFCWS, most nonresident fathers who were romantically involved with the mother bought children clothes, toys, medicine, or food at least sometimes, although fathers' in-kind assistance, like informal child support, was much less frequent when parents were not romantically involved.[65] In-kind contributions not only fill in essential gaps in the monthly budget, but also allow mothers to provide their children with nonessential items that enhance their own and their children's subjective sense of well-being.

Instrumental Assistance

In addition to direct forms of private cash and in-kind economic assistance, single mothers often rely on their private networks to provide instrumental assistance they might not otherwise afford. Edin and Lein emphasized the importance of emergency and regular child care that relatives provide. This care was most often provided by children's maternal grandmothers and was both low-cost and potentially preferable to the low-quality center-based care available in poor communities.[66] The vast majority of unwed mothers in the FFCWS—86 percent of cohabiting mothers and 91 percent of single mothers—reported someone in their social network would provide child care in an emergency, a necessity when regular child care arrangements fall through. Family and friends also provide mothers with transportation to and from work, which, for many mothers, can mean the difference between keeping and losing a job. Using data from the FFCWS, research by Michelle Livermore and Rebecca Powers[67] and also by Melissa Radey[68] found that mothers who received social support from family and friends to save money were more likely to be employed than mothers who received no such support, even when the mothers being compared had similar employment records in the previous year. Kristin Harknett reached similar conclusions examining employment patterns in a sample of former welfare recipients.[69] Overall, all of these forms of assistance—cash, in-kind economic support, and instrumental assistance—may serve two important economic purposes: to make ends meet and to facilitate employment.

Instability of Private Support

Although most mothers in fragile families receive some kind of help from social networks at some point, private forms of support differ from public benefits in that they are often unpredictable and inconsistent. Using both quantitative and qualitative data from the FFCWS (the latter drawn from a subsample of the larger study), Sarah Meadows documented the mismatch between unwed mothers' expectations of financial and instrumental support from family and friends and their actual receipt of it.[70] Approximately one-third of unwed mothers expected their social networks to provide financial and instrumental assistance in an emergency but did not receive help when they needed it, an experience strongly linked with the emergence of major depression five years after an unwed birth. To the extent that poorer mental health can undermine mothers' employability, the unpredictability and inconsistency of private support networks can place mothers in fragile families in double jeopardy.

Summary

Mothers in fragile families make ends meet by relying on many different sources of income and support. The vast majority are wage-reliant, in Edin and Lein's terms, meaning that the largest share of their income comes from own earnings. But because unwed mothers' incomes are low on average, most also depend on earnings from cohabiting partners and relatives. Mothers' and others' earnings, combined, make up more than half of the average household income in fragile families. Such dependency on others' earnings means that mothers' total incomes rise and fall with the economy. For families without wealth or assets to help weather unexpected adversity, instability could precipitate income shocks and financial crises with grave consequences for mothers and children.

To mitigate these shocks, the vast majority of mothers in fragile families rely on at least one public benefit. Since welfare was reformed in 1996, cash assistance, such as TANF, has become a less important source of income for fragile families, while in-kind assistance, such as food stamps, housing assistance, and Medicaid, has become more important. Thus, although roughly one-third of mothers in fragile families received welfare in the year after a nonmarital birth, cash assistance accounted for little of their average income package. By contrast, in-kind benefits accounted for nearly a quarter. More than cash programs, the invisible safety net of in-kind benefits safeguards mothers and children against the worst outcomes of life at the economic margins.

To close the economic gaps left by earnings and public support, mothers in fragile families sometimes receive help from partners, family, and friends. Periodic cash, in-kind, and instrumental assistance from private networks can prevent financial crises in times of need, and stable forms of assistance, such as child care, can promote job stability. In these ways, private support is essential to unwed mothers' economic survival. However, unlike public support, private safety nets are not always consistent and dependable. Thus, assistance from private sources may help mothers cope during stressful times but may not fundamentally improve their economic circumstances unless it is offered consistently and over long periods of time.

Conclusion

Mothers in fragile families experience higher rates of poverty and material hardship than their married counterparts. Although a large share of these mothers cohabit with their child's father, and many more live with other adults, unwed mothers have similar rates of economic hardship across a variety of living arrangements. Differences in economic well-being are far larger between mothers in fragile families and married mothers than among unwed mothers in different living arrangements, making clear that living arrangements do not primarily drive economic conditions in this population.

The primary cause of poverty and material hardship, instead, appears to be unwed mothers' (and fathers') low earnings. The limited ability of mothers in fragile families to command high wages stems from low education as well as physical, emotional, and mental health problems. Indeed, very few unmarried mothers in the FFCWS could support themselves and their children at more than twice the federal poverty level, given their average earnings. Moreover, mothers with low earnings are unlikely to be able to accumulate assets or purchase a home, and a lack of assets can exacerbate financial difficulties.

Given these economic challenges, how do mothers in fragile families make ends meet? As we have shown, various public programs, particularly those that provide in-kind assistance, do successfully lessen economic hardship in fragile families. However, many of the most effective programs, such as the EITC, hinge on mothers' employment. As the nation's economy emerges painfully slowly from recession, there is reason for concern about the stability of the public safety net for single mothers, particularly those with little education and other barriers to employment. Henceforth, single mothers may turn more often to private sources of support for cash, in-kind, and instrumental assistance. Although private safety nets are essential to many mothers' economic survival, they may not facilitate long-term economic mobility.

Among promising policy prescriptions to bolster fragile families' economic supports, perhaps the most important is to strengthen the public safety net, particularly the "invisible safety net" of in-kind benefits, to help families cope in an unstable economy. Moreover, as more single mothers enter the labor market in today's weak economy, it may become increasingly important to have a private safety net. A next step would thus be to strengthen the availability and efficacy of community-based programs that mimic private financial or instrumental support when mothers cannot receive it from their networks. Examples include programs that provide emergency cash assistance and food aid directly as well as programs to foster and perhaps formalize the provision of loans, child care, and in-kind assistance among families. Overall, it is important for policy makers to recognize that with rates of nonmarital childbirth at their current level, and potentially rising still, fragile families are likely an enduring fixture among U.S. families. It is thus essential to strengthen policies that both support their economic self-sufficiency and alleviate their hardship during inevitable times of economic distress.

Endnotes

1. Sara McLanahan, "Children in Fragile Families," Working Paper 09-16-FF (Princeton: Center for Research on Child Wellbeing, 2009).
2. Susan E. Mayer and Christopher Jencks, "Poverty and the Distribution of Material Hardship," *Journal of Human Resources* 24, no. 1 (1989): 88–114.
3. Julien O. Teitler, Nancy E. Reichman, and Lenna Nepomnyaschy, "Sources of Support, Child Care, and Hardship among Unwed Mothers, 1999–2001," *Social Service Review* 78, no. 1 (2004): 125–48.
4. Melissa Radey, "The Influence of Social Supports on Employment for Hispanic, Black, and White Unmarried Mothers," *Journal of Family and Economic Issues* 29 (2008): 445–60.
5. Carol Ann MacGregor, "Education Delayed: Family Structure and Postnatal Educational Attainment," Working Paper 09-07-FF (Princeton: Center for Research on Child Wellbeing, 2009).
6. Kristen Harknett and Jean Knab, "More Kin, Less Support: Multipartnered Fertility and Perceived Support among Mothers," *Journal of Marriage and Family* 69 (2007): 237–53.
7. Michelle DeKlyen and others, "The Mental Health of Married, Cohabiting, and Non-Coresident Parents with Infants," *American Journal of Public Health* 96, no. 10 (2006): 1836–41.
8. Aurora P. Jackson, Marta Tienda, and Chien-Chung Huang, "Capabilities and Employability of Unwed Mothers," *Children and Youth Services Review* 23, nos. 4–5 (2001): 327–51.
9. Wendy Sigle-Rushton and Sara McLanahan, "For Richer or Poorer? Marriage as an Anti-Poverty Strategy in the United States," *Population* 57, no. 3 (2002): 509–26.
10. Christine Percheski, "Maternal Employment after a Birth: Examining Variations by Family Structure," Working Paper 08-18-FF (Princeton: Center for Research on Child Wellbeing, 2008).
11. Rebecca Blank and Michael Barr, *Insufficient Funds: Savings, Assets, Credit, and Banking among Low-Income Households* (New York: Russell Sage Press, 2009).
12. Ibid.
13. Sigle-Rushton and McLanahan, "For Richer or Poorer?" (see note 9).
14. Wendy Sigle-Rushton and Sara McLanahan, "The Living Arrangements of New Unmarried Mothers," *Demography* 39, no. 3 (2002): 415–33.
15. Ibid.
16. Rebecca A. London, "The Interaction between Single Mothers' Living Arrangements and Welfare Participation," *Journal of Policy Analysis and Management* 19, no. 1 (2000): 93–117.
17. McLanahan, "Children in Fragile Families" (see note 1).
18. Cynthia Osborne and Sara S. McLanahan, "Partnership Instability and Child Wellbeing," *Journal of Marriage and Family* 69, no. 4 (2007): 1065–83.
19. Sarah Meadows, Sara McLanahan, and Jean Knab, "Economic Trajectories in Non-Traditional Families with Children," Working Paper 09-10-FF (Princeton: Center for Research on Child Wellbeing, 2009).

20. Kathryn Edin and Laura Lein, *Making Ends Meet: How Single Mothers Survive Welfare and Low-Wage Work* (New York: Russell Sage Foundation, 1997).

21. Qin Gao and Irwin Garfinkel, "Income Packaging among Unwed Fragile Families: Variation across 20 Large U.S. Cities," Working Paper (School of Social Work, Columbia University, 2004).

22. Sigle-Rushton and McLanahan, "The Living Arrangements" (see note 14).

23. Catherine Kenney, "Cohabiting Couple, Filing Jointly? Resource Pooling and U.S. Poverty Policies," *Family Relations* 53, no. 2 (2004): 237–47.

24. Jane Lawler Dye, "Participation of Mothers in Government Assistance Programs: 2004," Current Population Reports May 2008, U.S. Bureau of the Census (www.census.gov/prod/2008pubs/p70-116.pdf [accessed May 26, 2009]).

25. Julien O. Teitler, Nancy E. Reichman, and Lenna Nepomnyaschy, "Determinants of TANF Participation: A Multilevel Analysis," *Social Service Review* 81, no. 4 (2007): 633–56.

26. U.S. Department of Health and Human Services, "Public Assistance Use among Two-Parent Families: An Analysis of TANF and Food Stamp Program Eligibility and Participation," research brief (Office of the Assistant Secretary for Planning and Evaluation, 2005).

27. Gao and Garfinkel, "Income Packaging" (see note 21).

28. Ibid.

29. Tax Policy Center, "Earned Income Tax Credit: Number of Recipients and Amount of Credit, 1975–2007," Urban Institute and Brookings Institution (http://taxpolicycenter.org/taxfacts/displayafact.cfm?Docid=37 [accessed Sept. 22, 2009]).

30. Janet M. Currie, *The Invisible Safety Net: Protecting the Nation's Poor Children and Families* (Princeton University Press, 2006).

31. Ibid.

32. Gao and Garfinkel, "Income Packaging" (see note 21).

33. Currie, *The Invisible Safety Net* (see note 30).

34. House Ways and Means Committee, *Green Book 2004: Background Material and Data on the Programs within the Jurisdiction of the Committee on Ways and Means,* 108th Cong., 2nd sess. (Washington: Government Printing Office, 2004).

35. Teitler, Reichman, and Nepomnyaschy, "Sources of Support" (see note 3).

36. Gao and Garfinkel, "Income Packaging" (see note 21).

37. Daphne C. Hernandez and Kathleen M. Ziol-Guest, "Income Volatility and Family Structure Patterns: Association with Stability and Change in Food Stamp Program Participation," *Journal and Family Economic Issues* 30 (2009): 357–71.

38. Douglas J. Besharov and Peter Germanis, "Welfare Reform—Four Years Later," *Public Interest* 140 (2000): 17–35.

39. Teitler, Reichman, and Nepomnyaschy, "Sources of Support" (see note 3).

40. Gao and Garfinkel, "Income Packaging" (see note 21).

41. Joanna Turner, Michel Boudreaux, and Victoria Lynch, "A Preliminary Evaluation of Health Insurance Coverage in the 2008 American Community Survey," Working Paper, health insurance (U.S. Bureau of the Census, 2009).

42. Teitler, Reichman, and Nepomnyaschy, "Sources of Support" (see note 3).

43. Ibid.

44. Julia Overturf Johnson, "Who's Minding the Kids? Child Care Arrangements: Winter 2002," Current Population Reports, October 2005, U.S. Bureau of the Census (www.census.gov/prod/2005pubs/p70-101.pdf [accessed Sept. 22, 2009]).

45. Child Care Bureau, "Average Monthly Adjusted Number of Families and Children Served (FFY 2006)," U.S. Department of Health and Human Services, Administration for Children and Families (www.acf.hhs.gov/programs/ccb/data/ccdf_data/06acf800/table1.htm [accessed Sept. 22, 2009]).

46. Johnson, "Who's Minding the Kids?" (see note 44).

47. Nicole D. Forry, "The Impact of Child Care Subsidies on Low-Income Single Parents: An Examination of Child Care Expenditures and Family Finances," *Journal of Family and Economic Issues* 30, no. 1 (2009): 43–54.

48. Lisa A. Gennetian and others, "Can Child Care Assistance in Welfare and Employment Programs Support the Employment of Low-Income Families?" *Journal of Policy Analysis and Management* 23, no. 4 (2004): 723–43.

49. David Blau and Erdal Tekin, "The Determinants and Consequences of Child Care Subsidies for Single Mothers in the USA," *Journal of Population Economics* 20, no. 4 (2007): 719–41.

50. Gennetian and others, "Can Child Care Assistance in Welfare and Employment Programs" (see note 48).

51. Margaret L. Usdansky and Douglas A. Wolf, "When Child Care Breaks Down: Mothers' Experiences with Child Care Problems and Resulting Missed Work," *Journal of Family Issues* 29, no. 9 (2008): 1185–1210.

52. Nicole D. Forry and Sandra L. Hofferth, "Maintaining Work: The Influence of Child Care Subsidies on Child Care–Related Work Disruptions," Working Paper 09-09-FF (Princeton: Center for Research on Child Wellbeing, 2009).

53. Karen Schulman and Helen Blank, "State Child Care Assistance Policies 2008: Too Little Progress for Children and Families," issue brief (National Women's Law Center, 2008).

54. Gina Adams, Kathleen Snyder, and Jodi R. Sandfort, "Getting and Retaining Child Care Assistance: How Policy and Practice Influence Parents' Experiences," Occasional Paper 55, Assessing the New Federalism (Urban Institute, 2002).

55. Elizabeth Rigby, Rebecca M. Ryan, and Jeanne Brooks-Gunn, "Child Care Quality in Different State Policy Contexts," *Journal of Policy Analysis and Management* 26, no. 4 (2007): 887–908.

56. Edin and Lein, *Making Ends Meet* (see note 20).

57. Teitler, Reichman, and Nepomnyaschy, "Sources of Support" (see note 3).

58. Ibid.

59. Harknett and Knab, "More Kin, Less Support" (see note 6).

60. Edin and Lein, *Making Ends Meet* (see note 20).

61. Melissa Radey and Yolanda C. Padilla, "Kin Financial Support: Receipt and Provision among Unmarried Mothers," *Journal of Social Service Research* 35, no. 4 (2009): 336–51.

62. Julia R. Henly, Sandra K. Danziger, and Shira Offer, "The Contribution of Social Support to the Material Well-Being of Low-Income Families," *Journal of Marriage and Family* 67, no. 1 (2005): 122–40.

63. Edin and Lein, *Making Ends Meet* (see note 20).

64. Eboni C. Howard, "The Informal Social Support, Well-Being, and Employment Pathways of Low-Income Mothers," in *Making It Work: Low-Wage Employment, Family Life, and Child Development,* edited by Hirokazu Yoshikawa, Thomas S. Weisner, and Edward D. Lowe (New York: Russell Sage Foundation, 2006).

65. Rebecca M. Ryan, Ariel Kalil, and Kathleen M. Ziol-Guest, "Longitudinal Patterns of Nonresident Fathers' Involvement: The Role of Resources and Relations," *Journal of Marriage and Family* 70, no. 4 (2008): 962–77.

66. Susanna Loeb and others, "Child Care in Poor Communities: Early Learning Effects by Type, Quality, and Stability," *Child Development* 75, no. 1 (2004): 47–65.

67. Michelle M. Livermore and Rebecca S. Powers, "Employment of Unwed Mothers: The Role of Government and Social Support," *Journal of Family and Economic Issues* 27 (2006): 479–94.

68. Radey, "The Influence of Social Supports" (see note 4).

69. Kristen Harknett, "The Relationship between Private Safety Nets and Economic Outcomes among Single Mothers," *Journal of Marriage and Family* 68, no. 1 (2006): 172–91.

70. Sarah O. Meadows, "Is It There When You Need It? Mismatch in Perception of Future Availability and Subsequent Receipt of Instrumental Social Support," *Journal of Family Issues* 30 (2009): 1070–97.

Capabilities and Contributions of Unwed Fathers

Robert I. Lerman

Summary

Young, minority, and poorly educated fathers in fragile families have little capacity to support their children financially and are hard-pressed to maintain stability in raising those children. In this article, Robert Lerman examines the capabilities and contributions of unwed fathers, how their capabilities and contributions fall short of those of married fathers, how those capabilities and contributions differ by the kind of relationship the fathers have with their child's mother, and how they change as infants grow into toddlers and kindergartners.

Unwed fathers' employment and earnings vary widely among groups but generally rise over time. At the child's birth, cohabiting fathers earn nearly 20 percent more than noncohabiting unwed fathers, and the gap widens over time. Still, five years after an unwed birth, the typical unwed father is working full time for the full year. Although most unwed fathers spend considerable time with their children in the years soon after birth, explains Lerman, over time their involvement erodes. Men who lose touch with their children are likely to see their earnings stagnate, provide less financial support, and often face new obligations when they father children with another partner. By contrast, the unwed fathers who marry or cohabit with their child's mother earn considerably higher wages and work substantially more than unwed fathers who do not marry or cohabit. These results suggest that unwed fathers' earnings are affected by family relationships as well as their education and work experience.

Lerman notes that several factors influence the extent to which unwed fathers stay involved with their children. Better-educated fathers, those who most identify with the father's role, and those with good relationships with the child's mother, are most likely to sustain a relationship with their children. Some studies even find that strong child support enforcement increases father involvement. For many years, policy makers approached the problem of noncustodial, unwed fathers on a single track—by trying to increase their child support payments. Today's policy makers are recognizing the limits of that strategy. New programs focus on improving the relationship and communication skills of unwed fathers. In addition, targeted training programs, such as apprenticeships, enable unwed fathers to earn a salary while they learn skills.

www.futureofchildren.org

Robert I. Lerman is a professor of economics at American University and an institute fellow at the Urban Institute.

Unwed fathers are a heterogeneous and evolving group. Many become fathers when they are quite young and have little ability to support a family above the poverty threshold. About half begin their experience as a father living with their child and cohabiting with the child's mother. Although the rest do not live with their newborn child, most have a romantic relationship with their child's mother and are closely involved with the infant. Over time, however, the fathers' involvement with their children erodes; when the children reach age five, only about 36 percent of fathers live with their child and of those who live apart, half have not visited the child within the previous month.[1]

The majority of unwed fathers are men with a modest or poor education. Only about 12 percent have an associate's or bachelor's degree, a rate far below the 35 to 40 percent figure among all men. Only about one in four earns more than $25,000 a year. Young unwed fathers have extremely low earnings, and many survive economically by living with parents or other family members. They pay little in child support, but they do spend considerable time with their children in the years soon after birth. As their earnings increase, their financial support increases as well, but connections with their children often fray. Men who lose touch with their children often experience additional problems. They are likely to see their earnings stagnate, they are less likely to provide financial support, and they often find themselves with new obligations when they father children with another partner. Even when unwed fathers pay child support, their contributions—in cash and time—to their child's well-being are far less than they would be if they were resident fathers.

By contrast, the unwed fathers who marry or move in with their child's mother follow a more positive path. They earn considerably higher wages and work substantially more than unwed fathers who do not marry or cohabit. Among noncustodial fathers aged twenty-five to thirty-nine, married high school dropouts earn about $2,700 more than unwed high school graduates (with no college) and $16,000 more than unwed high school dropouts.[2] Although many unwed fathers marry or cohabit with their child's mother at least temporarily, most do not. The tendency of unwed fathers to increase their earnings substantially when they marry or cohabit indicates that many are not realizing their full earnings potential. Another possibility is that an unrelated improvement in their labor market situation made these fathers more successful in the marriage market.

The better educated the unwed father, the higher his earnings and the more rapidly his earnings grow; high school graduates earn 25 to 33 percent more than dropouts.[3] In the Fragile Families and Child Wellbeing Study sample of men who became fathers in the late 1990s, more than one-third of unwed fathers had not completed high school. In that sample, dropping out of school was closely associated with having been incarcerated; 45 percent of fathers who had been in prison previously had not earned a high school degree. Thus, a significant share of fathers faced two critical barriers to attaining adequate earnings—both poor education and a history of imprisonment. In a national sample of unwed fathers drawn from the Survey of Income and Program Participation (SIPP), nearly 25 percent lacked a high school diploma. In both the Fragile Families and SIPP samples, although few unwed fathers earned an associate's or bachelor's degree, those who did so achieved solid levels of earnings.

Perhaps not surprisingly, given their modest resources and increasing disengagement from their children and their children's mothers, one-half to two-thirds of unwed fathers provide little or no financial support to their children. Over the past fifteen years, the child support system has made great strides in establishing paternity among this group, but it has been less successful in increasing total support payments, both formal and informal. The system may, however, be imposing impossible arrearage burdens, especially on incarcerated men, and its increasingly rigorous efforts to enforce support may have contributed to declining employment among black men.

Cumulatively, these findings about unwed fathers represent a serious national problem. With annual nonmarital births reaching 1.7 million—and nearly 40 percent of all births—unwed fathers will bear at least partial responsibility for raising a major segment of the coming generation.[4] The young, minority, and less educated parents who are having a large share of these births have little capacity to support their children financially and lack stability in raising them.

In this article, I examine the capabilities and contributions of fathers who are unmarried when their children are born. I focus first on their capabilities and economic circumstances. How do their capabilities differ from those of married fathers? How do their capabilities differ by the kind of relationship they have with their child's mother? How do their capabilities and earnings change as their infants grow into toddlers and kindergartners? Next, I look at the contributions of unwed fathers. How much financial and other support do they provide around the time the child is born, and how do those contributions change over time? Again, how does their relationship with the child's mother affect their contributions? Finally, I examine the relationship between their capabilities and their contributions. How do weak capabilities and other constraints limit these fathers' contributions to their children? What role do poor education and earnings potential, previous incarceration, and responsibilities for other children, respectively, play in curtailing their contributions?

Policy makers can draw on several tools to help unwed fathers and their families improve their living standards and possibly their relationships as well. The most promising approaches involve training in a work-based context linked to careers. Sectoral strategies that involve close linkages between industries and workforce agencies have proved successful in raising the earnings of less-skilled men. Expanding apprenticeship training is an especially attractive option for unwed fathers since they can earn a salary while they undergo training that ultimately yields a valuable credential. Another approach, training in couple-relationship skills, could strengthen marriage and cohabiting relationships, which in turn could increase earnings. In addition, some of the skills learned to improve couple relationships, such as communication and problem solving, are applicable to many jobs. Couple-relationship skills training could thus raise fathers' earnings and ultimately the living standards of their children.

Earnings Capabilities of Unwed Fathers

Unwed fathers' earnings capabilities and actual earnings should be central concerns of policy makers committed to raising the living standards of children, especially children at risk of poverty. Raising the earnings of unwed fathers is likely to improve the living standards of children, not only by enabling these fathers to make formal and informal child support payments but also, potentially, by increasing the likelihood that unwed fathers will marry their child's mother or live with her and their children.

Marriage and Child Poverty

Men generally can help their children either by providing adequate child support as a nonresident father or by supporting them directly as a married or cohabiting father. Although child support can help families avoid poverty and hardship, the marriage option is most favorable for children for at least three reasons. First, married fathers are more likely than unmarried fathers to help parent their children and increase their chances of long-run success. Second, married fathers are more likely to provide a stable source of income. And, third, marriage is associated with higher earnings and may induce men to maximize their earnings capabilities, again benefiting the entire family.[5]

The role of marriage in easing child poverty has been addressed by two studies that examine how trends in child poverty over the past half-century would have differed had parents continued to marry at rates prevalent during the 1960s and 1970s.[6] Both studies, which took account of the incomes of the current pool of unmarried men and their likely spouses, found that the income pooling from the added marriages would have significantly reduced child poverty, even without the boost to men's earnings commonly associated with marriage.

Earnings Capacities and Earnings Levels of Unwed Fathers

Several sources of data offer evidence on unmarried fathers' earnings capabilities. One, the primary source in this review, is the Fragile Families and Child Wellbeing Study (FFCWS), which offers data on parents of children born in urban hospitals in twenty large cities between 1998 and 2000.[7] A second is the National Longitudinal Survey of Youth (especially the 1979 panel, NLSY79), which now provides data from 1979 to 2006 on the cohort of individuals aged fourteen to twenty-one in 1979.

One recent study using the FFCWS sample presents comprehensive data on the characteristics of unwed fathers at the time of the child's birth and on their earnings over time, making it possible to trace links between their characteristics and their earnings.[8] About 85 percent of unwed fathers in the sample were minority, with 56 percent black and 29 percent Hispanic; 15 percent were immigrants. About 40 percent of the unwed fathers had not completed high school, 40 percent had a high school degree or equivalent, and about 20 percent had some postsecondary education. By contrast, married fathers in the sample were far less likely to be black (27 percent) or Hispanic (24 percent) and were far better educated: only 17 percent were dropouts and 30 percent were college graduates. Age differences were also notable. The average age at the time of their child's birth was thirty-two among married men, twenty-seven among unwed fathers. When the men became fathers for the first time, only 13 percent of married fathers were under age twenty, compared with about 25 percent of unmarried men.[9] Not surprisingly, education and age turn out to be important factors in a father's earnings capabilities, as better educated and older men would be expected to have significantly higher earnings than their less educated and younger peers.

Several other factors were also potentially relevant to fathers' earnings capabilities. Less than half (42 percent) of unwed fathers lived with both their parents at age fifteen, a figure well below the 69 percent figure for married men. Unwed fathers were also significantly more likely than married fathers to have mental health problems, to have used illicit drugs, and to have served time in jail or in prison or both.[10]

Married fathers are more likely than unmarried fathers to help parent their children, increase their chances of long-run success, and provide a stable source of income. Marriage is associated with higher earnings and may induce men to maximize their earnings capabilities.

Another characteristic of fathers that was linked with their labor market outcomes was whether they were married. The earnings of married men were more than double those of unmarried men at the time of the child's birth.[11] Earnings averaged $33,572 among married fathers, compared with only $15,465 among unmarried men (the figures are in 2005 dollars). Hourly wage rates of unmarried men were only 60 percent of the rates of married men, though unmarried men worked only about 20 percent fewer hours each year.

Other tabulations for this sample indicate that the earnings of unwed fathers also vary by whether they cohabit with the mothers of their children. The annual earnings of married, cohabiting, and noncohabiting men whose age and education were comparable at the time of the child's birth vary considerably. Among whites and blacks, married fathers earned 51 percent more than noncohabiting unwed fathers; cohabiting unwed fathers earned 19 percent more than noncohabiting fathers. Among Hispanics, married men earned only 19 percent more than noncohabiting unwed fathers; the difference between cohabiting and noncohabiting unwed fathers was essentially zero.

By the child's first birthday, fathers who were married at baseline had increased their earnings by 15 percent, to $39,047; unmarried fathers had achieved an even more rapid 22 percent gain, to $19,219. Two years later, initially married fathers were earning nearly $47,000, a stunning 33 percent increase from their earnings at the child's birth. Unmarried fathers moved up as well but at a somewhat slower rate. Still, their earnings rose an impressive 30 percent over three years.[12] The earnings gains for initially married men took place entirely through hourly wage gains (from $15.85 to $20.68 over three years); most of the earnings growth for unmarried men also involved growth in wages (from $9.64 to $11.21), but some resulted from a 7 percent increase in hours worked over the year. Although unwed fathers worked about 20 percent fewer hours than married fathers in the year of their child's birth, they still averaged 1,823 hours a year, implying almost forty-six weeks of full-time work. By the fifth-year follow-up, men who were initially unmarried were working the equivalent of fifty weeks at forty hours a week. Thus, on average, unwed fathers quickly become full-time, year-round workers. A sizable share of unwed fathers, however, works much less than average.

One important fact relevant to fatherhood, employment levels, and employment growth is that 40 percent of unwed, nonresident fathers are teen fathers, compared with only about 16 percent of cohabiting fathers and 0.1 percent of married fathers. The weak job market outcomes of teen fathers—virtually none of whom are married—means that a large segment of unwed, nonresident fathers starts far behind other groups of fathers, but their earnings rise rapidly as they age into their twenties.

The link between men's earnings and their relationship status suggests that earnings capability and actual earnings may not always be the same. Fathers who work fewer hours, work at less demanding jobs, engage in less intensive job search, or work less hard at keeping a job may not realize their full earnings capability.

To examine whether the earnings of unwed fathers fall short of capacity, we compare their actual earnings to an estimate of what the earnings of unwed fathers would be if their education, work experience, and race or ethnicity matched those of married fathers. The outcomes from undertaking this exercise for fathers at baseline in the FFCWS indicate that differences in education, work experience, and race and ethnicity between married and unwed fathers accounted for only about half of the earnings gap.[13] Although cohabiting fathers earned more than noncohabiting fathers, the two groups were similar in terms of the proportion of their earnings shortfall (relative to married fathers) that was associated with education, work experience, and race or ethnicity. Of the earnings difference between cohabiting and noncohabiting unwed fathers, only about one-third was associated with education, work experience, and race or ethnicity. Because these estimates account for only some of the job market advantages that men who are married would have even if they were not married, they may overstate the gap between actual earnings and the earnings capabilities of unwed fathers. On the other hand, the estimates may understate the gap because wage rate differences may affect differences in effort.

The link between men's earnings and their relationship status suggests that earnings capability and actual earnings may not always be the same.

The concentration on average earnings masks wide variations in earnings among unwed fathers. In general, the earnings of noncohabiting fathers varied more widely than those of cohabiting men. Because the earnings gains for unwed noncustodial fathers were also uneven, with smaller gains for fathers at the 25th percentile, their earnings fell further behind those at the 75th percentile as time went by. By the child's fifth birthday, the average annual hours worked by unwed fathers were equivalent to fifty-two weeks at forty hours, or 2,080 hours. But at the 25th percentile, fathers not initially cohabiting worked only about 1,350 hours a year, while married fathers worked 2,080 hours, and initially cohabiting fathers worked 1,768 hours, or about halfway between the married and noncohabiting unwed fathers. The lower hours worked among unwed fathers could indicate that a significant share of fathers do not utilize their capacity or that they cannot find jobs because of shortfall in demand in their segment of the job market.

Earnings shortfalls at the bottom end of the distribution are particularly noticeable. At the child's fifth birthday, unwed fathers at the 25th percentile reported earning only $5,000 a year. Even among cohabiting fathers, those at the 25th percentile earned only $8,000.

Estimates based only on earnings in the formal sector of the economy understate the total earnings of unwed fathers.[14] A study based on the FFCWS examined formal and informal earnings one year after the child's birth and divided unwed fathers into cohabiting and noncohabiting fathers. Cohabiting fathers averaged about $24,500 a year in formal-sector earnings and another $1,700 in informal earnings. Other unwed fathers had similar formal earnings and nearly $3,000 in informal earnings.

Unwed Fathers and Other Groups of Young Men

The adults in the FFCWS are all parents. Other studies reveal how the capabilities of unwed fathers stack up against men with no children. In an early study using data from the NLSY79, I found that men who became unwed fathers during the 1980s had more educational and social shortcomings than did their childless peers.[15] The shortcomings were especially striking among white young men. For example, nearly 50 percent of white eighteen- to twenty-one-year-olds (as of 1979) who became unwed fathers by 1984 were high school dropouts, a rate far higher than the 10 percent of whites who had no children. Nearly one-third of white men who became unwed fathers by 1988 had been charged in an adult court as of 1982, compared with 5 percent of childless white young men. Black and Hispanic young men who became unwed fathers also performed more poorly in school and were more involved in drug and criminal activity than their counterparts who did not have children or who married. However, the differentials between unwed fathers and other young men were not as large for minorities as for whites.

The gaps in earnings and hours worked between unwed fathers and other groups of young men also varied by race and ethnicity. Black, white, and Hispanic unwed fathers all earned substantially less than married fathers but also far less than single men with no children. However, the size of the differences was much larger among white and Hispanic than among black young men.

When isolating the role of unwed father status from an extensive list of other factors associated with low earnings, I estimated that unwed fathers earned about $1,200 less a year than married, nonresident fathers and $3,800–$4,500 less than married resident men and married men with no children. As in the findings cited above from the FFCWS, unwed fatherhood was associated with earnings below what would be predicted on the basis of human capital characteristics. Again, the evidence indicates that although unwed fathers have lower education and experience than do other fathers, their actual earnings fall short of their earnings capabilities.

Child Support Effects on Unwed Fathers' Earnings

The earnings of unwed fathers not living with their children might be affected by child support obligations in several ways. If, for example, a nonresident father earns an additional $500 a month, his child support might increase by about $125. Together with higher taxes on the higher income, the increased child support orders could lower fathers' returns to earnings, perhaps causing them to reduce their work effort. A second possibility is that child support payments could make the father poorer and thus stimulate more work effort. A third possibility is that rigorous enforcement by the child support system could cause fathers to shift from the formal to the informal, or underground, work sector, where earnings are more difficult for the government to track.

The evidence on how child support enforcement affects earnings is quite mixed. Marianne Bitler finds that the earnings of noncustodial fathers increase as child support enforcement becomes stricter.[16] By contrast, Harry Holzer, Paul Offner, and Elaine Sorensen find that increasingly vigorous child support enforcement has contributed to the decline in employment of black men, especially men in their late twenties and early thirties, many of whom are unwed fathers.[17] Although Maureen Waller and Robert Plotnick report evidence from qualitative studies that rigorous child support enforcement induces men to shift from formal to informal labor markets,[18] Lauren Rich, Irwin Garfinkel, and Qin Gao, using the Fragile Families data, do not find substitution of this type.[19] In fact, they find that stronger child support enforcement reduces the informal working hours of fathers with earnings in both sectors.

Incarceration Effects on Unwed Fathers' Earnings

Another study drawn from the Fragile Families panel explores the effect of previous incarceration on the capabilities of unwed fathers.[20] The study finds that fathers who had never been incarcerated had $26,700 in total (regular plus underground) earnings, compared with $19,216 in total earnings for those who had previously been incarcerated. The study shows that having been incarcerated reduces the likelihood of employment, the number of weeks worked, and earnings, even net of education, race, drug and alcohol problems, depression, and poor health. The effects are quite large, nearly a 30 percent reduction in regular earnings, some of which is offset by earnings increases in underground employment. Prior incarceration may itself lower earnings or it may be a proxy for other characteristics, such as a poor work ethic and weak basic reading and math skills, that lower prospective earnings. Another possibility is that men who become incarcerated make other bad choices, including choices about how hard to work and what jobs to pursue.

Other research reports similar findings regarding the effects of prior incarceration on the capabilities and contributions of unwed fathers. At the time of the nonmarital birth, 42 percent of the Fragile Families sample of unwed fathers had spent time in jail. As Amanda Geller, Garfinkel, and Bruce Western point out, only 65 percent of these men were employed, and their average wage rate was only $8.50 an hour, well below the wage of men who had never been incarcerated.[21] By the five-year follow-up, a substantial majority of unwed, nonresident fathers had incarceration records, significantly reducing their earnings capabilities.

Marriage and Cohabitation Transitions

The earnings patterns of men in fragile families in part reflect the dynamics of their family circumstances. At the birth of nonmarital children, 82 percent of the couples in the Fragile Families panel were either cohabiting or in a close romantic relationship. Five years later, 15 percent were married and 21 percent were cohabiting or in a close romantic relationship. How did the marriage and cohabitation transitions affect men's job market outcomes? In a study of first-time fathers, Christine Percheski and Christopher Wildeman examine trajectories over time of weeks worked and hours worked per week.[22] They find that married fathers initially work several more weeks and longer hours than unwed, cohabiting fathers or unwed, noncohabiting fathers, but that the gaps in weeks worked and in hours worked per week narrow over the five-year period after the child's birth. Moreover, married fathers' initial advantage in weeks worked largely disappears when the fathers compared are similar in such characteristics as age, education, immigrant status, teenage fatherhood, health, criminal record, drug use, race, and Hispanic origin.

The study examines transitions both out of and into marriage and cohabitation. Married fathers and cohabiting fathers who separate from their children's mothers show declines in employment. Unwed fathers who marry and become resident fathers experience increases in weeks worked and hours worked. Overall, the study suggests, resident fatherhood itself stimulates unmarried men to work significantly more weeks and hours.

Additional evidence on the impacts of marriage and cohabitation transitions on labor market outcomes comes from two other studies of the FFCWS sample.[23] Garfinkel and others find that entering marriage between the birth of the child and one year later was associated with an earnings gain of 29 percent at the one-year point, 44 percent after three years, and 66 percent after five years. Entering cohabitation raised earnings almost as much. In all cases the increases are net of age, education, race, immigrant status, and prior relationship stability. Using a different methodology and focusing on race differences in responses, Ronald Mincy, Jennifer Hill, and Marilyn Sinkewicz show estimates indicating no statistically significant earnings gains from the transition to marriage. They argue that alternative approaches do not account sufficiently for differences between the characteristics of unwed fathers who subsequently marry and those who do not. Still, even their estimates indicate marriage-induced earnings gains of 40–50 percent for black unwed fathers. These gains are not so precisely estimated to yield statistical significance at the stringent 5 percent standard, but would be significant at the 10 percent level.

The studies by Percheski and Wildeman, by Garfinkel and his colleagues, and by Mincy, Hill, and Sinkewicz yield somewhat different conclusions about the persistence of a labor market disadvantage associated with unwed fatherhood. From the perspective of Percheski and Wildeman, the initial disadvantage linked to unwed fatherhood itself largely dissipates, at least with respect to weeks worked and hours worked. Yet some of the convergence results from the transition that some unwed, nonresident fathers make to become resident fathers. The picture painted by Garfinkel and his colleagues is more consistent with an enduring and substantial negative impact of unwed fatherhood on job market outcomes. Mincy, Hill, and Sinkewicz point to variations in earnings growth, mainly owing to differences in the initial characteristics of unwed fathers. Only black unwed fathers show consistent gains from marriage. Some differences in study methods may account for differences in results. The Garfinkel analysis uses data from all fathers, not just first-time fathers, and its sample of 4,897 fathers is more than four times the 1,086 fathers in the Percheski-Wildeman study. The Mincy, Hill, and Sinkewicz study focuses on race and ethnic differences and marriage transitions only up to three years after the child's birth, while Garfinkel and others use pooled estimates that account for marriage transitions up to five years after the child's birth. Also, while Percheski and Wildeman include teenage fatherhood as an independent variable, Garfinkel and his colleagues control only for age in a way that assumes changes in age have the same effect whether the starting point is eighteen or twenty-five.

An earlier study relevant to the issue of relationship transitions tracked the earnings and hours worked of unwed fathers aged twenty to twenty-seven in 1984 by their marital status in 1988.[24] In general, these unwed fathers experienced substantial increases in hours worked and earnings, regardless of their marital status in 1988. The nearly 70 percent of fathers who remained unmarried raised their annual hours of work from 1,078 to 1,428 and nearly doubled their earnings, from about $5,500 in 1983 to about $10,500 in 1987. The 22 percent of unwed fathers who married between 1984 and 1988, however, raised their annual earnings even more, from $7,370 to $17,699. The rapid economic growth from the mid-1980s to the late 1980s no doubt amplified the employment and earnings opportunities young men experienced as they matured and obtained adult jobs.

Contributions of Unwed Fathers

Two important—and measurable—ways in which fathers support their families are by contributing time and money. Although the quality of fathers' parenting and their relationships with children and partners are also no doubt critical contributions, they are difficult to measure. The increased emphasis by federal and state policy makers since the mid-1970s on using child support to help children escape poverty and on having fathers reimburse government welfare programs for supporting their children has led to many studies of child support payments. Studies of visitation and of time spent by fathers with their children followed shortly afterward. The less quantifiable contributions of fathers are now attracting some attention.[25]

Unwed Fathers' Monetary Contributions

National census data shed light on contributions by fathers who are not married at the time of the survey, while long-term data from the FFCWS and NLSY capture the contributions of all men who father children outside marriage, including men who subsequently cohabit and marry. Thus, the two types of information involve somewhat different groups of fathers.

The standard national estimates of the monetary contributions of fathers come from representative samples of custodial mothers and their children. Although many of these fathers were married at the time of the child's birth, others were and are still unmarried. In April 2008, the Census Bureau's Current Population Survey (CPS) obtained reports by custodial parents (usually custodial mothers) about the contributions of the noncustodial parents (usually fathers) of their children.[26] Although more than 60 percent of divorced custodial mothers had a formal agreement concerning child support payments, 56 percent of the 3.8 million unwed custodial mothers had no formal agreement. Of the 1.4 million unwed mothers with an award and a payment due in 2007, 558,000 received their full payment and 478,000 received a partial payment. The average payments received by never-married mothers amounted to about $250 a month ($3,040 a year). In addition, about 15 percent of unwed fathers included nonresident children in their health insurance coverage. Further, some of these custodial parents (about 8 percent) received child support payments even though they reported none was due through a child support agreement.[27] Others received noncash support.

The increased emphasis by federal and state policy makers since the mid-1970s on using child support to help children escape poverty and on having fathers reimburse government welfare programs for supporting their children has led to many studies of child support payments.

Another census survey, the Survey of Income and Program Participation (SIPP), asked noncustodial fathers about all payments for the "...support of your child or children under 21 years of age who live outside of this household...." About 900,000 unwed fathers reported providing support, with the median amount paid about $3,100 a year.[28] This figure is broadly consistent with the $3,040 mean annual amount reported in the CPS by never-married mothers, although the CPS figure includes only formal child support.

The child support provided by unwed fathers in the FFCWS was quite modest as well. Although legal paternity was established for 87 percent of children of cohabiting fathers, paternity was established for only 56 percent of children born to nonresident fathers. Support orders were much less frequently established, initially only for 20 percent of unwed, noncohabiting fathers and 6 percent of cohabiting fathers.[29] Lenna Nepomnyaschy and Garfinkel provide a detailed look at the unwed fathers' contributions using data from interviews with 1,326 unwed mothers who were not cohabiting with the father of a child born three years earlier.[30] Only 24 percent of the mothers reported receiving any formal support, but another 29 percent received some informal cash support. Although these figures are somewhat lower than reported in the CPS for a broader group of unwed mothers, they reinforce the importance of informal payments by many fathers. Fathers who have once lived with their children provide more informal cash support. Perhaps such men feel more closely linked to their children than do fathers who have never cohabited. In this sample, informal support often substitutes for formal support: mothers without a formal support order receive much more informal cash support than do mothers with an order. Indeed, mothers with no formal support order received almost $150 a month in informal support.

Unwed Fathers' Time Spent with Children

The usual metric for judging the involvement of nonresidential fathers with their children is the time they spend together. But, as Sandra Hofferth, Nicole Forry, and Elizabeth Peters point out, contact may not be the appropriate measure because studies find little or no effect of fathers' time on child well-being.[31] Positive and authoritative parenting may be more consequential than simple time spent together for better child outcomes. Of course, fathers will rarely be able to exert positive and authoritative parenting without spending time with their children.

Data on the time men spend with their children are available from mothers' reports on contact with fathers.[32] Some 3.7 million unwed mothers reported that roughly 40 percent of the men had no contact with their children during the previous year but most (2.2 million) fathers had some contact.[33] The amount of contact varied widely: the bottom quartile of fathers had 10 or fewer days of contact for the year; the top quartile, 120 days or more. Although men with more contact were more likely to provide support, the difference was modest. Those not paying formal support averaged about 48 days of contact, compared with 61 days among men who did pay support. In addition to visiting with their children, many fathers pay informal support. Unwed, custodial mothers reported that about half of fathers who paid no formal support made informal contributions, with one-third paying for clothing and about one-fourth paying for food.

Information from fathers is available for a representative sample of 470,000 nonresident fathers who report child support payments (out of the more than 2 million unwed, nonresident fathers in the SIPP panel). This group reported spending an average of fifty days a year with children living elsewhere—a figure similar to the median reported by unwed mothers as visiting.

One study uses mothers' reports of nonresident father involvement with a representative sample of children in 1997.[34] Of those fathers, 34 percent had no contact with the child's household at all, and 49 percent had no influence on decision making. Only 19 percent had a great deal of influence on issues involving their children. About 46 percent played with their children at least once a month, but only 15 percent spent time with them in school activities.

How Father Involvement Evolves

How does the involvement of unwed fathers change over time? In an analysis following young (nineteen- to twenty-six-year-old) fathers for eight years between 1984 and 1992, Elaine Sorensen and I found that most unwed fathers remained involved with at least one of their children.[35] Of men who had become unwed fathers by 1984, nearly half were living with at least one child in 1992. Moreover, as of 1992, only one in four reported either not visiting at all or visiting less than once a month. When the focus is on men's first nonmarital birth, however, involvement does erode. In the initial year, about 19 percent of fathers visited less than once a month or not at all; six years later, the proportion had jumped to 35 percent. Although overall involvement declined, increases in father involvement were associated with gains in fathers' earnings.

Studies based on father involvement for the Fragile Families sample have so far been able to examine only the first five years after the nonmarital births. Over this period, the involvement of unwed fathers with their children has eroded in two ways. First, the share of unwed fathers living with their children declined from 52 percent at one year after the child's birth to 44 percent after three years and to 37 percent after five years. Second, unwed fathers not living with their children reduced their visitation and child contacts over time. During thirty days before an interview at the one-year point, 62 percent of unwed fathers had been in contact with their child, but the share fell to 56 percent at the three-year follow-up.[36] Put another way, 44 percent of unwed fathers had no contact with their children in the previous month. This pattern is similar to that for young unwed fathers in the NLSY.[37]

Father involvement continues to erode as children age from three to five. Forty-seven percent of unwed fathers saw their three-year-olds more than once a month, compared with 43 percent by the time the child reached age five.[38] At that point, 49 percent of fathers had not seen their children in the previous month, and 37 percent had had no contact with the child in the previous two years. Forty-three percent of fathers, however, still had regular enough contact to see their five-year-olds an average of twelve days a month.

Most unwed fathers (64 percent) remained in contact with their children at least through the age of five; 37 percent lived with their children, and another 27 percent visited more than once a month. But the share of children not seeing their father more than once a month rose from 18 percent at age one to 36 percent at age five. One may view this glass as being half full (after all, most unwed fathers do not abandon their children), but it is worrying that by age five more than one-third of children born outside marriage have minimal or no involvement with their fathers. Moreover, father-child contacts are likely to erode further as children move through elementary and high school.

Factors Influencing Father Involvement

Several factors influence the extent to which unwed fathers stay involved with their children. A variety of studies find that better educated fathers and those who most identify with the father's role are more likely to sustain a relationship with their children. Not surprisingly, so too are fathers with good relationships with their child's mother. At the same time, fathers who subsequently have children with other partners are likely to reduce their contact with previous children.[39]

Black fathers are more likely than white and Hispanic fathers to maintain close contact with their children, especially in cases when the father neither marries nor cohabits with the mother. Mincy and Hillard Pouncy find, in a study of low-income families in Louisiana, that many black fathers retain their involvement with their child, despite having only intermittent or no romantic relationships with the child's mother.[40] Other studies indicate that black fathers and mothers maintain better relationships after separation and, in turn, have improved relationships with their children.[41] Although divorced fathers are generally more likely than unwed fathers to pay child support and to have frequent contact with their children, black unwed fathers have greater contact with their children than black divorced fathers.[42] One possible explanation is that black mothers and nonresident fathers live closer to each other than other unwed parents.

Quantitative as well as qualitative studies based on the FFCWS reinforce earlier findings and document other factors affecting fathers' involvement.[43] Unwed fathers who participated at the time of the birth in parenting and providing financial support were more likely to remain involved with their children. Problematic behaviors by the fathers, such as violence or drug or alcohol abuse, generally led to less involvement, largely because of mothers' efforts to protect their children. Not surprisingly, close relationships between unwed mothers and unwed fathers led to greater father involvement. The quality of the parental relationship is measured not only in terms of whether they are cohabiting or in a close romantic relationship at the time of birth, but also in terms of how well they communicate, support each other, and get along. The linkages between relationship quality and father involvement remain even after the parents are no longer romantically involved.

On the basis of in-depth and repeated interviews with a subset of the FFCWS sample, Waller finds that some unwed fathers were closely enough involved to become the primary caregiver or to share equally in the care of young children.[44] The reasons varied. Some chose to do so because of experience and strong preferences for fathering; others, because of problems that mothers were facing; still others, because they were out of work and could best contribute to the household by caring for their children. When their relationships with the mothers ended, some fathers ended their caregiver role. But others began doing more with their children, especially when they had good jobs or were responding to the mother's loss of a job, substance abuse, or other problems. Because research on these patterns comes mainly from ethnographic studies, it is not clear how many low-income fathers are highly active caregivers and what the potential is for expanding the share of fathers taking on these responsibilities.

When the parents separate, some men and women start new dating and cohabiting relationships and have children with new partners. These changes can complicate fathers' involvement with their children, as a study by Laura Tach, Mincy, and Kathryn Edin reveals.[45] The authors find that new relationships and childbearing by mothers lowers the number of days fathers see their children by more than one-third; smaller reductions in involvement also take place as a result of fathers' new partnerships. Other factors lowering father involvement include the amount of time elapsed since the parents lived together, fathers' drug use and recent time in jail or prison, and joblessness or low earnings of fathers.

How the Child Support System Affects Fathers' Financial and Time Contributions

Much of the detailed research on unwed fathers' contributions to their children has focused on the impact of the child support enforcement system and on the interactions between child support and welfare assistance. Other studies focus on the effect of incarceration, the links between support payments and contact with children, and the involvement of more than one custodial parent.

Several studies have analyzed the relationship between fathers' contributions through visitation and child support payments. Fathers induced to pay support may take an increasing interest in how their child is reared and do more to involve themselves in the lives of their children. Mothers may also be more receptive to the involvement of fathers who are contributing financial support to their children. Another possibility is that involved fathers are more willing to provide financial support. Yet another is that fathers may see financial support as substituting for contributions of their time.

Fathers induced to pay support may take an increasing interest in how their child is reared and do more to involve themselves in the lives of their children.

Empirical studies yield mixed findings on the child support–visitation linkage for all noncustodial parents. Some find that strong child support enforcement influences both support payments and father involvement. Using state differences in enforcement to help identify potential effects, Chien-Chung Huang finds that more rigorous child support enforcement raises child support payments and increases visitation.[46] In fact, Huang estimates that 45 percent of the increase in visitation he finds is explained by the increased rigor of the child support enforcement system. In a study of unwed fathers one year after their children's births, Mincy, Garfinkel, and Nepomnyaschy found, using Fragile Families data, that strong enforcement, measured as a city or state's commitment to establishing paternity, increased the chance that fathers had seen their child in the past thirty days and that they had received an overnight visit from their child in the past year.[47] A nuanced set of findings emerges from a separate study by Nepomnyaschy of the interactions between father involvement, and formal and informal support payments.[48] Both formal and informal support payments one year after a child's birth raise the likelihood of father contact two years later. But although early contact has no effect on later formal payments, father visits at year one do increase informal payments in year three.

These and other estimates showing that child support enforcement increases formal support payments generally do not take into account possible indirect effects on informal payments. Rigorous child support enforcement, for example, could mainly shift payments from informal to formal without increasing what mothers receive. In fact, the shift could even reduce mothers' receipts because the formal payments sometimes go to reimburse the government. In a striking finding based on the Fragile Families sample and child support enforcement variables at the city level, Nepomnyaschy and Garfinkel find that strong enforcement raises formal child support payments but that the increase is fully offset by reductions in the amount of informal support.[49] It is not clear, however, how far this finding can be generalized. Child support enforcement may be increasing the support provided by the broader population of nonresident fathers. And the shift from informal to formal support may itself be a positive change in that it contributes to the integrity of the child support system. Nonetheless, the Nepomnyaschy-Garfinkel study suggests that past studies may have overstated the gains from strong child support enforcement by failing to account carefully for informal payments.

Unwed Fathers' Earnings and Child Support Obligations

One primary purpose of research on the earnings of unwed fathers is to determine both the potential scope for increasing child support payments and the current burdens of child support on unwed fathers. In general, the approach is to develop accurate estimates of the incomes of fathers and what they should pay under sensible child support guidelines—as well as the gap between the two. With this approach comes the presumption that actual earnings represent earnings capabilities. My focus here is on unwed fathers not living with their children, because cohabiting fathers are providing direct support to the family budget.

Some studies call attention to how hard it is for many such fathers to make reasonable financial contributions. Only 10 percent of poor, young nonresident fathers paid support in 1990, for example, while half of those with incomes above the poverty level paid support.[50] Payments reported by fathers who had not graduated from high school were one-third less than payments by fathers with at least a high school diploma (U.S. census). Young fathers earn less and pay less than other fathers.

In a recent paper, Garfinkel and Marilyn Sinkewicz estimate the earnings relevant to the typical child owed child support from a nonresident father.[51] Excluding fathers who have died, who have no knowledge of their fatherhood, or who are otherwise ineligible, the authors estimate that the mean annual earnings of unwed, nonresident fathers eligible to pay child support is about $18,000 one year after the child's birth. In calculating potential child support, Garfinkel and Sinkewicz include the obligations of unwed fathers to more than one mother. These additional obligations, along with improved earnings estimates, reduce the capability of unwed fathers to pay child support to current children from 60 to 33 percent. Obligations differ significantly by race. Although earnings differences between white and black unwed fathers are modest ($19,324 vs. $16,927), black fathers have an average of 1.2 children from a previous partner, as compared with 1.0 for whites.

Another study highlights the large number of children to whom unwed fathers must pay support out of their typically modest incomes. Using Wisconsin data on welfare recipients, Daniel Meyer, Maria Cancian, and Steven Cook find that only 26 percent of fathers have children with only one mother who has established connections only with that one father.[52] Another 28 percent have children with only one mother who has connections with multiple fathers; 9 percent have children with two or more mothers who have connections with only that one father; and 37 percent have children with two or more mothers who have connections with multiple fathers. The study examines connections between mothers and fathers with legally established paternity. The authors find that fathers who have children with multiple mothers pay significantly greater support, mainly because they owe more. Controlling for total support owed, however, fathers who have children with multiple mothers pay less support.

Whatever their actual contributions, many unwed fathers face child support obligations that represent a very large share of their incomes. Those with children on welfare confront the additional disincentive of knowing that much of their support payment reimburses the government instead of improving their child's standard of living.[53] In a study of all Wisconsin children on welfare, Cancian and Meyer reported that about 25 percent of all noncustodial fathers (most of whom were unwed) were ordered to pay more than 40 percent of their reported personal income in child support.[54] In 1999, one-third of fathers reported incomes below the poverty line. More than half the fathers were living with children other than the child on welfare. The authors estimated that if child support orders reflected Wisconsin standards (guidelines for the percent of income noncustodial parents should pay), the poverty rate among nonresident fathers would increase from 34 percent (before paying child support) to 39 percent (after paying child support).

Incarceration as a Barrier to Fathers' Contributions

Another critical barrier to fathers' contributions is incarceration, past and present. In 2007, about 750,000 inmates in state or federal prisons were fathers to 1.7 million children.[55] Few of these men can pay any support while in prison, but many face support obligations anyway. The time spent in prison thereby increases the arrearages that must be paid off when they leave. High arrearages, together with current obligations, mean that fathers will face such high deductions from any post-incarceration earnings that they will be discouraged from participating in the formal job market. Given their limited job skills, lack of recent work experience, and their criminal record, it is not surprising that fathers who have been in prison pay far less than other fathers. Five years after a nonmarital birth, the annual contribution of unwed fathers who had never been in prison averaged nearly $2,700, about 2.7 times the $964 average annual payment by unwed fathers who had been imprisoned.[56] Net of other social and personal characteristics, previously incarcerated fathers are 36 percent less likely to make financial contributions to their children, and when they do, they contribute less than other nonresident fathers. Almost 80 percent of the effect of incarceration on financial contributions can be accounted for by two factors: performance in the labor market and relationship instability after incarceration. Previously incarcerated fathers are far more likely to remain nonresident fathers than to live with their children.

Implications for Research and Policy

Unwed mothers and fathers are now bearing 40 percent of the nation's children. Despite the severe problems presented by this new reality—especially high poverty and bleak outlooks for children—past efforts by policy makers to stem the tide have proved largely unsuccessful. Most policy interventions have targeted women. Some discourage teen pregnancy; others (such as an expanded earned income tax credit, child care subsidies, child health insurance, and work requirements) try to raise the work effort and incomes of single mothers.

The primary initiative focused on men has been to increase child support collections from noncustodial fathers. Steps such as improving the rate of paternity establishment, increasing both the number and size of child support awards, and reliably collecting amounts due have had two goals—to increase the incomes of single parents and their children and to discourage men from becoming unwed fathers or separating from the mother of their children. Although initiatives in the child support arena have achieved some income gains for single parents, they have proved less successful in lowering nonmarital births. Moreover, further tightening the child support program is likely to yield diminishing returns. More rigorous child support enforcement seems to increase fathers' formal payments, but not the total amount paid. Strict enforcement of obligations—including the buildup of arrearages when fathers are in jail and unable to earn anything—can prove counterproductive, as men facing enormous debts relative to their incomes become discouraged and fail to earn up to their potential.

Reducing the financial disincentives to marry that are built into public tax and benefit programs is another potential option. But notwithstanding modest recent changes that lower marriage penalties, efforts to tilt benefits further toward two-parent families would either be prohibitively expensive in this era of enormous government deficits or would lower benefits to the poorest families, most of which are single-parent families.

Some research findings on unwed fathers point toward policies that involve few such difficult tradeoffs. One effort already under way consists of programs to improve the relationship and communication skills of unwed fathers and mothers and, in turn, increase the likelihood of marriage and marital stability. Nonexperimental evidence suggests that enhanced couple relationships, particularly marriage, will increase the earnings of fathers as they utilize more of their capabilities. Even if participating individuals ultimately separate, an improved relationship between parents is likely to increase fathers' contributions of money and time, thereby improving the capacity of parents to raise healthy children. Many low-income fathers already spend much time caring for their children. Improving parental relationships could enhance their parenting. Initial results from the Building Strong Families experiment, which provided group sessions on communication, conflict resolution, intimacy, trust, and other relationship skills to unwed couples, show no significant increases for the full sample in terms of parents living together or relationship quality.[57] Modest, statistically significant improvements did occur in one site and for black couples. Moreover, these programs are still in their early stages and the actual hours of group sessions were small. As additional research and demonstration evidence accumulates, researchers will learn whether relationship skills training can play a constructive role in helping couples and children.

Central to improving family outcomes on a long-term basis is increasing the earnings capacities of unwed fathers, especially those with the least education. Although gains from training programs are uneven, especially among men, evidence shows substantial increases in earnings associated with years of general and vocational education. Sectoral strategies are emerging as a promising way to link training with employer demands and careers. These sectoral programs target an industry (or subset of an industry), become a strategic partner by learning about the industry's workforce policies, reach out to low-income job seekers, and work with other labor market groups, such as community colleges, community nonprofits, employer groups, and policy makers. Nonexperimental evidence indicates that six sectoral programs taking part in the Sectoral Employment Development Learning Project (SEDLP) yielded earnings gains of more than 70 percent for the participants employed for two years.[58]

A traditional sector-based approach with a long track record of success in raising earnings through targeted training is the apprenticeship system. Apprenticeships involve intensive work-based learning and classroom courses. Employers are central to the process, setting up the programs and paying the apprentices during their work-based learning. Apprenticeships are particularly well suited to many unwed fathers, who can earn a salary while they learn skills. The learning takes place mostly at workplaces in the context of real production, relieving apprentices from having to spend much time in classrooms. Completing an apprenticeship yields a respected, portable credential, a sense of pride, and participation in a community of occupational practice. Finally, empirical evidence shows that apprenticeships substantially raise the earnings of workers and result in high levels of satisfaction among employers.[59]

Another broad option is to add employment components to current marriage education initiatives. One possibility is a joint couple-based employment program that allows both partners to understand what the other is undertaking. The concept showed promise as part of a job readiness and job search assistance program for seventeen- to twenty-four-year-old couples.[60]

Helping young people get off to a solid start in careers can be important for improving couple outcomes and avoiding nonmarital births. Career Academies, for example, not only raised the earnings of young men, especially those with a high or medium risk of dropping out of high school, but also generated gains in marriage as well.[61] Complementing the Career Academies with training in relationships skills might reinforce their pro-family outcomes. Adding relationship-skills components to other highly touted youth programs, including Job Corps, YouthBuild, and the National Guard ChalleNGe Academy, would be a low-cost way to recognize close linkages between careers and family dynamics.

Finally, child support programs should do more to recognize inequities and inefficiencies. It should be easier for fathers to adjust awards when they are the primary caregiver and when they are involuntarily unemployed. The data document a wide dispersion of earnings and household incomes of unwed fathers, with some fathers capable of making appropriate payments, some having obligations to multiple partners, others facing extremely low earnings and incomes, and still others having low earnings but living in moderate-income households. A collection focus may be sensible for the high earners and for others with high earnings capabilities. But for low earners, partnering with responsible father programs and incorporating employment and relationship-skills programs show more promise in achieving child support and broader social objectives.

Endnotes

1. Lenna Nepomnyaschy and Irwin Garfinkel, "Child Support, Fatherhood, and Marriage: Findings from the First 5 Years of the Fragile Families and Child Wellbeing Study," *Asian Social Work and Policy Review* 1 (2007): 1–20.

2. Author's tabulations from the Survey of Income and Program Participation (SIPP), 2004 panel, topical module 3.

3. Author's tabulations of earnings by education of unwed fathers as of the baseline and fourth follow-up of the Fragile Families and Child Wellbeing Study data.

4. Stephanie Ventura, *Changing Patterns of Nonmarital Childbearing in the United States,* NCHS Data Brief 18 (National Center for Health Statistics: Centers for Disease Control and Prevention, 2009).

5. Avner Ahituv and Robert I. Lerman, "How Do Marital Status, Work Effort, and Wage Rates Interact?" *Demography* 44, no. 3 (2007): 623–47; Irwin Garfinkel and others, "Unmarried Fathers' Earnings Trajectories: Does Partnership Status Matter?" (Princeton University: Center for Research on Child Wellbeing, 2009).

6. Robert I. Lerman, "The Impact of Changing U.S. Family Structure on Child Poverty and Income Inequality," *Economica* 63, no. 250 (1996) S: S119–39; Adam Thomas and Isabel Sawhill, "For Richer or Poorer: Marriage as an Antipoverty Strategy," *Journal of Policy Analysis and Management* 21, no. 4 (2002): 587–600.

7. For detail on this data set, see the description in the article by Sara McLanahan and Audrey Beck, titled "Parental Relationships in Fragile Families," in this volume.

8. Garfinkel and others, "Unmarried Fathers' Earnings Trajectories" (see note 5).

9. Marcia Carlson and Sara McLanahan, "Fathers in Fragile Families," Working Paper 09-14-FF (Princeton: Center for Research on Child Wellbeing, 2009).

10. Ibid.

11. Garfinkel and others, "Unmarried Fathers' Earnings Trajectories" (see note 5).

12. Ibid.

13. For these calculations, the author first estimated a regression of log earnings of married men on education, potential work experience, potential work experience squared, and black and Hispanic status. Using these estimates for how these variables affect earnings, the author predicted log of earnings of cohabiting and noncohabiting unwed fathers. The author then compared the percentage differences in actual earnings with the percentage differences in predicted earnings for each group.

14. Lauren M. Rich, Irwin Garfinkel, and Qin Gao, "Child Support Enforcement Policy and Unmarried Fathers' Employment in the Underground and Regular Economies," *Journal of Policy Analysis and Management* 26, no. 4 (2007): 791–810.

15. Robert Lerman, "Employment Patterns of Unwed Fathers and Public Policy," in *Young Unwed Fathers: Changing Roles and Emerging Policies,* edited by Robert Lerman and Theodora Ooms (Temple University Press, 1993).

16. Marianne Bitler, "Microeconomics of the Family: Three Essays" (Ph.D. dissertation, Cambridge, Mass.: Massachusetts Institute of Technology, 1998).

17. Harry Holzer, Paul Offner, and Elaine Sorensen, "Declining Employment among Young Black Less-Educated Men: The Role of Incarceration and Child Support," *Journal of Policy Analysis and Management* 24, no. 2 (2005): 329–50.

18. Maureen Waller and Robert Plotnick, "Effective Child Support Policy for Low-Income Families: Evidence from Street-Level Research," *Journal of Policy Analysis and Management* 20, no. 2 (2001): 89–110.

19. Rich, Garfinkel, and Gao, "Child Support Enforcement Policy and Unmarried Fathers' Employment in the Underground and Regular Economies" (see note 14).

20. Charles E. Lewis, Irwin Garfinkel, and Qin Gao, "Incarceration and Unwed Fathers in Fragile Families," *Journal of Sociology & Social Welfare* XXXIV, no. 3 (2007): 22–94.

21. Amanda Geller, Irwin Garfinkel, and Bruce Western, "Incarceration and Support for Children in Fragile Families," Working Paper 08-090-FF (Princeton: Center for Research on Child Wellbeing, 2008).

22. Christine Percheski and Christopher Wildeman, "Becoming a Dad: Employment Trajectories of Married, Cohabiting, and Nonresident Fathers," *Social Science Quarterly* 89, no. 2 (2008): 482–501.

23. Ronald Mincy, Jennifer Hill, and Marilyn Sinkewicz, "Marriage: Cause or Mere Indicator of Future Earnings Growth?" *Journal of Policy Analysis and Management* 28, no. 3 (2009): 417–439; Garfinkel and others, "Unmarried Fathers' Earnings Trajectories" (see note 5).

24. Lerman, "Employment Patterns of Unwed Fathers and Public Policy" (see note 15).

25. See, for example, Maureen Waller, "Family Man in the Other America: New Opportunities, Motivations, and Supports for Paternal Caregiving" (Princeton University: Center for Research on Child Wellbeing, 2009).

26. Timothy S. Grall, *Custodial Mothers and Fathers and Their Child Support: 2005,* Current Population Reports (Washington: U.S. Bureau of the Census, 2007). The detailed tables on child support payments in 2007 are available on the census website at www.census.gov/hhes/www/childsupport/cs07.html.

27. Heather Koball, Laura Wheaton, and Elaine Sorensen, *Child Support Trends in the CPS-CSS: The Role of Allocation and Survey Design* (prepared for the Office of Child Support Enforcement, Department of Health and Human Services: Urban Institute, 2002).

28. See the census report based on wave 5 of the 2004 SIPP panel collected in June–September 2005.

29. Fragile Families Research Brief Number 15, "Child Support Enforcement and Fragile Families" (Princeton University: Center for Research on Child Wellbeing, 2003)

30. Lenna Nepomnyaschy and Irwin Garfinkel, "Child Support Enforcement and Fathers' Contributions to Their Nonmarital Children," Working Paper 06-09-FF (Princeton: Center for Research on Child Wellbeing, 2007).

31. Sandra Hofferth, Nicole Forry, and Elizabeth Peters, "Child Support, Contact, and Involvement with Children after Relationship Dissolution," Working Paper (University of Maryland: Maryland Population Research Center, 2008).

32. The data come from the April 2006 CPS.

33. These results come from tabulations by the author from the April 2006 Current Population Survey. The data were drawn from the NBER website.

34. Sandra Hofferth and others, "The Demography of Fathers: What Fathers Do," in *Handbook of Father Involvement: Multidisciplinary Perspectives,* edited by Catherine Tamis-Lemonda and Natasha Cabrera (Mahwah, N.J.: Lawrence Erlbaum Associates, 2002), pp. 63–90; The authors use the PSID for their analysis.

35. Robert Lerman and Elaine Sorensen, "Father Involvement with Their Nonmarital Children: Patterns, Determinants, and Effects on Their Earnings," *Marriage and Family Review* 29, no. 2/3 (2000): 137–58; the authors use the NLSY79 for their analysis.

36. Lenna Nepomnyaschy, "Child Support and Father-Child Contact: Testing Reciprocal Pathways," *Demography* 44, no. 1 (2007): 93–112.

37. Lerman and Sorensen, "Father Involvement with Their Nonmarital Children" (see note 35).

38. Carlson and McLanahan, "Fathers in Fragile Families" (see note 9).

39. Ibid.

40. Ronald Mincy and Hillard Pouncy, *Baby Fathers and American Family Formation: Low-Income, Never-Married Parents in Louisiana before Katrina* (New York: Center for Marriage and Families, Institute for American Values, 2007).

41. Hofferth, Forry, and Peters, "Child Support, Contact, and Involvement with Children after Relationship Dissolution" (see note 31).

42. L. M. Agrys, H. E. Peters, and J. R. Smith, "The Impact of Child Support on Cognitive Outcomes of Young Children," *Demography* 35, no. 2 (1998): 159–73.

43. Carlson and McLanahan, "Fathers in Fragile Families" (see note 9).

44. Waller, "Family Man in the Other America" (see note 25).

45. Laura Tach, Ronald Mincy, and Kathryn Edin, "Parenting as a 'Package Deal': Relationships, Fertility, and Nonresident Father Involvement among Unmarried Parents," *Demography* 47, no. 1 (2010): 181–204.

46. Chien-Chung Huang, "Child Support Enforcement and Father Involvement for Children in Never-Married Mother Families," *Fathering: A Journal of Theory, Research, & Practice about Men as Fathers* 4, no. 1 (2006): 97–11.

47. Ronald Mincy, Irwin Garfinkel, and Lenna Nepomnyaschy, "In-Hospital Paternity Establishment and Father Involvement in Fragile Families," *Journal of Marriage and Family* 67, no. 3 (2005): 611–26.

48. Nepomnyaschy, "Child Support and Father-Child Contact" (see note 36).

49. Nepomnyaschy and Garfinkel, "Child Support Enforcement and Fathers' Contributions to Their Nonmarital Children" (see note 30).

50. Ronald Mincy and Elaine Sorensen, "Deadbeats and Turnips in Child Support Reform," *Journal of Policy Analysis and Management* 17, no. 1 (1998): 44–51.

51. Marilyn Sinkewicz and Irwin Garfinkel, "Unwed Fathers' Ability to Pay Child Support: New Estimates Accounting for Multiple-Partner Fertility," *Demography* 46, no. 2 (2009): 245–63.

52. Daniel R. Meyer, Maria Cancian, and Steven T. Cook, "Multiple Partner Fertility: Incidence and Implications for Child Support Policy," *Social Service Review* 79, no. 4 (2005): 577–601.

53. Waller and Plotnick, "Effective Child Support Policy for Low-Income Families" (see note 18).

54. Maria Cancian and Daniel R. Meyer, "Fathers of Children Receiving Welfare: Can They Provide More Child Support?" *Social Service Review* 78, no. 2 (2004): 179–206.

55. Lauren Glaze and Lauran Maruschak, *Parents in Prison and Their Minor Children,* Special Report (Washington: Bureau of Prison Statistics, 2008).

56. Geller, Garfinkel, and Western, "Incarceration and Support for Children in Fragile Families" (see note 21).

57. Robert G. Wood and others, *Strengthening Unmarried Parents' Relationships: The Early Impacts of Building Strong Families* (Princeton, N.J.: Mathematica Policy Research, 2010).

58. Amy J. Blair, *Measuring Up and Weighing In: Industry-Based Workforce Development Training Results in Strong Employment Outcomes* (Washington: Aspen Institute, 2002).

59. Kevin Hollenbeck, "State Use of Workforce System Net Impact Estimates and Rates of Return" (Los Angeles: Association for Public Policy and Management Meetings, 2008); Robert Lerman, Lauren Eyster, and Kate Chambers, "The Benefits and Challenges of Registered Apprenticeship: The Sponsor's Perspective" (Washington: U.S. Department of Labor, Employment and Training Administration, 2009).

60. Rachel Gordon and Carolyn Heinrich, "The Potential of a Couples' Approach to Employment Assistance: Results of a Nonexperimental Evaluation," *Review of Economics of the Household* 7, no. 2 (2009): 133–58.

61. James Kemple, with Cynthia Willner, *Career Academies: Long-Term Impacts on Labor Market Outcomes, Educational Attainment and Transitions to Adulthood* (New York: MDRC, 2008).

Fragile Families and Child Wellbeing

Jane Waldfogel, Terry-Ann Craigie, and Jeanne Brooks-Gunn

Summary

Jane Waldfogel, Terry-Ann Craigie, and Jeanne Brooks-Gunn review recent studies that use data from the Fragile Families and Child Wellbeing Study (FFCWS) to examine why children who grow up in single-mother and cohabiting families fare worse than children born into married-couple households. They also present findings from their own new research.

Analysts have investigated five key pathways through which family structure might influence child well-being: parental resources, parental mental health, parental relationship quality, parenting quality, and father involvement. It is also important to consider the role of the selection of different types of men and women into different family types, as well as family stability. But analysts remain uncertain how each of these elements shapes children's outcomes.

In addition to providing an overview of findings from other studies using FFCWS, Waldfogel, Craigie, and Brooks-Gunn report their own estimates of the effect of a consistently defined set of family structure and stability categories on cognitive, behavioral, and health outcomes of children in the FFCWS study at age five. The authors find that the links between fragile families and child outcomes are not uniform. Family instability, for example, seems to matter more than family structure for cognitive and health outcomes, whereas growing up with a single mother (whether that family structure is stable or unstable over time) seems to matter more than instability for behavior problems. Overall, their results are consistent with other research findings that children raised by stable single or cohabiting parents are at less risk than those raised by unstable single or cohabiting parents.

The authors conclude by pointing to three types of policy reforms that could improve outcomes for children. The first is to reduce the share of children growing up in fragile families (for example, through reducing the rate of unwed births or promoting family stability among unwed parents). The second is to address the pathways that place such children at risk (for example, through boosting resources in single-parent homes or fostering father involvement in fragile families). The third is to address directly the risks these children face (for example, through high-quality early childhood education or home-visiting policies).

www.futureofchildren.org

Jane Waldfogel is a professor of social work and public affairs at Columbia University, Terry-Ann Craigie is a postdoctoral research associate at the Center for Research on Child Wellbeing, Princeton University, and Jeanne Brooks-Gunn is the Virginia and Leonard Marx Professor of Child Development and Education at Teachers College and the College of Physicians and Surgeons, Columbia University.

For much of the nation's history, the vast majority of American children were born into and spent their childhood in intact married-couple families. Almost the only exceptions were children whose families suffered a parental death. Over the course of the twentieth century, however, as divorce became more common, an increasing share of children experienced a breakup in their families of origin and went on to spend at least some portion of their childhood or adolescence living with just one parent or with a parent and stepparent. A large research literature developed examining the effects of such living situations on child outcomes.

More recently, as unwed births have risen as a share of all births, family structure in the United States has increasingly featured "fragile families" in which the mother is unmarried at the time of the birth. Children born into fragile families spend at least the first portion of their lives living with a single mother or with a mother who is residing with a partner to whom she is not married. For simplicity, we will refer to the first of these types of fragile family as single-mother families and the second as cohabiting-couple families.[1]

An astonishing 40 percent of all children born in the United States in 2007 were born to unwed parents and thus began life in fragile families. That share was more than twice the rate in 1980 (18 percent) and an eightfold increase from the rate in 1960 (5 percent).[2] Half of the children born to unwed mothers live, at least initially, with a single mother who is not residing with the child's biological father (although about 60 percent of this group say they are romantically involved with the father), while half live with an unwed mother who is cohabiting with the child's father.[3] These estimates imply that today one-fifth of all children are born into single-mother families, while another fifth are born into cohabiting-couple families. Therefore, in examining the effects of unwed parenthood on child outcomes, it is important to consider both children living with single mothers and those living in cohabiting-couple families.

Single parenthood and cohabitation have lost much of their stigma as their prevalence has increased. But there are still many reasons to be concerned about the well-being of children in fragile families, and, indeed, research overwhelmingly concludes that they fare worse than children born into married-couple households.[4] What remains unclear is how large the effects of single parenthood and cohabitation are in early childhood and what specific aspects of life in fragile families explain those effects.

In this article, we review what researchers know about the effects of fragile families on early child development and health outcomes, as well as what they know about the reasons for those effects. Many underlying pathways or mechanisms might help explain the links between fragile families and children's cognitive, behavioral, and health outcomes. Identifying these mechanisms is important to efforts by social scientists to understand how family structure affects child outcomes and to develop policies to remedy negative effects. A challenge that must be addressed is the role of "selection." The characteristics of young women and men who enter into single parenthood or cohabiting relationships differ from those of men and women in married-couple families, and those pre-existing characteristics might lead to poorer outcomes for children regardless of family structure. Parents in fragile families, for example, tend to be younger and less educated than those in married-couple families, and they may also differ in ways that cannot readily be observed even using detailed survey data. A final question is the degree to which the stability of the family setting affects how well children fare. In fact, recent research holds that it is in large part the stability of the traditional family structure that gives it its advantage.

We highlight new answers to these questions from studies using data from the Fragile Families and Child Wellbeing Study (FFCWS)—a data set designed specifically to shed new light on the outcomes of children born into single-mother and cohabiting families and how they compare with those of children in married-couple families. The study follows children from birth and collects data on a rich array of child health and developmental outcomes, thus providing evidence on how children's outcomes differ depending on whether they grow up in single and cohabiting versus married-couple families and on the factors that might underlie those differences.

We review the evidence on the effects of fragile families on child well-being by comparing outcomes for three types of families. The first type is families where children live with two married parents (for simplicity, we refer to these as traditional families). In this category are children living with their married biological parents as well as children living with married stepparents. (Research has documented differences in outcomes between these two subgroups of children, but those differences are not our focus here.) Rather, we are interested in two other types of families—both fragile families—that have become increasingly prevalent in recent years. One is single-mother families in which the mother was not married at the time of the birth and in which she is not currently living with a boyfriend or partner. The other is cohabiting-couple families in which the mother was not married at the time of the birth but is currently cohabiting with a boyfriend or partner, who might be either the child's biological parent or a social parent (someone who is not biologically related to the child but who functions at least partially in a parental role). We do not distinguish between families that share and do not share households with extended family members or with other families or friends. We also do not distinguish between single mothers who are in a dating or visiting relationship and those who are not. Such distinctions likely matter, but our focus is on the three more general family types: traditional married-couple family, single-mother family, and cohabiting-couple family.

Explaining the Links between Fragile Families and Poorer Child Well-Being

Many studies, reviewed below, concur that traditional families with two married parents tend to yield the best outcomes for children.[5] But the specific pathways by which growing up in traditional families lead to this advantage are still being debated. The key pathways, or mechanisms, that likely underlie the links between family structure and child well-being include: parental resources, parental mental health, parental relationship quality, parenting quality, and father involvement. As noted, the selection of different types of men and women into the three different family types also likely plays a role, as does family stability and instability. We discuss each of these mechanisms in turn.

The Role of Parental Resources

One clear explanation for the poorer outcomes of children in fragile families is that fewer resources are available to these families, particularly single-mother families.[6] As Ariel Kalil documents in her article in this volume, single-mother households face a disproportionate risk of economic disadvantage in a variety of ways—from having less money for books, clothes, and extracurricular activities to living in poorer school districts and neighborhoods. Even with child support enforcement, single parents are substantially more likely to be poor than their married-couple counterparts, and many children living with single mothers receive no child support.

In large part, the sparse resources available to children in single-mother homes reflect the fact that these homes have only one adult who can work and bring in income (and the benefits that often go along with employment, the most important of which is health insurance). Having two adults in the home could clearly make more resources available to children (assuming that adults pool their resources and use them on behalf of the family). It matters, however, who the adults are. Although cohabiting-couple families (by definition) have two adults living with the children, the characteristics of these adults do not particularly resemble those of the adults in traditional families. Cohabiting parents tend to be less educated than married parents, and as a consequence they also have lower incomes.[7] There is also evidence that cohabiting couples are less likely to share their income or invest in joint household goods than are married-couple families.

Parents invest not only economic resources in their children, but time resources as well. Particularly in early childhood, parental time is important to child health and development, and even in middle childhood and adolescence, parental time matters. Children in fragile families are likely to be shortchanged in terms of time resources too. A single mother, particularly if she is working, will not have as much time to give to her children as would two parents in a married-couple family. There can be no division of labor within her household—the single mother bears all the burden associated with child care, the financial and organizational logistics of the household, and her own welfare.[8] At the same time, children growing up with single mothers get less time with their fathers than they would in homes where the father is present.

Although cohabiting-couple families have two adults living with the children, the characteristics of these adults do not particularly resemble those of the adults in traditional families.

Cohabiting-couple families should have more parental time available for children than single-mother families. But particularly when the cohabiting partner is not the biological father, he is likely to invest less time in the children than he would in a married-couple family where he is their biological parent.

The Role of Parents' Mental Health

Parental mental health is also an important influence on child well-being, and one that differs across family types. Single mothers report more depression and psychological problems than married mothers and undoubtedly function less well as parents as a result.[9] Cohabiting mothers have also been found to suffer more from depression than married mothers, which again would directly interfere with their ability to display good parenting skills.[10] It is important to note that these differences may be the result of these mothers' living situation or may reflect pre-existing differences between the types of women who have children out of wedlock rather than in marriage (as we discuss in the section on selection below).[11]

The Role of Parental Relationship Quality

It has long been recognized in the research on divorced parents that the quality of parents' relationships (for example, how well they get along and how much conflict they experience) would be a key intervening variable explaining links between divorce or separation and poorer child outcomes. Clearly, the adjustments and conflict associated with divorce or separation would be a source of stress, which might in turn impair parental mental health or detract from parenting quality. In addition, parental conflict fosters dysfunctional social interactions in children, leading to emotional and behavioral problems.[12] Children whose parents do not have a positive relationship may harbor anger and anguish, which may subsequently threaten their academic success and provide the impetus behind early family formation. Indeed, some researchers have argued that leaving the nest and starting a family is a direct response to less than ideal circumstances at home.[13]

It is likely that the quality of parents' relationship influences child outcomes in fragile families, although the direction of its effects is not clear.[14] One theory is that poor relationship quality (for example, parents not getting along and experiencing significant conflict) is likely to spill over to parenting, lowering its quality. Another theory is that parents who have poor relationships with adult partners might compensate by engaging more positively in their relationships with their children.

As discussed in the article by Sara McLanahan and Audrey Beck in this volume, parents in fragile families—both cohabiting couples and single mothers—tend to have poorer relationship quality than do those in married families and to report more conflict and less cooperation in parenting. (Single mothers report on the quality of their dating or visiting relationship.)[15] One situation that adversely affects parental relationship quality in fragile families is having children with multiple partners.[16]

The Role of Parenting Quality

Particularly for young children, but also for older children and adolescents, at least as consequential as the time that parents spend with them is the quality of their parenting during that time. In early childhood, two key dimensions of parenting quality are sensitivity and responsiveness to the child. Children's outcomes are better when parents are warm and nurturing, and children fare worse when parents are either harsh and punitive or detached and neglectful. Parents also engage in a range of activities that may promote or impair children's health—among them, arranging for their health care, managing family meals and nutrition, providing direction regarding exercise and television watching, and being attentive to safety hazards.

Although there is no reason why unwed parents would necessarily have poorer parenting skills, there are many reasons why they might. As noted, single parents, on average, have fewer resources, are in poorer mental health, and have more problematic relationships with their partners—any of which might in turn affect the quality of parenting that single mothers provide for their children.

Cohabiting mothers might also be expected to have poorer parenting skills than married mothers, but are likely to have better parenting skills on average than single mothers do.

The Role of Father Involvement

Also of interest is how father involvement may affect child well-being, particularly in families where the father does not live in the home. While in principle a nonresident father could still be involved in the care of his child, in fact his involvement will often, though by no means always, diminish as the child gets older. Marcia Carlson and Sara McLanahan find that by age five, nearly two-fifths of children of unwed parents had no regular contact with their fathers in the past two years, while another two-fifths were seeing their father on a regular basis (the remaining one-fifth fell somewhere in between).[17] Having a father who is actively involved in the child's upbringing even though he is not residing in the household could yield numerous benefits in terms of child health and development. Nonresident father involvement might also benefit children by raising the quality of mothers' parenting. Nonresident father involvement could also, however, be detrimental if fathers acted in ways that interfered with child health and development or if poor relationship quality between the father and mother led to lower-quality parenting behaviors on her part.

The involvement of resident biological fathers and social fathers in cohabiting-couple families is also of interest. As discussed, particularly when a father is resident, the quality of his parenting is likely to be an important input into child health and development. So too is the quality of his relationship with the mother.

Father involvement has been linked with fewer child behavioral problems, even when the father is a social father only (that is, the romantic partner of the mother living in the child's household).[18] The quality of a father's involvement has also been associated with child cognitive development and language competence.[19]

The Role of Selection

A common challenge in research in this area is that parents who are single or cohabiting may have attributes (both observed and unobserved) that differ from those of married parents and that also foster adverse child and adolescent outcomes. Men who choose to cohabit, for example, may not have the same family values that men who choose to marry do. As a consequence of such attributes, the negative "effects" being ascribed to single parenthood and cohabitation may be explained by the pre-existing attributes of members of these families, rather than reflecting an effect of the family type. Although some of these differing attributes can be controlled for using survey data on characteristics such as age and education, other differences may be harder to measure even in a detailed study such as FFCWS. A parental characteristic such as a lack of strong family values is hard to observe in survey data but it may be at work within the family system, simultaneously influencing both the structure of the family and child well-being.

Most research has not been able to address selection in a very convincing way. Studies typically include extensive controls for observed characteristics, often including controls for characteristics before the child's birth or the family's entry into a particular family structure. Accounting for such observed differences in parental and economic resources, however, is not sufficient, because there are likely to be unobserved differences as well. Couples that engage in out-of-wedlock childbearing as opposed to childbearing within marriage may differ from each other fundamentally, in ways that are not observed in typical survey data.[20]

Because controlling for selection is so important in obtaining unbiased estimates of the effects of fragile families, we pay particular attention in this review to studies that have attempted to do so. One method that has been used often is sibling comparisons (comparing the outcomes of siblings born to married parents with the outcomes of siblings born to parents whose family status differed at the time of their birth). This method, however, is limited in that it derives its findings from blended families and also in that it is not able to control for other factors that may have changed at the same time the family's status changed.[21] Another frequently used method is comparing outcomes for the same child at different points in time, when family circumstances have changed. But this method too derives its findings from families experiencing change and is unable to control for other factors that may have changed at the same time the family's status changed. Another way to address selection is instrumental variables (IV) estimation. This estimation strategy uses variation in family structure that is predicted by a variable that is external to the family, that influences family structure, and that is not otherwise associated with child outcomes (for example, state laws or tax policies). In theory, this method is well suited to address selection, but in practice, it can be difficult to identify such an external variable.[22]

The Role of Family Stability

A further challenge in identifying exactly how family structure shapes child well-being is the difficulty of distinguishing the effects of family structure from the effects of family stability. Family stability refers to whether children grow up with the same parent(s) that were present at their birth. The assumption is that children will do better, on average, with stable parents because change can be disruptive to children and families and also because new partners coming into the household may be not as good caretakers as parents who have been with the children since birth. Poor outcomes related to instability may be explained by the stress that accompanies changes in family structure for both parent and child; moreover, changing family circumstances may confound the status quo of authority within the household.[23]

Particularly in earlier research on family structure, the vast majority of nontraditional families had been formed through divorce, and thus family structure was typically conflated with family stability or instability. To the extent that stability matters for child well-being, the effects of family structure on child outcomes might be due, at least in part, to its association with stability.[24]

Single-parent and cohabiting-couple families are both more susceptible to family instability than are traditional married-couple families. Studies have shown that family structure at birth is highly predictive of family instability, affirming that cohabiting couples experience the most instability, followed by single-parent families, and then traditional two-parent families.[25] However, it remains challenging to determine the importance of family stability relative to family structure. As we discuss below, one recent study found that family stability trumps family structure as it pertains to early cognitive development even after controlling for economic and parental resources.[26] It has been shown that children living in stable single-parent families (that is, families that were headed by a single parent throughout childhood) do better than those living in unstable two-parent families (that is, families that had two parents present initially but then experienced a change in family structure).[27] Another study finds that children living in stable cohabiting homes (that is, families where two parents cohabit throughout the child's life) do just as well as children living with cohabiting parents who eventually marry.[28] But other research challenges the conclusion that it is family stability that is crucial for child well-being. One study, for instance, found that children who experience two or more family transitions do not have worse behavioral problems or cognitive test scores than children who experience only one or no family transitions. The same study found that children living in stable single-parent homes had the worst behavioral and cognitive outcomes.[29]

The effects of family structure as distinct from instability have been the focus of much of the recent research in this area. We provide a review of the most recent studies, and also offer some evidence from our own new analyses below.

Past Research on the Links between Family Structure and Child Outcomes

An extensive body of work has examined the effects of parental divorce on child outcomes. As noted, however, most of this work was published before the massive increase in unwed parenthood that now characterizes American families. Thus, informative as it was about the effects of divorce, this early wave of research lacked data to explain how unwed parenthood might affect child outcomes.

The classic study by Sara McLanahan and Gary Sandefur, published in 1994, bridged the gap by bringing together an array of evidence on how growing up in various types of nontraditional families—including both divorced families and unwed-mother families—affected child well-being. Even after controlling for the selection of different types of individuals into different types of family structure, the authors concluded that children who spent time in divorced- or unwed-mother households fared considerably worse than those remaining in intact two-parent families throughout their childhood and adolescence. While they were still in high school, they had lower test scores, college expectations, grade-point averages, and school attendance, and as they made the transition to young adulthood, they were less likely to graduate from high school and college, more likely to become teen mothers, and somewhat more likely to be "idle" (a term that refers to those who are disengaged from both school and work).

In addition, although the differences were not large (and not always statistically significant), children of unwed parents tended to fare worse than those with divorced parents, even after taking into account differences in basic demographic characteristics such as race, sex, mother's and father's education, number of siblings, and residence. For example, although the risk of dropping out of high school was 31 percent for children whose parents had divorced, it was 37 percent for children whose parents were unwed; similarly, although the risk of a teen birth for children whose parents had divorced was 33 percent, it was 37 percent for children whose parents were unwed.[30]

With regard to mechanisms, McLanahan and Sandefur found that income was an important explanatory factor for the poorer outcomes of children in single-parent families (but not for children in stepparent families). On average, single-parent families had only half the income of two-parent families, and

Although an earlier generation of researchers had debated whether or not divorce affected children's well-being, McLanahan and Sandefur's findings left little doubt that children of unwed parents were worse off than other groups.

this difference accounted for about half the gap between the two sets of children in high school dropout and nonmarital teen birth rates (in regression models that also controlled for race, sex, mother's and father's education, number of siblings, and residence).[31] The other important mechanism was parenting. When McLanahan and Sandefur entered parenting into the regressions (instead of income), they found that the poorer parenting skills and behaviors in single-parent families explained about half the gap in high school dropout rates, but only a fifth of the gap in teen birth rates (again controlling for race, sex, mother's and father's education, number of siblings, and residence). Because the authors did not control for income and parenting in the same models, the question of how much overlap there was in their effects remains.

Although child health was not a focus in the McLanahan and Sandefur analysis, other analysts have consistently found effects of family structure on children's health outcomes.[32] Janet Currie and Joseph Hotz found that children of single mothers are at higher risk of accidents than children of married mothers, even after controlling for a host of other demographic characteristics.[33] Anne Case and Christina Paxson showed that children living with stepmothers receive less optimal care and have worse health outcomes than otherwise similar children living with their biological mothers (whether married or single).[34] An extensive body of research also links single-parent and cohabiting-family structures with higher risk of child abuse and neglect.[35]

As McLanahan and Sandefur noted at the time, their findings were worrisome given the burgeoning growth in unwed parenthood in the United States at the time. Although an earlier generation of researchers had debated whether or not divorce affected children's well-being, McLanahan and Sandefur's findings left little doubt that children of unwed parents were worse off than other groups. Concern about how children would fare in unwed families ultimately led to the Fragile Families and Child Wellbeing Study.[36]

The Fragile Families and Child Wellbeing Study

The Fragile Families and Child Wellbeing Study is a new data set that follows a cohort of approximately 5,000 children born between 1998 and 2000 in medium to large U.S. cities.[37]

Approximately 3,700 of the children were born to unmarried mothers and 1,200 to married mothers.[38] The study initiated interviews with parents at a time when both were in the hospital for the birth of their child and therefore available for interviews.[39] As a consequence, FFCWS is able to comprehensively detail the characteristics of both parents and the nature of their relationship at the time of the child's birth.

Table 1. Summary of Fragile Families and Child Wellbeing Findings on Various Child Outcomes

Author	Outcomes	Addresses selection	Positive effect of traditional two-parent family	Negative effect of nontraditional families	Negative effect of family instability
Berger, Paxson, and Waldfogel (2009)	Child abuse	Yes		Yes	
Bzostek (2008)	Behavior problems and health			No (positive)	
Bzostek and Beck (2008)	Obesity/asthma/health	Yes	Yes	Yes	Yes
Cooper and others (2008)	PPVT-R/behavior problems				Yes
Craigie (2008)	PPVT-R	Yes	Yes	Yes	Yes
Fomby and Osborne (2008)	Behavior problems				Mixed
Guterman and others (2009)	Child abuse	Yes	Yes		
Harknett (2005)	Asthma		Yes	Yes	
Liu and Heiland (2007)	Asthma	Yes		Yes	Yes
Liu and Heiland (2008)	PPVT-R/asthma/behavior problems	Yes	Yes		
Osborne and others (2004)	Behavior problems	Yes	Yes	Yes	
Osborne (2007)	Behavior problems		Yes	Yes	
Osborne and McLanahan (2007)	Behavior problems				Yes
Padilla and Reichman (2001)	Low birth weight			Yes	

The study also contains extensive information on early child developmental and health outcomes. The Peabody Picture Vocabulary Test–Revised (PPVT-R) is administered to children aged three or older as a measure of their receptive vocabulary capabilities for Standard English as well as their academic readiness.[40] The Woodcock-Johnson Tests of Achievement Letter-Word Identification subtest, another measure of cognitive development, is administered at the age-five assessment. At the same time, interviewers assess children's sustained attention, a key skill that has been linked to school readiness and success in school, using the Leiter International Performance Scale-Revised.

Interviewers gather data on children's behavior problems by asking mothers questions from the Child Behavior Checklist about both externalizing and internalizing behaviors—that is, both outward displays of emotion, including violence and aggression, and introverted behavioral tendencies, including anxiety, withdrawal, and depression. The study assesses prosocial behavior (which includes the child's ability to get along in social situations with adults and peers) by asking the mother questions using the Adaptive Social Behavior Inventory.

Finally, FFCWS includes several measures of child health. The initial survey records whether a child had a low birth weight. In addition, at the age-three and age-five in-home assessment, the interviewer records physical measurements of the child's height and weight to make it possible to calculate the child's BMI and to determine whether the child is overweight or obese. At the same interviews, the mother is asked about four other health outcomes: whether the child has ever been diagnosed with asthma; the child's overall health, from the mother's perspective; whether the child was hospitalized in the past year; and whether the child had any accidents or injuries in the past year. The study also includes fairly extensive information on child abuse and neglect, which captures another aspect of child health and well-being. The primary caregiver's use of discipline strategies is measured by the Conflicts Tactics Scale (including the child neglect supplement). Parents are also asked whether their family has ever been reported to child protective services for child abuse or neglect.

Studies using data from FFCWS have found that in general, children in traditional married-couple families fare better than children living in single-mother or cohabiting families. We summarize separately below the evidence on cognitive development, child behavior, and child health (see table 1 for details).

Fragile Families and Child Cognitive Development

Several FFCWS studies have specifically focused on the effects of family structure on children's cognitive development and also confirmed the importance of stability as an explanatory factor. Shirley Liu and Frank Heiland find that among couples unmarried at the time of the child's birth, marriage improved cognitive scores for children whose parents later married.[41] Terry-Ann Craigie distinguishes among stable cohabiting unions, stable single-mother homes, and stable married-couple families, as well as unstable cohabiting families and unstable married-couple families. She finds no difference in children's vocabulary scores at age three between stable two-parent families (whether cohabiting or married) and stable single-mother families, but she finds that scores are lower in unstable families (whether cohabiting or married) than in stable families.[42] Carey Cooper and co-authors also highlight the role that partnership instability plays in the link between family structure and child cognitive development, although these links are much weaker than those they find for behavioral development (discussed below).[43]

Fragile Families and Child Behavior Problems

Several studies using FFCWS data confirm that child behavior problems are elevated in both single-parent and cohabiting families. Cynthia Osborne and her co-authors, for instance, found that children living with cohabiting parents have more externalizing and internalizing behavioral problems than children living with married parents, even at age three. One explanation may be the pre-existing risks that accompany nontraditional families.[44] In addition, research by Rebecca Ryan, Ariel Kalil, and Lindsey Leininger suggests that resources are one mechanism underlying these links: when single mothers have more material and instrumental support, children have fewer behavior problems and more prosocial behavior.[45] Relationship quality may also play a role. Several FFCWS studies offer evidence that poorer relationship quality is linked with less parental engagement with children. Paula Fomby and Cynthia Osborne find that relationship conflict exacerbates externalized behavioral problems in children regardless of past family structure transitions.[46]

The deleterious effects of family instability on behavior problems are also highlighted in the FFCWS studies. Osborne and McLanahan show that behavioral problems are intensified with each additional change in family structure the child experiences (changing from single to cohabiting parent, or cohabiting to single, for example), with this association mediated at least in part by differences in maternal stress and parenting quality.[47] Cooper and co-authors also find a link between instability and behavior problems, with children who experience instability in the people with whom they live going on to display more externalizing, attention, and social problems, and again find that these effects are mediated, at least in part, by mothers' problematic mental health and harsh parenting.[48] Audrey Beck and her co-authors' analyses of both cohabiting and dating mothers confirm that mothers experiencing instability in their relationships go on to report more stress and to engage in harsher parenting.[49]

It appears, however, that there is an important interaction between family structure and stability. Several studies find that behavior problems are more serious in both stable single-mother families and unstable cohabiting families than in stable married-couple families.[50] In contrast, children living with stable cohabiting-couple families do not display more behavior problems than children living with stable married-couple families. Thus, stability seems to matter in cohabiting families, but not in single-mother families, where the risk of behavior problems is elevated even if that family structure is stable. Osborne and McLanahan find that about half the association between family structure and behavior problems is attributable to mothers' higher levels of stress and poorer parenting skills and behaviors. In a study of father involvement, Sharon Bzostek shows that having a social father involved in a child's life can lower behavioral problems just as having an involved biological father can.[51]

Some studies find no evidence that family structure affects child behavioral problems. An analysis by Liu and Heiland indicates that marriage up to three years after a child's birth does not significantly improve behavioral problems.[52]

Fragile Families and Child Health

In a comprehensive analysis of the effects of nontraditional family structure on child health using data from FFCWS, Bzostek and Beck consider five health outcomes: whether the child is overweight or obese, whether the child has ever been diagnosed with asthma, the mother's overall assessment of the child's health, whether the child was hospitalized in the past year, and whether the child had any accidents or injuries over the past year.[53] Overall, they find, consistent with earlier research, that children born to unwed mothers have worse health across a range of outcomes, even after controlling for other differences in characteristics such as maternal age, race and ethnicity, and education. Children living with single mothers have worse outcomes on all five health measures than children living with married parents, while children in cohabiting-couple families tend to have worse outcomes on some but not all measures. The authors also consider the effect of instability. In contrast to some past research, they find that instability for the most part does not affect children's health outcomes (the exception is hospitalizations, where they find, unexpectedly, that children who experienced more instability are less likely to have been hospitalized).[54] These findings suggest that what negatively affects health among children in fragile families has to do with living with single or cohabiting parents (rather than experiencing changes in family structure).

Bzostek and Beck also consider several mechanisms that might account for the links between family structure and child health. Although no single factor is strongly linked with all the health outcomes, together the intervening variables (or mediators) they examine do help explain some of the differences in health outcomes across family structure type. However,

Bzostek and Beck find evidence that at least a portion of the family structure effects they estimate likely reflects selection. Their models examining the effect of changes in family structure on changes in outcomes for a child over time suggest weaker effects on child health than do their snapshot-in-time cross-sectional models.[55]

Studies have consistently found that children born to unwed parents are at higher risk of low birth weight, and analyses from FFCWS confirm this finding.[56] Further, FFCWS analyses by Nancy Reichman and her co-authors suggest some of the mechanisms that link unwed parenthood with greater risk of low birth weight. They find that women who are not married at the time of the birth are more likely to smoke cigarettes and use illicit drugs during pregnancy, and less likely to receive prenatal care in the first trimester of their pregnancy, all of which are associated with low birth weight (use of illicit drugs is also associated with other infant health problems).[57] Yolanda Padilla and Reichman find that unwed mothers who received support from the baby's father are less likely to have a low-birth-weight baby, as are those who cohabited with the father.[58]

Studies based on FFCWS also confirm earlier research finding that children living with single mothers are at higher risk of asthma. For instance, Kristen Harknett finds that the likelihood that children have been diagnosed with asthma by age fifteen months is highest for children with single mothers, next highest for those with cohabiting mothers, and lowest for those with married mothers. Although differences in characteristics account for the gap between married and cohabiting families, they do not fully account for why children with single mothers are more likely to have been diagnosed with asthma.[59] Liu and Heiland, following children to age three, find that children whose parents had been cohabiting but then separated have a higher risk of asthma than otherwise comparable children whose parents remained together.[60]

A few studies have taken advantage of the data in FFCWS to examine the effects of family structure on child abuse and neglect. Neil Guterman and his co-authors look at whether mothers are less likely to be physically aggressive or punitive with their children if they are in a married household and find that, although marriage appears to be protective in the raw data, that effect disappears in models that control for parental and family characteristics.[61] Lawrence Berger and his co-authors examine the effect of family structure on whether a family has been reported to child protective services for abuse or neglect and find that both single-mother families and cohabiting families where the mother is living with a man who is not the biological father of all her children are at higher risk of having been reported than are families where the mother is living with the biological father of all her children.[62] This latter finding is robust to extensive controls for factors associated with selection into different family types, leading the authors to conclude that the presence of a social father in the home is associated with increased risk of abuse or neglect.[63]

Our Own Analyses of FFCWS

The many studies in this area, including the recent ones using FFCWS data, do not always define family structure or stability in a consistent way. Studies also vary in the extensiveness of other controls that are included in the analyses. These differences across studies can make it difficult to generalize across studies and to summarize their results.

Figure 1. Variation in Predicted Values for Scores on the Peabody Picture Vocabulary Test–Revised, by Family Type

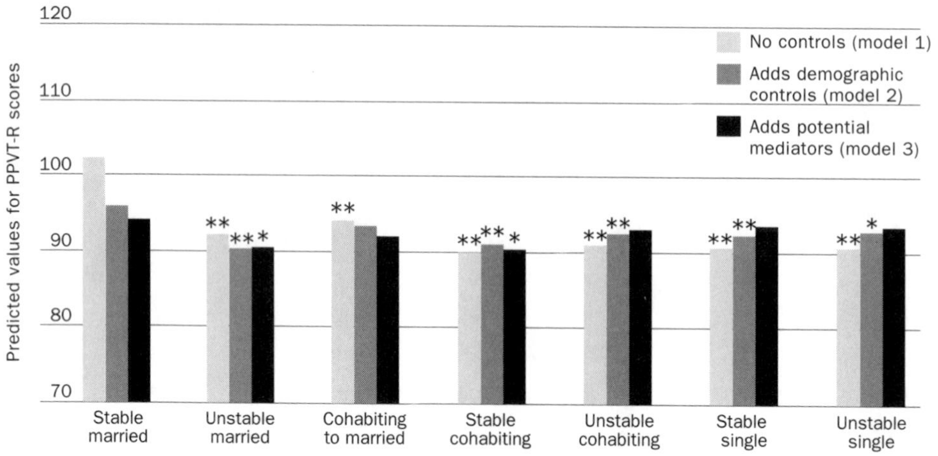

* p<0.05, ** p<0.01
Asterisks indicate that each group is statistically significantly different from the stable married group (the reference category).

Accordingly, we carried out our own analyses of FFCWS data, estimating the effect of a consistently defined set of family structure and stability categories on a set of child cognitive, behavioral, and health outcomes at age five. The family categories we defined account for both family structure at birth and stability since birth. We divide families into the following six categories: stable cohabitation, stable single, cohabitation to marriage, married at birth (unstable), cohabiting at birth (unstable), and single at birth (unstable). We then contrast them with the traditional family reference group (that is, families in which parents were married at the child's birth and have remained so).

We estimate three sets of regression models. In model 1, we control only for the family structure and stability categories; thus, these results tell us the association between family type and child outcomes without controlling for any of the differences in other characteristics between families. Model 2 adds controls for a commonly used set of demographic characteristics—the child's gender, mother and father's race and ethnicity, mother and father's education, and mother and father's age. Thus the results from model 2 regressions tell us the effect of family structure and stability holding constant these demographic differences. Model 3 further adds controls for possible mediating variables that might help explain the links between family structure and stability and child outcomes. We do not have controls for all the possible mediators of interest but we do include here controls for several important ones—mother's income, father involvement, parenting quality, and maternal and paternal depression. Thus, the results for model 3 tell us whether and how much family structure and stability matter for child well-being after controlling for demographic differences and these possible mediators.

We estimated these models for two cognitive outcomes, the Peabody Picture Vocabulary Test–Revised (PPVT–R) and Woodcock-Johnson test; two behavioral outcomes: the

Figure 2. Variation in Predicted Values for Aggression, by Family Type

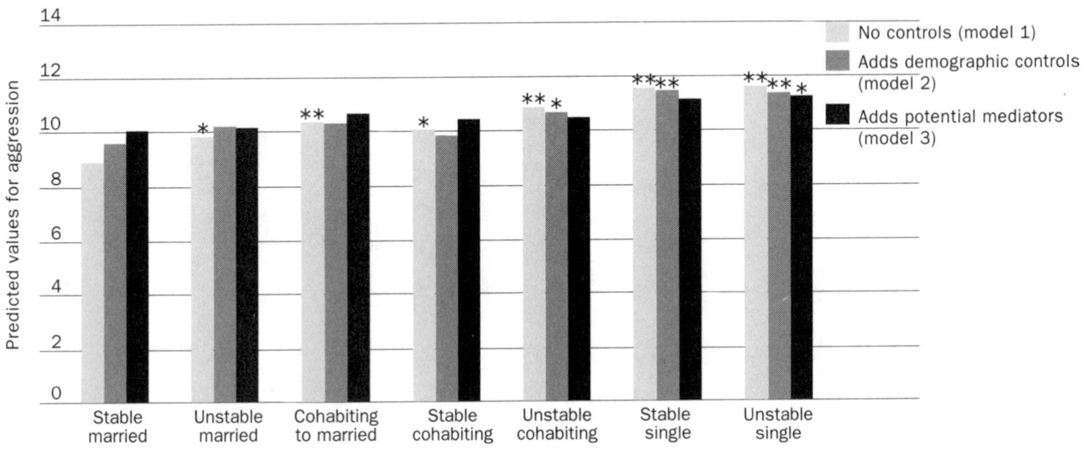

* p<0.05, ** p<0.01
Asterisks indicate that each group is statistically significantly different from the stable married group (the reference category).

child's score on a measure of aggressive behavior and the child's score on a measure of anxiety and depression; and two health outcomes: obesity and asthma. Details on all the outcome variables are provided in Appendix 1; means for all the variables in our models are listed in Appendix 2.

We show selected results in figures 1 through 3.[64] In these figures, we show how children's predicted scores on the outcome measures vary as a function of their family type. Figure 1 displays results for the PPVT–R. In model 1, all types of nontraditional or unstable families are associated with lower scores. Results for model 2 are similar, with the exception of the cohabitation to marriage category, which is now no longer significantly different from the stable married category. In model 3, the possible mediators explain some, but not all, of these negative effects.

The findings for aggressive behavior are shown in figure 2. In model 1, just as with the results for cognitive outcomes, all types of nontraditional or unstable families are associated with worse scores (in this case, because the outcome variables are ratings of behavior problems, higher scores indicate worse outcomes). However, in contrast to the results for cognitive outcomes, it appears that for aggressive behavioral problems, growing up with a single mother (stable or unstable) is worse than growing up with a cohabiting mother. The effects of growing up with a single mother are larger in model 1 and are more likely to remain significant after controlling for demographic differences (model 2) or demographic differences plus possible mediators (model 3).

Results for the health outcomes reveal a different pattern. Figure 3 shows that for obesity, the worst outcomes, across all three models, are associated with growing up with a single parent (whether stable or unstable) or an unstable cohabiting parent. This pattern is true as well for asthma,[65] although after controlling for demographic differences (or demographic differences plus the possible

Figure 3. Variation in Predicted Values for Obesity, by Family Type

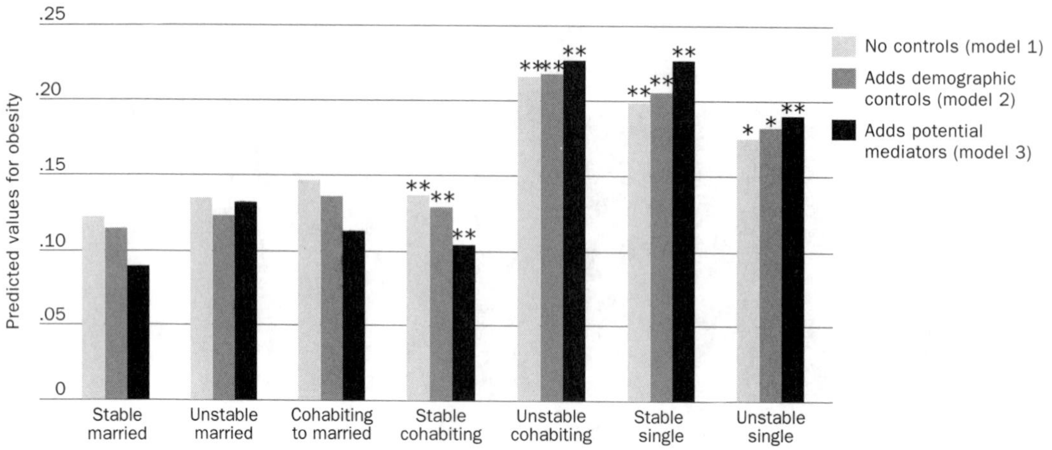

* p<0.05, ** p<0.01

Asterisks indicate that each group is statistically significantly different from the stable married group (the reference category).

mediators), instability appears to be most important (with the worst outcomes found for children of unstable single or unstable cohabiting mothers).

These results suggest that the relative importance of family structure versus family instability matters differently for behavior problems than it does for cognitive or health outcomes. That is, instability seems to matter more than family structure for cognitive and health outcomes, whereas growing up with a single mother (whether that family structure is stable or unstable over time) seems to matter more than instability for behavior problems.

Summary and Conclusions

In this article we summarize the findings from prior research, as well as our own new analyses, that address the question of how well children in fragile families fare compared with those living in traditional married-parent families, as well as what mechanisms might explain any differences. We pay particular attention to studies that use the data from FFCWS to examine the effects of family structure in early childhood.

The FFCWS studies add to a large body of earlier work that suggested that children who live with single or cohabiting parents fare worse as adolescents and young adults in terms of their educational outcomes, risk of teen birth, and attachment to school and the labor market than do children who grow up in married-couple families. Until recently, most of this research focused on divorced parents. The sharp rise over the past few decades in births to unwed mothers, however, has shifted the focus to unmarried single and cohabiting parents. These demographic changes make it difficult to compare research done even ten or fifteen years ago with research on cohorts from the beginning of this century. Rapid changes in the characteristics of parents over time also could result in different selection biases in terms of which parents (both mothers and fathers) have children when married or when unmarried (for example, as the pool of parents having unwed births grows, the characteristics of unwed parents may become more similar to those of married parents, which would result in smaller estimated associations between fragile families and child outcomes). And given that recent cohorts of children born to single and cohabiting parents are relatively young, an additional complication involves comparing outcomes across studies (that is, analysts cannot yet estimate effects of family structure on adolescent and adult outcomes for cohorts such as FFCWS). Therefore, although growing up with single or cohabiting parents rather than with married parents is linked with less desirable outcomes for children and youth, comparisons of the size of such effects, across outcomes, ages, and cohorts, is not possible. In addition, analysts have used vastly different controls to estimate family structure effects, again complicating the quest for integration across studies. We addressed this latter problem by carrying out our own analyses using a consistent set of controls across outcomes.

Current and past research points to several mechanisms that likely underlie the links between family structure and child well-being, including: parental resources, parents' relationship quality, parents' mental health, parenting quality, and father involvement. The selection of different types of men and women into these family types also likely plays a role. Currently, researchers are examining the role of family instability as well as family structure, allowing in some cases for estimates of the influence of both on children.

As noted, past research focused mainly on children whose parents were married when they were born but then separated or divorced (and subsequently lived on their own or remarried). Today, an increasing share of American children is being born to unwed mothers and thus the children are spending the early years of their lives in fragile families, with either a single mother or a cohabiting mother.

That worrisome change informed the launch of the Fragile Families and Child Wellbeing Study a decade ago. Today FFCWS provides a wealth of policy-relevant data on the characteristics and nature of relationships among unwed parents. It also provides extensive data on early child health and development, currently available through age five. A new wave of studies from FFCWS data has enriched understanding of how unwed parenthood affects child well-being.

Studies using the FFCWS data have shed new light on how family structure affects child well-being in early childhood. The findings to date confirm some of the findings in earlier research, but also provide some new insights. In terms of child cognitive development, the FFCWS studies are consistent with past research in suggesting that children in fragile families are likely at risk of poorer school achievement. Of particular interest are analyses suggesting that some of these effects may be due to family instability as much as, or more than, family structure. That is, some studies find that being raised by stable single or cohabiting parents seems to entail less risk than being raised by single or cohabiting parents when these family types are unstable. Because findings are just emerging, the relative risks of unmarried status and turnover in couple relationships cannot be specified yet. Nor do researchers yet know the mechanisms through which family structure and instability influence children or whether the intervening mechanisms are similar or different.

With regard to child behavior problems, evidence is consistent that children in fragile families are at risk for poorer social and emotional development starting in early childhood. In contrast to the results for cognitive outcomes, it appears that behavioral development is compromised in stable single-mother families, but, in common with the results for cognitive outcomes, such problems are aggravated by family instability for children in cohabiting families. The research also sheds a good deal of light on mechanisms, such as maternal stress and mental health as well as parenting, that might help explain why behavior problems are more prevalent in fragile families.

FFCWS is also providing some new insights on the effects of family structure on child health. Across a range of outcomes, findings suggest that children of single mothers are at elevated risk of poor health; evidence of health risks associated with living with cohabiting parents is less consistent. Findings for child abuse and neglect are also intriguing and suggest that children of single mothers and cohabiting mothers are at elevated risk of maltreatment, although marital status per se may be less consequential than whether a man who is not the child's biological father is present in the home.

These findings clearly are cause for concern. Although the children in FFCWS are still quite young, these early gaps in child cognitive, behavioral, and health outcomes do not bode well for these children's long-run prospects.[66] As the children in this cohort age, researchers will be able to study how growing up in fragile families is affecting well-being in middle childhood and adolescence for children who began life with unwed parents. Particularly important in this regard will be studies that take into account the mechanisms we discuss in this article as well as the role of selection and instability.

To the extent that children in fragile families do have poorer outcomes than children born into and growing up in more stable two-parent married-couple families, what are the policy implications? In principle, the findings summarized here point to three routes by which outcomes for children might be improved. The first is to reduce the share of children growing up in fragile families (for example, through policies that reduce the rate of unwed births or that promote family stability among unwed parents). The second is to address the mediating factors that place such children at risk (for example, through policies that boost resources in single-parent homes or that foster father involvement in fragile families). The third is to address directly the risks these children face (for example, through high-quality early childhood education policies or home-visiting policies).

Appendices

Appendix 1. Dependent Variables

Measures of Child Cognitive Ability

1. Peabody Picture Vocabulary Test–Revised (Standardized)
2. Woodcock-Johnson Letter-Word Recognition Test

Measures of Child Behavioral Problems

1. Aggressive Behavior: selected items from the Child Behavior Checklist (20 items) [see page 49 of Five-Year In-Home Longitudinal Study of Pre-School Aged Children User's Guide[1]]
2. Anxiety/Depression: selected items from the Child Behavior Checklist (14 items) [see page 50 of Five-Year In-Home Longitudinal Study of Pre-School Aged Children User's Guide[2]]

Measures of Child Health

1. Obesity [Five-Year In-Home Longitudinal Study of Pre-School Aged Children]: BMI equal to or greater than the 95th percentile
2. Asthma: "During past 12 months, has child had episode of asthma or an asthma attack?" [Mother's Fifth-Year Interview]

Potential Mediators

- Income: Fifth-year household income (in tens of thousands)
- Father's Involvement: "During the last 30 days, on how many days has father seen child?"
- Parenting Quality: "Mother's Aggravation in Parenting" [see Scales Documentation and Question Sources for Five-Year Questionnaires (page 16)[3]]
- Depression: "Constructed—Parent meets depression criteria (liberal) at five-year (Composite International Diagnostic Interview)"

1. See www.fragilefamilies.princeton.edu/documentation.asp.

2. Ibid.

3. Ibid.

Appendix 2. Means of Independent Variables, by Family Structure/Stability Group

	General	Stable married	Stable cohabiting	Stable single	Cohabiting to married	Unstable married	Unstable cohabiting	Unstable single
	N=4,032	*N*=733	*N*=265	*N*=571	*N*=281	*N*=269	*N*=900	*N*=1,013
Independent variable	Mean	Mean	Mean	Mean	Mean	Mean	Mean	Mean
Male	0.53	0.54	0.51	0.54	0.51	0.48	0.50	0.55
Mother white	0.21	0.49	0.17	0.10	0.27	0.28	0.15	0.11
Mother black	0.49	0.21	0.40	0.69	0.30	0.35	0.53	0.64
Mother Hispanic	0.27	0.22	0.42	0.19	0.40	0.32	0.30	0.22
Other	0.04	0.07	0.02	0.02	0.03	0.06	0.03	0.03
Father of different race	0.12	0.09	0.11	0.12	0.14	0.14	0.13	0.13
Mother is high school dropout	0.38	0.15	0.46	0.40	0.35	0.25	0.48	0.48
Mother has high school diploma	0.26	0.15	0.31	0.30	0.29	0.25	0.27	0.28
Mother has some college	0.25	0.27	0.22	0.26	0.31	0.31	0.23	0.22
Mother has college degree	0.11	0.42	0.02	0.03	0.05	0.20	0.02	0.02
Father has same education	0.52	0.60	0.55	0.50	0.50	0.51	0.50	0.49
Father has less education	0.23	0.22	0.20	0.24	0.24	0.32	0.21	0.23
Father has more education	0.25	0.18	0.25	0.26	0.26	0.16	0.28	0.28
Mother's age	30.29	35.05	29.85	29.73	29.53	32.74	29.04	27.95
Father's age	32.89	37.26	32.83	32.71	32.43	35.42	31.51	30.50
Mother's income (in 10,000)	3.79	7.89	3.33	2.09	4.48	4.45	2.60	2.60
Father involvement	17.18	29.89	30.00	5.24	29.79	14.72	12.16	12.92
Parenting quality	2.82	2.87	2.87	2.75	2.90	2.90	2.80	2.79
Mother depressed	0.16	0.11	0.09	0.17	0.19	0.22	0.20	0.17
Father depressed	0.08	0.05	0.09	0.07	0.06	0.12	0.11	0.08

Data: Fragile Families and Child Wellbeing Study.

Endnotes

1. It is important to note that both types of families may spend at least some time as part of larger households that include other family members or friends.
2. Stephanie Ventura, "Changing Patterns of Nonmarital Childbearing in the United States," NCHS Data Brief 18 (Hyattsville, Md.: National Center for Health Statistics, 2009) (www.cdc.gov/nchs/data/databriefs/db18.htm [accessed October 2, 2009]). The share of children born to unwed parents is considerably higher among African Americans, and somewhat higher among Hispanics, than for non-Hispanic whites; see Robert A. Hummer and Erin R. Hamilton, "Race and Ethnicity in Fragile Families," in this volume.
3. See Sara McLanahan and Audrey Beck, "Parental Relationships in Fragile Families," in this volume.
4. Wendy Sigle-Rushton and Sara McLanahan, "Father Absence and Child Well-Being: A Critical Review," Working Paper 02-20-FF (Princeton: Center for Research on Child Wellbeing, October 2002); Sara McLanahan and Gary Sandefur, *Growing Up with a Single Parent: What Hurts, What Helps?* (Harvard University Press, 1994); Sara McLanahan and others, "Unwed Fathers and Fragile Families," Working Paper 98-12-FF (Princeton: Center for Research on Child Wellbeing, March 1998).
5. See review in Paul Amato, "The Impact of Family Formation Change on the Well-Being of the Next Generation," *Future of Children* 15, no. 2 (2005): 75–96. Amato also provides a useful overview of mechanisms that might account for the benefits associated with marriage.
6. See Adam Thomas and Isabel Sawhill, "For Love and Money? The Impact of Family Structure on Family Income," *Future of Children* 15, no. 2 (2005): 57–74. For evidence from FFCWS, see Sara McLanahan, Jean Knab, and Sara Meadows, "Economic Trajectories in Non-Traditional Families with Children," Working Paper 09-10-FF (Princeton: Center for Research on Child Wellbeing, September 2009).
7. Susan L. Brown, "Family Structure and Child Well-Being: The Significance of Parental Cohabitation," *Journal of Marriage and Family* 66 (2004): 351–67; Deborah R. Graefe and Daniel T. Lichter, "Life Course Transitions of American Children: Parental Cohabitation, Marriage, and Single Motherhood," *Demography* 36 (1999): 205–17.
8. McLanahan and Sandefur, *Growing Up with a Single Parent* (see note 4).
9. Steven Friedlander, Daniel S. Weiss, and John Traylor, "Assessing the Influence of Maternal Depression on the Validity of the Child Behavior Checklist," *Journal of Abnormal Psychology* 14 (1986): 123–33; Cynthia Osborne, Sara McLanahan, and Jeanne Brooks-Gunn, "Young Children's Behavioral Problems in Married and Cohabiting Families," Working Paper 03-09-FF (Princeton: Center for Research on Child Wellbeing, September 2004).

10 Brown, "Family Structure and Child Well-Being" (see note 7).

11. Analyses from FFCWS suggest that exits from cohabitation or marriage between the year-one and year-three interviews are associated with deteriorating mental health for men, but not for women, whose mental health seems to be less sensitive to family structure changes (except that women who exit from cohabitation do have larger increases in anxiety than other groups). See Claire Kamp Dush and Kate Adkins, "The Mental Health of Mothers and Fathers before and after Cohabitation and Marital Dissolution," Working Paper 09-03-FF (Princeton: Center for Research on Child Wellbeing, January 2009).

12. E. Mark Cummings and Patrick T. Davies, "Effects of Marital Conflict on Children: Recent Advances and Emerging Themes in Process-Oriented Research," *Journal of Child Psychology and Psychiatry* 43 (2002): 31–63; James L. Peterson and Nicholas Zill, "Marital Disruption, Parent-Child Relationship, and Behavioral Problems in Children," *Journal of Marriage and the Family* 48 (1986): 295–307; Osborne, McLanahan, and Brooks-Gunn, "Young Children's Behavioral Problems in Married and Cohabiting Families" (see note 9).

13. McLanahan and Sandefur, *Growing Up with a Single Parent* (see note 4).

14. See discussion in Marcy Carlson and others, "Couples as Partners and Parents over Children's Early Years," Working Paper 09-12-FF (Princeton: Center for Research on Child Wellbeing, September 2009).

15. Osborne, McLanahan, and Brooks-Gunn, "Young Children's Behavioral Problems" (see note 9); Susan Brown and Alan Booth, "Cohabitation versus Marriage: A Comparison of Relationship Quality," *Journal of Marriage and Family* 58 (1996): 668–78.

16. Marcy Carlson and Frank Furstenberg, "The Consequences of Multi-Partnered Fertility for Parental Involvement and Relationships," Working Paper 06-28-FF (Princeton: Center for Research on Child Wellbeing, May 2007).

17. Marcia Carlson and Sara McLanahan, "Fathers in Fragile Families," Working Paper 09-14-FF (Princeton: Center for Research on Child Wellbeing, 2009). Forthcoming in Michael E. Lamb, ed.,*The Role of the Father in Child Development,* fifth edition (New York: Wiley and Sons).

18. Sharon Bzostek, "Social Fathers and Child Wellbeing," *Journal of Marriage and Family* 70, no. 4 (2008): 950–61; Maureen Black, Howard Dubowitz, and Raymond Starr Jr., "African American Fathers in Low-Income, Urban Families: Development, Behavior, and Home Environment of Their Three Year Old Children," *Child Development* 70, no. 4 (1999): 967–78. See also review by Carlson and McLanahan (note 17).

19. Black, Dubowitz, and Starr, "African American Fathers in Low-Income, Urban Families" (see note 18). See also review by Carlson and McLanahan (note 17).

20. Frank Heiland and Shirley H. Liu, "Family Structure and Wellbeing of Out-of-Wedlock Children: the Significance of the Biological Parents' Relationship," *Demographic Research* 15 (2005): 61–104.

21. See, for example, Eirik Evenhouse and Siobhan Reilly, "A Sibling Study of Stepchild Well-Being," *Journal of Human Resources* 39, no. 1 (2004): 248–76; Sigle-Rushton and McLanahan, "Father Absence and Child Well-Being" (see note 4); Gary Sandefur and Thomas Wells, "Using Siblings to Investigate the Effects of Family Structure on Educational Attainment," Discussion paper 1144-97 (Madison, Wis.: Institute for Research on Poverty, 1997); Lawrence L. Wu, "Effects of Family Instability, Income and Income Instability on the Risk of a Premarital Birth," *American Sociological Review* 61 (1996): 386–406.

22. For instance, some studies have used as an instrument an indicator for the gender of the oldest child, on the grounds that a family is more likely to stay intact if the oldest child is a boy. See Kelly Bedard and Olivier Deschenes, "Sex Preferences, Marital Dissolution, and the Economic Status of Women," *Journal of Human Resources* 40, no. 2 (2005): 411–34; and Elizabeth O. Ananat and Guy Michaels, "The Effect of

Marital Breakup on the Income Distribution of Women with Children," *Journal of Human Resources* 43, no. 3 (2008): 611–29.

23. See, for example, Paula Fomby and Andrew J. Cherlin, "Family Instability and Child Wellbeing," *American Sociological Review* 72 (April 2007): 181–204; Cynthia Osborne and Sara McLanahan, "Partnership Instability and Child Well-Being," *Journal of Marriage and Family* 69 (November 2007): 1065–83.

24. Shannon Cavanagh and Aletha C. Huston, "Family Instability and Children's Early Problem Behavior," *Social Forces* 85, no. 1 (2006): 551–81; Cynthia Osborne, Wendy D. Manning, and Pamela J. Smock, "Married and Cohabiting Parents' Relationship Instability: A Focus on Race and Ethnicity," *Journal of Marriage and Family* 69, no. 5 (2007): 1345–66; Osborne and McLanahan, "Partnership Instability and Child Well-Being" (see note 23).

25. Terry-Ann Craigie, "Effects of Paternal Presence and Family Instability on Child Cognitive Performance," Working Paper 08-03-FF (Princeton: Center for Research on Child Wellbeing, November 2008).

26. Cavanagh and Huston, "Family Instability and Children's Early Problem Behavior" (see note 24); Fomby and Cherlin, "Family Instability and Child Wellbeing" (see note 23).

27. Heiland and Liu, "Family Structure and Wellbeing of Out-of-Wedlock Children" (see note 20).

28. Marcy J. Carlson and Mary Corcoran, "Family Structure and Children's Behavioral and Cognitive Outcomes," *Journal of Marriage and Family* 63 (2001): 779–92.

29. Cynthia Osborne, "Maternal Stress and Mothering Behaviors in Stable and Unstable Families," Working Paper 03-08-FF (Princeton: Center for Research on Child Wellbeing, May 2004); Cavanagh and Huston, "Family Instability and Children's Early Problem Behavior" (see note 24).

30. McLanahan and Sandefur, *Growing Up with a Single Parent* (see note 4).

31. Ibid. Differentials in income also accounted for nearly half the lower school performance of children in single-parent versus two-parent families, although they explained relatively little of the gap in behavior problems between the two groups. Other studies examining the mediating role of income include: Elizabeth Thomson, Thomas L. Hanson, and Sara S. McLanahan, "Family Structure and Child Well-Being: Economic Resources vs. Parental Behavior," *Social Forces* 73 (1994): 221–42; Brown, "Family Structure and Child Well-Being" (see note 7); Osborne, McLanahan and Brooks-Gunn, "Young Children's Behavioral Problems in Married and Cohabiting Families" (see note 9).

32. This research is reviewed by Sharon Bzostek and Audrey Beck, "Family Structure and Child Health Outcomes in Fragile Families," Working Paper 08-11-FF (Princeton: Center for Research on Child Wellbeing, 2008); and by Robert Wood, Brian Goesling, and Sarah Avellar, "The Effects of Marriage on Health: A Synthesis of Recent Research Evidence," report prepared by Mathematica Policy Research for U.S. Department of Health and Human Services, Assistant Secretary for Planning and Evaluation, 2007 (http://aspe.hhs.gov/hsp/07/marriageonhealth/report.pdf [accessed October 4, 2009]).

33. Janet Currie and V. Joseph Hotz, "Accidents Will Happen? Unintentional Injury, Maternal Employment, and Child Care Policy," *Journal of Health Economics* 23, no. 1 (2004): 25–59.

34. Anne Case and Christina Paxson, "Mothers and Others: Who Invests in Children's Health?" *Journal of Health Economics* 20 (2001): 301–28.

35. This literature is reviewed in Lawrence Berger, Christina Paxson, and Jane Waldfogel, "Mothers, Men, and Child Protective Services Involvement," *Child Maltreatment* 14 (2009): 263–76. See also Jane Waldfogel, *The Future of Child Protection* (Harvard University Press, 1998).

36. See also discussion in Sara McLanahan, "Fragile Families and the Reproduction of Poverty," *Annals of American Academy of Political and Social Science* 62, no. 1 (2009): 111–31; and Sara McLanahan and Christine Percheski, "Family Structure and the Reproduction of Inequality," *Annual Review of Sociology* 34 (2008): 257–76.

37. Nancy Reichman, Julien Teitler, and Sara McLanahan, "Fragile Families: Sample and Design," *Children and Youth Services Review* 23, nos. 4/5 (2001): 303–26.

38. Osborne, McLanahan, and Brooks-Gunn, "Young Children's Behavioral Problems in Married and Cohabiting Families" (see note 9); Carlson and Corcoran, "Family Structure and Children's Behavioral and Cognitive Outcomes" (see note 28).

39. Reichman, Teitler, and McLanahan, "Fragile Families" (see note 37).

40. Craigie, "Effects of Paternal Presence and Family Instability on Child Cognitive Performance" (see note 25).

41. Shirley Liu and Frank Heiland, "Should We Get Married? The Effect of Parents' Marriage on Out-of Wedlock Children," Working Paper 07-02-FF (Princeton: Center for Research on Child Wellbeing, 2008).

42. Craigie, "Effects of Paternal Presence and Family Instability on Child Cognitive Performance" (see note 25).

43. Carey Cooper and others, "Partnership Instability and Child Wellbeing during the Transition to Elementary School," Working Paper 08-08-FF (Princeton: Center for Research on Child Wellbeing, April 2010).

44. Osborne, McLanahan, and Brooks-Gunn, "Young Children's Behavioral Problems in Married and Cohabiting Families" (see note 9); Cynthia Osborne, "Is Marriage Protective for All Children? Cumulative Risks at Birth and Subsequent Child Behavior among Urban Families," Working Paper 07-09-FF (Princeton: Center for Research on Child Wellbeing, April 2007).

45. Rebecca Ryan, Ariel Kalil, and Lindsey Leininger, "Low-Income Mothers' Private Safety Nets and Children's Socioemotional Wellbeing," *Journal of Marriage and the Family* 71, no. 2 (2009): 278–98.

46. Marcy Carlson, Sara McLanahan, and Jeanne Brooks-Gunn, "Do Good Partners Make Good Parents? Relationship Quality and Parenting in Two-Parent Families," Working Paper 06-34-FF (Princeton: Center for Research on Child Wellbeing, November 2006); Marcy Carlson and others, "Couples as Partners and Parents over Children's Early Years" (see note 14); Paula Fomby and Cynthia Osborne, "The Relative Effects of Family Instability and Mother/ Partner Conflict on Children's Externalizing Behavior," Working Paper 08-07-FF (Princeton: Center for Research on Child Wellbeing, May 2008).

47. Cynthia Osborne and Sara McLanahan, "Partnership Instability and Child Wellbeing," *Journal of Marriage and Family* 69 (2007): 1065–83. This result was also found in a study using data from the NICHD Study of Early Child Care and Youth Development, which is important since that study included a measure of teacher-reported behavior problems (whereas the measure in FFCWS is mother-reported). See Cavanagh and Huston, "Family Instability and Children's Early Problem Behavior" (see note 24).

48. Carey Cooper and others, "Partnership Instability and Child Wellbeing during the Transition to Elementary School" (see note 43).

49. Audrey Beck and others, "Relationship Transitions and Maternal Parenting," Working Paper 08-12-FF (Princeton: Center for Research on Child Wellbeing, January 2009).

50. Cynthia Osborne and Sara McLanahan, "Partnership Instability and Child Wellbeing" (see note 47).

51. Bzostek, "Social Fathers and Child Wellbeing" (see note 18).

52. Liu and Heiland, "Should We Get Married?" (see note 41).

53. Bzostek and Beck, "Family Structure and Child Health Outcomes in Fragile Families" (see note 32).

54. See also a FFCWS study that finds that instability is associated with mothers' obesity but not with children's obesity; see Earle Chambers, Christiane Duarte, and Frances Yang, "Household Instability, Area Poverty, and Obesity in Urban Mothers and Their Children," *Journal of Health Care for the Poor and Underserved* 20, no. 1 (2009): 122–34.

55. They also examine the role of reverse causality and find some evidence that children who are in poorer health are less likely to have their parents cohabiting at the next survey wave.

56. Lisa Bates and Julien Teitler, "Immigration and Low Birthweight in the US: The Role of Time and Timing," Working Paper 08-15-FF (Princeton: Center for Research on Child Wellbeing, July 2008). In this study and others, low birth weight is typically defined as a birth weight of less than 2,500 grams.

57. Nancy Reichman and others, "Infant Health Production Functions: What a Difference the Data Make," *Health Economics* 18, no. 7 (2009): 761–82.

58. Yolanda Padilla and Nancy Reichman, "Low Birthweight: Do Unwed Fathers Help?" *Children and Youth Services Review* 23, nos. 4/5 (2001): 505–30. See also Julien Teitler, "Father Involvement, Child Health, and Maternal Health Behavior," *Children and Youth Services Review* 23, nos. 4/5 (2001): 403–26.

59. Kristen Harknett, "Why Are Children with Married Parents Healthier? The Case of Pediatric Asthma," *Population Research and Policy Review* 28, no. 3 (2009): 347–65; Kristen Harknett, "Children's Elevated Risk of Asthma in Unmarried Families: Underlying Structural and Behavioral Mechanisms," Working Paper 05-01-FF (Princeton: Center for Research on Child Wellbeing, July 2005).

60. Shirley Liu and Frank Heiland, "New Estimates of the Effect of Parental Separation on Child Health," in *Causal Analysis in Population Studies: Concepts, Methods, and Applications,* edited by Henriette Engelhardt, Hans Peter Kohler, and Alexia Furnkranz-Prskawetz (Vienna: Springer, 2009), pp. 167–99.

61. Neil Guterman and others, "Fathers and Maternal Risk for Physical Child Abuse," *Child Maltreatment* 14 (2009): 277–90.

62. Berger, Paxson, and Waldfogel, "Mothers, Men, and Child Protective Services Involvement" (see note 35).

63. The authors were not able to determine whether the increased risk was due to abuse or neglect on the part of the mother, the social father, or another caregiver.

64. See Terry-Ann Craigie, Jane Waldfogel, and Jeanne Brooks-Gunn, "Family Structure, Stability, and Early Child Health and Development," Princeton University and Columbia University mimeo, 2010, for full results.

65. Ibid.

66. See, for example, Janet Currie, "Healthy, Wealthy, and Wise: Socioeconomic Status, Poor Health in Childhood, and Human Capital Development," *Journal of Economic Literature* 47, no. 1 (2009): 87–122; and Janet Currie and others, "Child Health and Young Adult Outcomes," *Journal of Human Resources,* forthcoming.

Race and Ethnicity in Fragile Families

Robert A. Hummer and Erin R. Hamilton

Summary

Robert Hummer and Erin Hamilton note that the prevalence of fragile families varies substantially by race and ethnicity. African Americans and Hispanics have the highest prevalence; Asian Americans, the lowest; and whites fall somewhere in the middle. The share of unmarried births is lower among most foreign-born mothers than among their U.S.-born ethnic counterparts. Immigrant-native differences are particularly large for Asians, whites, and blacks.

The authors also find racial and ethnic differences in the composition and stability of fragile families over time. Although most parents of all racial and ethnic groups are romantically involved at the time of their child's birth, African American women are less likely to be in a cohabiting relationship than are white and Hispanic mothers. Over time, these racial and ethnic differences become more pronounced, with African American mothers having the lowest rates of marriage and cohabitation and the highest breakup rates, and Mexican immigrant mothers having the highest rates of marriage and cohabitation and the lowest breakup rates.

Fragile families have far fewer socioeconomic resources than married families, though resources vary within fragile families by race and ethnicity. White mothers, in general, have more socioeconomic resources than black, Mexican American, and Mexican immigrant mothers; they are more likely to have incomes above the poverty limit, more likely to own a car, less likely to have children from a prior relationship, and more likely to report living in a safe neighborhood. Access to health care and child care follows a similar pattern. The exception is education; black and white unmarried mothers are equally likely to have finished high school, and Mexican immigrant and Mexican American mothers are less likely to have done so.

The authors argue that socioeconomic differences are by far the biggest driver of racial and ethnic differences in marriage and family stability, and they support reforms to strengthen parents' economic security. They also discuss how sex ratios and culture affect family formation and stability. In particular, they note that despite severe poverty, Mexican immigrant families have high rates of marriage and cohabitation—an advantage that erodes by the second generation with assimilation. To address the paradox that marriage declines as socioeconomic status improves, they support policies that reinforce rather than undermine the family ties of Mexican immigrants.

www.futureofchildren.org

Robert A. Hummer is the Centennial Commission Professor of Liberal Arts in the Department of Sociology and Population Research Center at the University of Texas–Austin. Erin R. Hamilton is an assistant professor of sociology at the University of California–Davis.

One of the most striking demographic trends in the United States over the past half-century has been the increasing share of children born to unmarried parents. Nonmarital births accounted for 39.7 percent of all U.S. births in 2007,[1] up from 18.4 percent in 1980 and just 5.3 percent in 1960.[2] Current percentages are highest among African Americans, American Indians, and Hispanics, and lowest among Asian Americans. A major component of the growth in nonmarital childbearing has been births to unmarried but cohabiting parents; during the late 1990s, births to cohabiting parents made up about half of all nonmarital births.[3]

A second striking demographic trend in American society over the past half-century has been the racial and ethnic diversification of the population. The U.S. population grew from roughly 200 million during the mid-1960s to more than 300 million in 2006, with immigration—immigrants themselves, plus their U.S.-born children—accounting for 55 percent of this increase.[4] Because nearly 80 percent of immigrants to the United States since 1965 have come from Latin America and Asia, the growth of the Hispanic and Asian American populations has been especially rapid, with Hispanics now accounting for 15 percent of the total U.S. population and Asian Americans, nearly 5 percent, compared with approximately 4.7 percent for Hispanics and 0.8 percent for Asian Americans in 1970. The share of the population that is African American or black, now 13 percent, has also continued to grow, although more slowly. In contrast, the non-Hispanic white population—while continuing to grow in absolute terms—has dropped from 83.2 percent of the total in 1970 to an estimated 67 percent in 2006.[5] Population projections suggest that the non-Hispanic white population share will fall to less than 50 percent by the middle of the twenty-first century, while the Hispanic and Asian American populations will continue to grow especially rapidly.[6]

Demographic changes like increases in the share of children born to unmarried parents (with particularly high levels among some racial and ethnic minority groups) and diversification of the population would have less meaning if they were not accompanied by differences across racial and ethnic groups in resources available to children. But these resources vary greatly from one group to another. Because children from most racial and ethnic minority groups are much more likely than white and Asian American children to be born to unmarried parents, and children of unmarried parents are substantially disadvantaged relative to those in married households, family structure is a key mechanism through which racial and ethnic inequality persists across generations.[7] Parental resources—particularly socioeconomic and health care resources—also vary quite extensively by race and ethnicity within unmarried families, as we document below.

In this paper, we review racial and ethnic differences in fragile families—those families in which the parents are unmarried at the time of their child's birth. First, we document racial and ethnic differences and trends in the prevalence, composition, and stability of fragile families. Second, we examine the extent to which parental resources differ by race and ethnicity within fragile families themselves and between fragile families and married families. Third, we review explanations for the racial and ethnic differences in the prevalence of, and trends in, fragile families. We conclude with a discussion of

Figure 1. Share of Births to Unmarried Mothers by Race/Ethnicity and Nativity, 2006

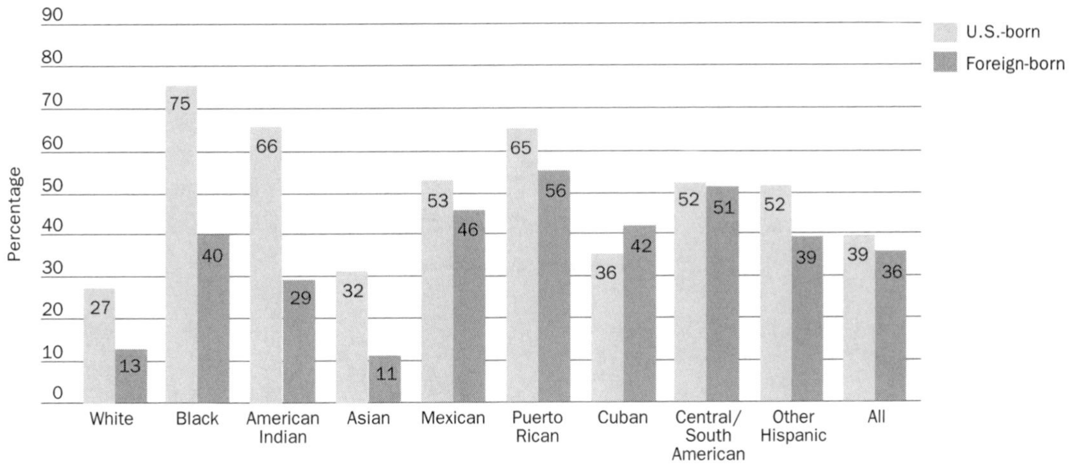

Source: National Center for Health Statistics, Vital Statistics.

policy implications. Throughout the review, we compare immigrant and nonimmigrant families to the extent data allow because nativity is an important axis of differentiation for many social and demographic phenomena in the United States.

Prevalence, Composition, and Stability of Fragile Families by Race and Ethnicity

The prevalence of nonmarital childbearing, as well as trends in such childbearing over time, differs considerably across racial and ethnic groups, as does the relationship type and the level of instability among fragile families during their children's early years.

Unmarried Births: Prevalence and Trends

Recent national data on nonmarital births show large racial and ethnic differences in the prevalence of fragile families. In 2006, the share of births to unmarried mothers ranged from a high of 75 percent among non-Hispanic U.S.-born black women to a low of 11 percent among immigrant Asian women (see figure 1). Children of U.S.-born black women were thus more than six times as likely as children of immigrant Asian American women to be born into fragile families; they were more than two and a half times as likely as children of U.S.-born non-Hispanic white women to be born into fragile families (the share of unmarried births to white women was 27 percent in 2006). Figure 1 also shows substantial diversity in the share of unmarried births among Hispanics by national origin group, ranging from a high of 65 percent among mainland-born Puerto Rican women to a low of 36 percent among U.S.-born Cuban women. Roughly half of children born to Mexican-origin women—46 percent among Mexican immigrant women and 53 percent among Mexican American women—were born in fragile families in 2006.

The share of unmarried births is lower among most foreign-born (that is, immigrant) groups of women than among their U.S-born co-ethnic counterparts,[8] even though the difference in the share of such births to the two groups as a whole is narrow (39 percent, compared with 36 percent). The

Figure 2a. Change in the Share of Births to Unmarried Mothers by Race/Ethnicity, 1970–2006

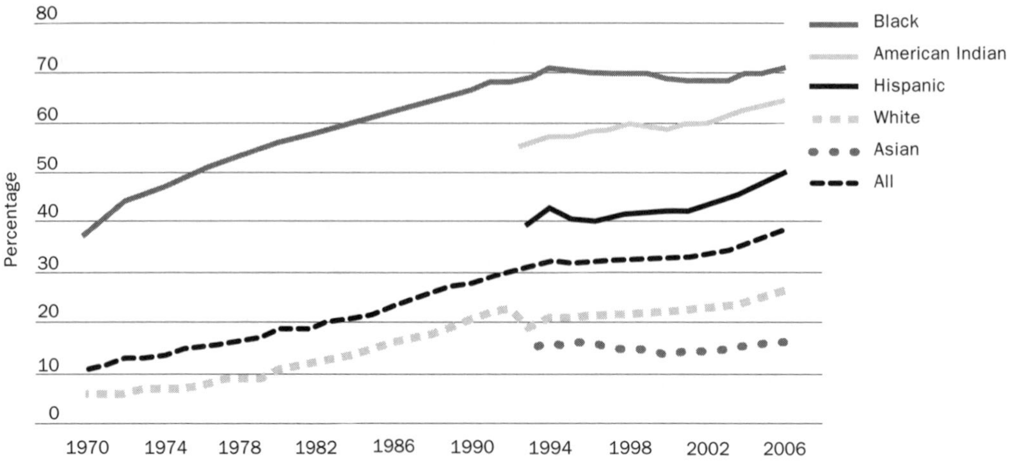

Source: National Center for Health Statistics, Vital Statistics.

immigrant-native difference is particularly large among Asian Americans: births to unmarried women are 11 percent among immigrants, but 32 percent among those born in the United States. The immigrant-native difference is also large among non-Hispanic whites and non-Hispanic blacks; in both these groups, the share of unmarried births among immigrant women is about half that among U.S.-born women. Immigrant-native differences in the share of births to unmarried women tend to be smaller among the Hispanic national origin groups.

The share of births to unmarried women has been growing steadily over the past four decades. In 1970, fewer than one in ten U.S. births was to an unmarried mother, compared with 39 percent in 2006 (figure 2a).[9] Figure 2a also shows that the share of births to unmarried women increased for both white and black women over this period, although that for black women has remained steady at around 70 percent since the mid-1990s.[10] Among white women, the share of unmarried births in 1970 (6 percent) more than quadrupled by 2006 (27 percent). Data for Hispanics, American Indians, and Asian Americans were not available until the 1990s. Although the share of unmarried births to Asian American women held fairly steady between 1993 and 2002, it has increased each year since then, up to almost 17 percent in 2007. The share of unmarried births increased rapidly for Hispanics (up to 50 percent) and American Indians (up to 65 percent) from 1993 until 2007.

The share of unmarried births reflects a mix of the birth rates for unmarried and married women in each racial and ethnic group, as well as the proportion of childbearing-aged women that is married in each racial and ethnic group. The share of unmarried births for a group can increase, for example, through a decline in the marital birth rate, an increase in the nonmarital birth rate, or both. Moreover, the share of unmarried births for a group can increase through a shift in the proportion of women of childbearing age who are not married. In the United States, the increasing proportion of both black and white

Figure 2b. Change in the Nonmarital and Marital Birth Rates by Race, 1970–2006

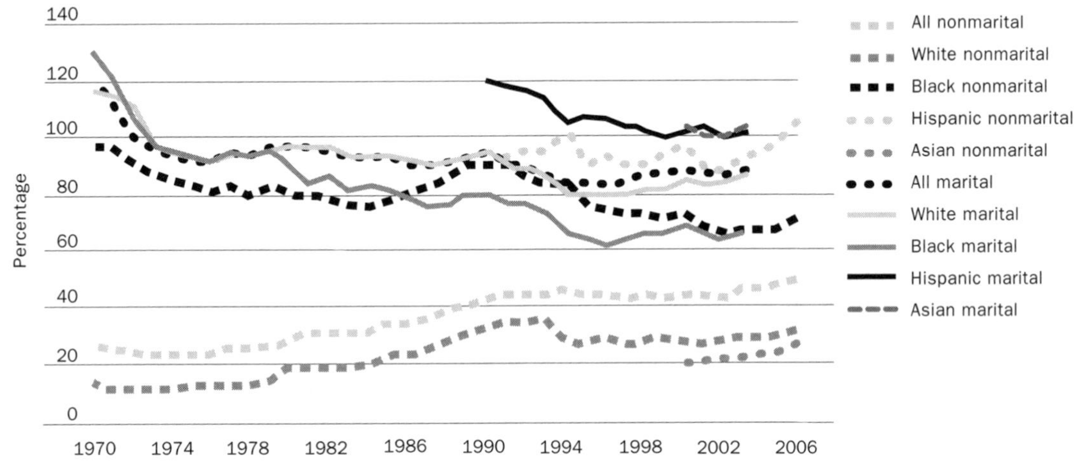

Source: National Center for Health Statistics, Vital Statistics.

women of childbearing age who were unmarried in recent decades has been important in helping to explain the rise in the share of unmarried births among both groups.[11]

Beyond shifts in the share of unmarried childbearing-aged women, trends in marital and nonmarital birth rates among women have also been important in explaining the overall rising share of nonmarital births among each racial and ethnic group. Figure 2b shows trends in both the nonmarital and marital birth rates by race and ethnicity and for all U.S. women since 1970. The nonmarital birth rate is equal to the number of nonmarital births in a year per 1,000 unmarried women, while the marital birth rate is the number of marital births in a year per 1,000 married women. Figure 2b clearly shows that, for the whole population, marital birth rates have sharply declined since 1970 while nonmarital birth rates have sharply increased. Nonmarital birth rates have been rising for most racial and ethnic groups except for blacks. Among blacks, the nonmarital birth rate declined from nearly 100 in 1970 to a low of 66 in 2002; there has been a slight upturn over the past few years. In contrast, the nonmarital birth rates for whites rose from 14 in 1970 to 32 in 2006. Unmarried black women today are thus having fewer births than they did in 1970, while unmarried white women are having more. Hispanic women now have the nation's highest nonmarital birth rate (106) and, together with Asian American women, the highest marital birth rate (101).[12] The high level of marital fertility among Hispanic women is important in producing an overall percentage of nonmarital births (50 percent) that is lower than that among blacks, in spite of the higher nonmarital birth rate among Hispanics.

Relationship Types and Family Stability over Time

Fragile families are more complex than data on unmarried birth percentages and rates suggest, and their compositional complexity too varies across racial and ethnic groups. Figure 3 shows the distribution of relationship type among unmarried families included in the Fragile Families and Child Wellbeing Study.

Figure 3. Unmarried Parents' Relationship Status at the Birth of a Child and Three and Five Years Following the Birth, by Mother's Race/Ethnicity

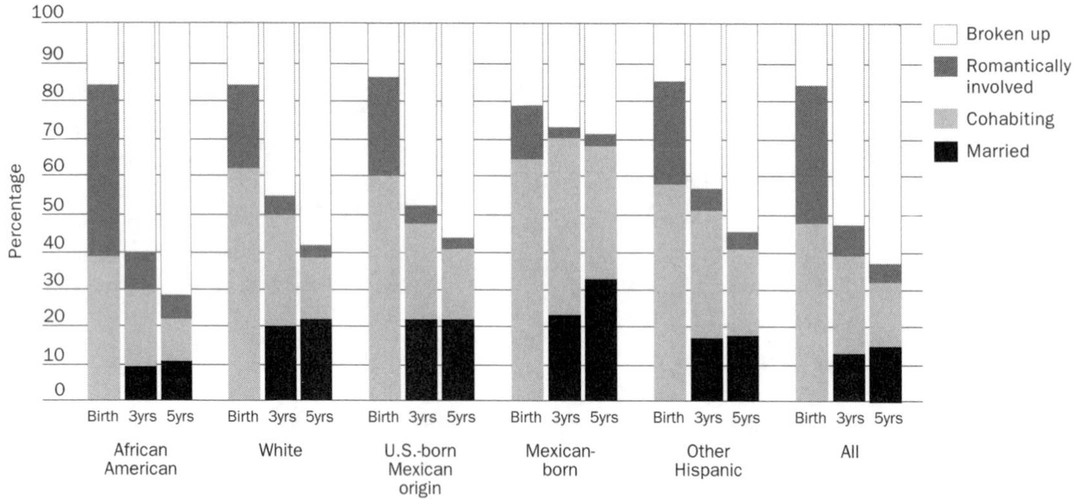

Source: Fragile Families and Child Wellbeing Study.
Note: This presentation mimics figure 2 from Kristen Harknett and Sara McLanahan, "Racial and Ethnic Differences in Marriage after the Birth of a Child," *American Sociological Review* 69 (2004): 790–811.

The first bar for each group shows relationship type among unmarried parents at the birth of their child. A commonality across all groups is that a large majority—between 79 and 86 percent—of parents are romantically involved at the time of the birth of their child. Among romantically involved parents, African American mothers are more likely to be in a noncohabiting union than other mothers, whereas white, Mexican-origin, and other Hispanic mothers are more likely to be cohabiting with the child's father at the time of the birth.

Figure 3 also shows that there is substantial relationship instability among unmarried parents in the five years following the birth of a child and that there are profound racial and ethnic differences in these compositional shifts over time. At the two extremes are African American and Mexican immigrant women. Five years following unmarried births, African American mothers have the lowest rates of marriage (9 percent) and cohabitation (13 percent) and the highest relationship breakup rate (71 percent). They also are most likely (6 percent) to maintain a noncohabiting romantic union with the child's father. Mexican immigrant unmarried mothers, on the other hand, have the highest rates of marriage (33 percent) and cohabitation (36 percent) over the next five years, and the lowest relationship breakup rate (29 percent). These differences mean that children born to unmarried Mexican immigrant mothers are three times more likely than children born to unmarried African American mothers to be living with both biological parents at age five. Five years after the birth of a child, between 55 and 59 percent of white, Mexican American, and other Hispanic unmarried mothers have broken up with the child's father—a sharp contrast with the 14–17 percent who had broken up at the time of the child's birth. Clearly, instability among fragile families is very high, even within the first five years of a child's life.

Figure 4. Relationship Status Three and Five Years Following the Birth, by Mother's Race/Ethnicity, among Parents Who Were Cohabiting at Birth

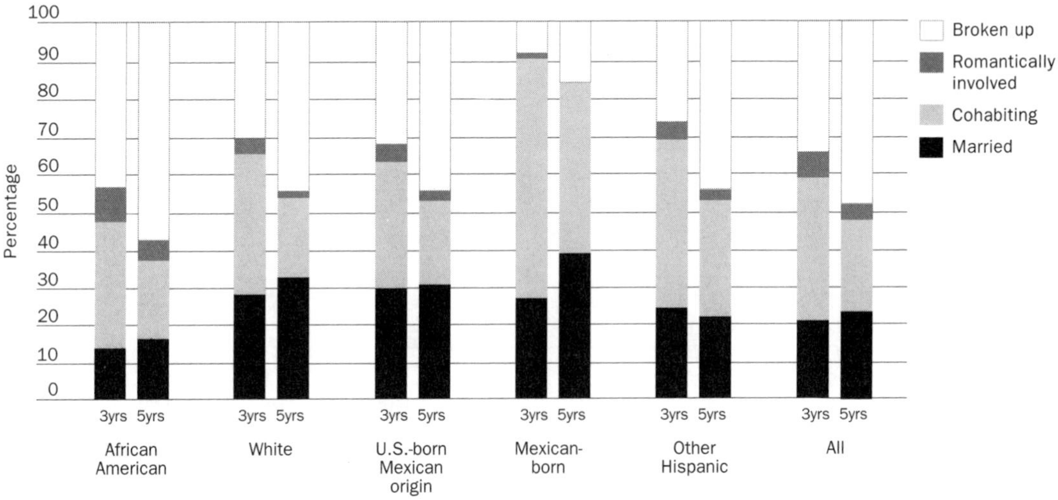

Source: Fragile Families and Child Wellbeing Study.
Note: This presentation mimics figure 2 from Kristen Harknett and Sara McLanahan, "Racial and Ethnic Differences in Marriage after the Birth of a Child," *American Sociological Review* 69 (2004): 790–811.

Figure 4 further illustrates instability in fragile families, and racial and ethnic variations within those families, by showing relationship change among unmarried mothers who were cohabiting at the time of the child's birth. Among all such women, less than half were still cohabiting (24 percent) or were married (23 percent) by the time the child reached age five, while 48 percent had separated. Mexican immigrant women were by far the least likely to separate from the father—only 9 percent by the time the child was three and 16 percent by the time the child was five. For all the other racial and ethnic groups shown, more than 40 percent of mothers cohabiting at birth had separated by the time their child was five. The share was highest among African American mothers, at 57 percent.

Racial and Ethnic Differences in Resources among Fragile Families

Resources available to fragile families vary by race and ethnicity in ways that generally favor white women and that illustrate the difficult socioeconomic circumstances faced by most unmarried black, Mexican American, and Mexican immigrant mothers. Table 1 summarizes these racial and ethnic differences in socioeconomic, social support, and health care and child care resources among single (that is, noncohabiting), cohabiting, and married mothers at the time of birth.[13] Baseline (at time of birth) national data from the Fragile Families and Child Wellbeing Study (FFCWS) are used for these comparisons because the survey contains in-depth information regarding parental resources among fragile families along with a comparison sample of married mothers.[14] Because of the relatively small sample sizes available for some groups in the survey, racial and ethnic categories must be limited. Thus, our discussion focuses on resource comparisons between non-Hispanic black, non-Hispanic white, Mexican American, and Mexican immigrant women and their families.

Table 1. Resource Differentials, by Maternal Race/Ethnicity and Nativity among Fragile Families and Married Families at Child's Birth

	Single mothers				Cohabiting mothers				Married mothers			
Percent unless otherwise indicated	Non-Hispanic black	Mexican American	Mexican immigrant	Non-Hispanic white	Non-Hispanic black	Mexican American	Mexican immigrant	Non-Hispanic white	Non-Hispanic black	Mexican American	Mexican immigrant	Non-Hispanic white
Socioeconomic resources												
Mother lacks high school degree	44.2	53.1*	82.4*	37.4	39.6	56.7*	75.2*	39.8	13.9*	35.3*	70.2*	8.1
Father lacks high school degree	31.1	36.2	52.9*	29.6	29.6	46.0*	77.6*	30.1	11.9*	33.8*	73.7*	6.1
Household in poverty	52.6*	41.5*	45.9*	29.1	41.5*	42.8*	48.5*	21.3	14.2*	23.5*	39.5*	3.0
Household near poverty	27.0	28.5	44.7*	24.3	25.7*	30.0	33.3	28.5	23.1*	20.6*	37.7*	10.1
Receipt of public assistance in past year	48.9	40.8	31.8*	47.1	47.2*	45.5*	18.2*	36.4	16.3*	22.1*	21.1*	4.9
Own car	23.6*	26.2*	10.6*	44.7	38.7*	38.5*	29.1*	57.7	66.8*	60.3*	39.5*	84.4
Live in safe neighborhood	78.4*	79.2*	77.7*	88.4	78.4*	84.5	72.7*	86.8	86.8*	94.1	73.7*	95.1
Mother under age 20	26.1	25.4	16.5	25.2	16.8	23.5	14.0	21.0	1.4	11.8*	3.5	2.4
Mother has other children	60.3*	50.0	55.3	44.2	72.2*	68.5*	58.8	49.8	77.0*	67.7	66.7	60.7
Partner and social support												
Father visited hospital at birth	61.1	55.4	40.0*	56.3	91.4*	94.7	94.6	96.9	92.2*	97.1	93.0*	98.6
Father wants involvement	89.8*	77.7	68.2	76.7	99.9	99.5	100.0	100.0	N/A	N/A	N/A	N/A
Grandparent in home	45.4	55.4	23.5*	47.1	16.0	21.4	12.1	15.4	10.2*	13.2*	7.1	5.5
Access to support if needed:												
Financial help ($200)	87.5	90.8	83.5	89.8	85.7	91.4	84.9	89.3	92.2*	95.6	90.4*	98.0
Place to live	91.4	95.4	92.9	92.2	89.5	94.1	81.2*	91.9	91.9*	95.6	88.6*	97.4
Health care and child care resources												
Health insurance at birth												
Private or HMO	18.7*	24.6	7.2*	28.9	23.2*	20.9*	14.1*	31.9	62.3*	58.8*	30.1*	87.6
Medicaid	77.4*	73.9	81.9*	66.7	73.1*	76.5*	79.8*	62.5	35.3*	41.2*	62.8*	9.5
None	3.9	1.5	10.8*	4.4	3.7	2.7	6.1	5.7	2.4	0.0	7.1*	2.8
Help with child care during child's first year	92.8	93.1	84.7*	94.2	90.6	94.1	79.4*	94.0	89.2*	97.1	86.0*	96.4
Primary source of child care during child's first year†												
Parents	53.1*	50.4	60.0*	42.8	53.0	54.7	71.9*	56.8	44.1*	59.3	80.4*	59.0
Family	20.4*	26.5	20.0	27.2	22.1	22.4	18.0	19.7	20.9*	27.1*	10.3	12.6
Neighborhood	7.5*	5.8	20.0	12.2	8.7	7.7	7.9	12.8	16.0	6.8	7.2	13.5
Center	19.0	17.4	0.0*	17.8	16.3*	15.3	2.2*	10.7	19.0	6.8	2.1*	15.0
Sample size	1,226	130	85	206	790	187	165	319	295	68	114	494
Distribution	53.1	33.8	23.4	20.2	34.2	48.6	45.3	31.3	12.8	17.7	31.3	48.5

* $p<.05$, indicates statistically significant difference in comparison to non-Hispanic white women based on a two-sided t-test of equal means.
† Reported at year 1 by mothers completing year 1 follow-up survey.

Source: Authors' analysis of the Fragile Families and Child Wellbeing Study baseline survey (see note 14).

Socioeconomic Resources

As table 1 shows, unmarried new mothers (both single, or noncohabiting, and cohabiting) in each racial and ethnic group are much more likely to have less than a high school education, have a partner with less than a high school education, and to live in or near poverty than married new mothers in the same group. Further, unmarried women in each racial and ethnic group are less likely to own a car or report that they live in a safe neighborhood than married women. These fundamental socioeconomic disadvantages for unmarried mothers are apparent for every racial and ethnic category and are especially pronounced among single (that is, noncohabiting) mothers compared with married mothers.[15] For example, 37.4 percent of white women in the FFCWS who were single (again, noncohabiting) at the time of their child's birth had no high school degree compared with just 8.1 percent of married white women. Likewise, 52.6 percent of single (noncohabiting) black women were living in poverty at the time of their child's birth, compared with 14.2 percent of married black women.

Within groups of cohabiting and single mothers, white women have greater socioeconomic resources than black, Mexican American, and Mexican immigrant mothers. In particular, white single and cohabiting new mothers are far less likely to have household incomes below the federal poverty limit, are much more likely to own a car, are somewhat less likely to have other children, and are more likely to report living in a safe neighborhood than their black, Mexican American, and Mexican immigrant counterparts. Likely as a result of their lower incidence of poverty, cohabiting white mothers are also less likely to have received public assistance in the past year than cohabiting black or Mexican American women (although a relatively high share of single white women reports receiving public assistance). The share of Mexican American and Mexican immigrant unmarried women without a high school degree is high, ranging from 53.1 percent among single Mexican American mothers to 82.4 percent among single Mexican immigrant mothers. By contrast, much lower shares of black and white unmarried women lack a high school degree and, for unmarried mothers in the same category of family relationship (that is, single or cohabiting), the shares of black and white women without a high school degree exhibit only minor differences. Patterns of paternal education largely reflect those of maternal education, with Mexican immigrant and Mexican American unmarried women reporting the highest shares of less than a high school degree among their children's fathers.

The share of mothers younger than age twenty at time of birth does not vary much between racial and ethnic groups within the same category of family relationship, with the share of Mexican immigrant teen mothers being modestly lower than those of other racial and ethnic groups within each family relationship category. Thus, racial and ethnic differences in socioeconomic resources among single, cohabiting, or married mothers are not attributable to maternal age disparities across groups.

All told, then, Mexican immigrant and Mexican American single and cohabiting women are particularly disadvantaged along most socioeconomic characteristics, with Mexican immigrants the most socioeconomically disadvantaged. About 80 percent of Mexican immigrant cohabiting mothers and about 90 percent of Mexican immigrant single mothers are in or near poverty, and more than 75 percent of single and cohabiting

Mexican immigrant new mothers have less than a high school degree. But Mexican immigrant women also have the lowest rates of public assistance receipt, likely because undocumented and recently arrived documented immigrants are ineligible for many public services. Black single and cohabiting women are also disadvantaged compared with white single and cohabiting women, respectively, especially in terms of poverty. More important even than these socioeconomic disparities between unmarried black and white mothers, though, is the much higher prevalence of births to unmarried black than white women.

Partner and Social Support Resources

Table 1 shows that differences in partner and social support across racial and ethnic groups are far less pronounced than differences in socioeconomic resources. Women cohabiting at the time of their children's birth in all racial and ethnic groups report (in a pattern virtually identical with that of married women) that fathers nearly universally want involvement with their children and have visited the hospital shortly after the birth. Cohabiting mothers in all groups also report very good access to social support at the time of their children's birth, a pattern that, again, differs little from that reported by married mothers. Among cohabiting women, reported social supports are modestly lower among Mexican immigrants, which might be expected given that some of their most important support networks may be in Mexico.

Single mothers report generally less partner support than cohabiting or married mothers among all racial and ethnic groups. Single mothers are, however, about twice as likely as cohabiting mothers to report having a grandparent of their new child living with them, likely because more single mothers live with their parents for financial support and child care absent a cohabiting partner. Mexican immigrant single mothers are least likely to report having a grandparent of their children in the home, again most likely because parents of Mexican immigrant new mothers may be living in Mexico. Within the category of single mothers, however, most racial and ethnic differences in partner and social support are not large; for example, racial and ethnic groups report no differences in access to financial support or to a place to live in emergency situations. One pattern that does turn up among mothers who are not cohabiting at the time of birth is that black mothers are somewhat more likely to report that the fathers of their children visited the hospital and want to be involved in their children's lives than are other racial and ethnic groups. This finding is consistent with other recent evidence that black fathers' roles outside of marriage may be more strongly institutionalized than those of unmarried white fathers.[16] Overall, though, reported partner and social support differences across racial and ethnic groups are modest in comparison to the wide differences in socioeconomic resources across groups.

Health Care and Child Care Resources

As with socioeconomic resources, health care and child care resources available to women differ by race and ethnicity at the time of their children's birth, even within family structure categories. As table 1 shows, across all groups, single and cohabiting women are far less likely to have private or health maintenance organization (HMO) health care coverage than are married women and are far more likely to rely on Medicaid or to be completely uninsured. But single white women in fragile families are the most likely to be privately or HMO insured, while single Mexican immigrant women in fragile families are the least likely to have private or HMO

Research on explanations for the racial and ethnic differences in fragile families is complex because such differences involve historical patterns of family formation across groups, the effects of immigration and assimilation trends, and economic and social changes over time.

coverage and are most likely to be uninsured. For example, table 1 shows that 29 percent of single white mothers reported private or HMO insurance coverage at the time of their child's birth compared with just 7 percent for single Mexican immigrant mothers. This pattern is consistent with earlier work using the FFCWS and suggests that young children of Mexican immigrant women are especially at risk of not having insurance coverage and of not seeing physicians when ill or after accidents.[17] Black and Mexican American single and cohabiting mothers are also more likely to rely on Medicaid than white single and cohabiting mothers, which is not surprising given the reported racial and ethnic differences in household income.

Racial and ethnic differences in child care arrangements also reflect to some degree the particular socioeconomic and geographic disadvantages for Mexican immigrant single and cohabiting new mothers, who are least likely to have someone available to help them with care early in their children's lives and are most likely to be, themselves, their primary source of child care. Related work using FFCWS data finds that, among unmarried mothers who work outside the home, Hispanics are most apt to use maternal relatives for care, while blacks are most likely to use day care centers, and whites, to use their children's fathers.[18] Such racial and ethnic differences reflect both socioeconomic differences across groups and culturally based preferences for child care arrangements.

Explanations for Racial and Ethnic Differences in Fragile Families

Research on explanations for the racial and ethnic differences in fragile families is complex because such differences involve historical patterns of family formation across groups, the effects of immigration and assimilation trends, and economic and social changes over time, including changing norms regarding the American family. We focus here on three themes prevalent in the research literature. The first is the effect of structurally based socioeconomic barriers to marriage and family stability. The second is the effect of sex ratios. The third is the effect of culture and norms on patterns of family formation and stability among some racial and ethnic groups. Although our review suggests that all three explanations are important for understanding racial and ethnic differences in fragile families, we believe the first—the effect of structurally based socioeconomic disadvantages—best explains current racial and ethnic differences in the formation, resource disparities, and stability of fragile families.

Structurally Based Socioeconomic Disadvantages as Barriers to Marriage and Family Stability

One important strand of research strongly suggests that structural conditions of socioeconomic disadvantage make marriage a milestone that is harder to achieve for African Americans and other disadvantaged minority groups, such as American Indians and some Hispanic groups, than for whites and Asian Americans. In its most basic sense, the argument is that racial and ethnic differences in family structure reflect class differences in family structure and the differing distribution of racial and ethnic groups across classes.[19] Research focused on the early twentieth century convincingly showed large black-white differences in family structure that parallel much more recent patterns, strongly suggesting that persistent socioeconomic disparities are responsible for understanding long-term race differences in the formation and stability of fragile families.[20]

More recent changes in family structure among racial and ethnic groups since the middle of the past century, particularly the growth in the percentage of unmarried births for all groups over this time frame, can be attributed to several important economic and social factors.[21] First, economic inequality in both yearly income and wealth accumulation increased quite substantially between 1975 and 2000 as the U.S. economy became more technologically, informationally, and financially oriented. With this shift in the economy, particularly the accompanying loss of unionized manufacturing jobs, employment that offers wages adequate to support a family now depends to a much greater extent on postsecondary education. Second, tax policies were altered to provide increased advantages to the affluent, while government supports to protect the less well off, such as the minimum wage, stagnated or were sometimes even reduced in value. Third, rates of incarceration among young men soared.

These structural changes affected all racial and ethnic groups, including low-income whites. In particular, economic reorganization away from manufacturing work disproportionately affected poorly educated working-class whites who had previously benefited from unionized labor.[22] In other words, the structural changes of the second half of the twentieth century affected all groups and, in the case of some measures of family structure, served to make racial and ethnic differences in family structure less, rather than more, pronounced.

Structural disadvantages in each group strongly influence marriage prospects and family stability. Recent work by Linda Burton and Belinda Tucker, for example, has documented that young women who are living in or near poverty (and possibly even some middle-class women, given uncertain employment and economic prospects in today's economy) face substantial uncertainty in their lives that makes marriage a less realistic option for them than for higher-income young women.[23] Such uncertainties, or insecurities, include intermittent employment for themselves as well as for their potential partners, the time demands of night and weekend jobs, concerns over caring for older relatives, burdensome debt, high costs and instability in housing, poor health or lack of access to affordable health care, neighborhood violence, and even public and partner scrutiny over the use of their time. While Burton and Tucker focus on socioeconomically disadvantaged African American women in describing the ways that uncertainty frames their attitudes toward, perceptions about, and decisions about forming marital unions, they also make clear that such uncertainty is common to all groups of socioeconomically disadvantaged women. But it is important to note that black, Hispanic, and American Indian women face much greater structural socioeconomic disadvantage than white and Asian American women.

Research also shows that although socioeconomically disadvantaged women often postpone or forsake marriage in the context of substantial uncertainty, they value motherhood highly and see no need to postpone motherhood until marriage, even if they view marriage as the preferred context for childbearing.[24] Indeed, through extensive interviews with low-income women in Philadelphia, Kathryn Edin and Maria Kefalas found that socially disadvantaged women value marriage symbolically as a milestone to be achieved by economically viable and stable couples.[25] Survey data also support this finding. Among low-income women surveyed in Boston, San Antonio, and Chicago in the Three-City Study, 80 percent disagreed or strongly disagreed that nonmarital childbearing is embarrassing or harmful for future chances of marriage, and 70 percent agreed or strongly agreed that a woman does not have to be married to have a child.[26] At the same time, two-thirds of urban, unmarried mothers in the Fragile Families and Child Wellbeing Study felt that married parents are better for children.[27]

Sex Ratios

Another important barrier to marriage that influences racial and ethnic differences in family formation is the limited supply of partners for young women. Given a high degree of racial endogamy in marriage—intra-racial marriages are far more common than interracial marriages—differences in race- and ethnic-specific marriage markets are another primary structural reason for racial and ethnic differences in marriage.[28] Research shows that marriage markets—measured with race-, ethnic-, and age-specific ratios of non-incarcerated men to women in a given geographical area—help to account for racial and ethnic differences in marriage.[29] Ratios of men to women are substantially lower for blacks than they are for whites, meaning that black women have far fewer marriageable partners within their race group from which to choose. Moreover, women of all racial and ethnic groups who live in a geographic area with a low sex ratio are less likely to marry than comparable women in a geographic area with higher sex ratios.

Sex ratios of men to women are also substantially higher for Hispanics than for blacks, meaning that Hispanic women have more marriageable partners to choose from. Kristen Harknett and Sara McLanahan show that although African American men are in short supply in local marriage markets, Hispanic men tend to outnumber women in those same markets.[30] These differential sex ratios are very important in helping to explain lower marriage rates among African Americans in comparison to Hispanics. Marriage markets also seem to matter more for Mexican immigrant women than for Mexican American women, perhaps because language barriers help to define a more restrictive supply of potential partners among Mexican immigrants.[31] The fact that racial and ethnic differences in the supply of marriageable partners account in significant ways for racial and ethnic differences in marriage implies that women of all racial and ethnic groups share a similar aspiration for marriage—that they would marry if they could find a suitable partner.

Cultural Explanations of Racial and Ethnic Differences in Fragile Families

The structurally based socioeconomic explanation of racial and ethnic differences in fragile families cannot account for the fact that some disadvantaged immigrant groups, such as Mexican immigrants, engage in less nonmarital childbearing and have more stable relationships as unmarried parents than do

Our findings clearly show that cohabiting Mexican immigrants have the highest rates of marriage following a nonmarital birth and the highest rate of relationship stability of all cohabiting couples, despite their pronounced socioeconomic disadvantages.

U.S.-born disadvantaged racial and ethnic groups. For example, although Mexican immigrants as a group have the poorest education and highest poverty rates in the Fragile Families data, they are also the most likely of all racial and ethnic groups to be married by age twenty-four, they have fewer nonmarital births as a proportion of all births than do U.S.-born Mexican Americans, and they are less likely than whites, blacks, or native-born Mexicans to divorce.[32] These patterns may be attributed to a Mexican cultural orientation known as familism, which strongly values family roles and elevates family responsibilities over individual needs.[33] Familism also emphasizes traditional gender roles that favor marriage and high fertility, as well as familial responsibility that translates into more stable relationships. Although some research has questioned the role that familism might play in the unique patterns of family formation and stability of Mexican immigrants, our findings from the Fragile Families data clearly show that cohabiting Mexican immigrants have the highest rates of marriage following a nonmarital birth and the highest rate of relationship stability of all cohabiting couples, despite their pronounced socioeconomic disadvantages.[34] This finding indicates how powerful a family-centric cultural orientation such as familism can be in the face of socioeconomic disadvantage.

Another research finding regarding the respective roles of socioeconomic resources and culture (including norms) in explaining racial and ethnic differences in fragile families is that U.S.-born Mexican American women have higher levels of nonmarital births and lower levels of stability in their relationships than do Mexican immigrant women, even though they have much higher levels of socioeconomic resources. Familism, then, appears to erode over time in the United States.[35] And, in fact, all U.S.-born racial and ethnic groups have higher shares of nonmarital childbearing than the immigrant generation; as noted, the share of nonmarital births among U.S.-born Asian Americans is about three times that among Asian immigrants. Thus, to the extent that contemporary immigrants can be compared with the descendants of earlier-arriving immigrants, this more general pattern across all racial and ethnic groups—that is, that fragile families form more commonly in the generations that follow the initial immigrant generation—reflects a process of convergence to current U.S. norms that may not always be in the best interests of second-generation immigrants and their children.[36] The fading influence of familism may represent one example of how, more generally, the process of assimilation among all immigrant groups to current American family structures involves a shift away from particular family forms that are brought to the United States by immigrant families.

Since 1960, Americans' attitudes toward marriage and childbearing have also become much more flexible, shifting substantially away from stigmatization of nonmarital childbearing and toward greater acceptance of it.[37] That attitudinal shift began earlier, and has been accepted more broadly, among blacks than among other racial and ethnic groups.[38] If the shift continues, racial and ethnic gaps in patterns of family formation and stability may narrow in the coming decades. But the continuing socioeconomic disadvantages of black, Mexican American, and American Indian populations and advantages of white and Asian American populations will most likely keep family formation and stability gaps from closing.

Policy Implications

Racial and ethnic differences in fragile families continue to be strongly influenced by socioeconomic inequality across groups. In all racial and ethnic groups, less education strongly predicts nonmarital childbearing, both planned and unplanned.[39] Perhaps even more important, uncertainties surrounding employment prospects, the cost of housing, health and access to health care, neighborhood violence, the criminal justice system, and other day-to-day stresses of coping with life in poverty or near-poverty conditions predict racial and ethnic patterns in forming fragile families, as well as the relative lack of available resources in, and the marked instability of, fragile families. This socioeconomic-based understanding of racial and ethnic differences in fragile families implies that such policy goals as increasing the rates of marriage and decreasing nonmarital childbearing will require structural change to improve opportunities—particularly educational and employment opportunities—for black, Hispanic, and American Indian men. Also important for marriage prospects are policies that directly or indirectly reduce the high rates of incarceration among disadvantaged minority group members. Addressing these structural barriers to marriage among the socioeconomically disadvantaged will also reduce racial and ethnic inequality and, ultimately, racial and ethnic differences in family structure.

Policies that target particular communities might also assuage racial and ethnic differences in socioeconomic resources among fragile families. Data from the Fragile Families and Child Wellbeing Study show that black and Mexican American unmarried mothers are more likely than white unmarried mothers to be in poverty, to depend on public assistance, to live in unsafe neighborhoods, not to own a car, and not to have private health insurance. Social policies must continue to address racial and ethnic inequalities in basic socioeconomic resources: employment and income, access to quality health insurance, access to credit, and access to quality housing in safe neighborhoods. Policies that build certainty and stability into the lives of U.S. young adults will raise marriage rates and reduce racial and ethnic disparities in fragile families.

The structural explanation for racial and ethnic differences in fragile families cannot, however, explain why some highly socioeconomically disadvantaged immigrant groups, such as Mexican immigrants, have higher rates of marriage and, among unmarried parents, of relationship stability, than some U.S.-born racial and ethnic groups. Here the explanation seems to be the strong role of family life in Mexican culture. Overall, because Hispanics are expected to make up nearly one-third of the U.S. population by 2050, they represent a very important group in terms of future social service provision.[40] Policy programs serving the Hispanic community should explicitly acknowledge—indeed, embrace and encourage—approaches to marriage and childbearing that draw on the unique strengths of the Mexican family.

That the prevalence of childbearing is lower in almost all immigrant groups than in their U.S.-born co-ethnic counterparts suggests a different set of policy needs specific to immigrants. Policies that restrict undocumented and recently documented immigrants from public services, together with policies that criminalize, disenfranchise, and restrict the cross-border mobility of nominally undocumented immigrants, contribute to downward assimilation and instability in the lives of immigrants. Instead, U.S. immigration policy should embrace the strengths of immigrant family ties, thus keeping immigrant families together and helping them to stabilize their lives in the United States and to develop greater trust in U.S. institutions. Taking advantage of immigrants' strong family ties would also enable them to assimilate more effectively into the United States and create upwardly mobile prospects for the second generation and beyond.

In closing, we note that normative attitudes toward marriage and nonmarital childbearing in the United States have changed over the past few decades and show few if any signs of reverting to old patterns. Although policies to promote marriage among racial and ethnic groups are important in that most young U.S. men and women continue to regard marriage as an important goal, marriage promotion cannot be the only goal of effective family policy. Indeed, policy should stress tolerance—and support—for all types of family forms, particularly in the interest of child well-being, rather than attempting to turn back the clock. Greater acceptance of and attention to the needs of diverse family structures will also be another step toward racial and ethnic equality.

Endnotes

1. Stephanie J. Ventura, "Changing Patterns of Nonmarital Childbearing in the United States," *Data Brief* 18 (Hyattsville, Md.: National Center for Health Statistics, 2009).
2. Joyce A. Martin and others, *Births: Final Data for 2006,* National Vital Statistics Report 48, no. 16. (Hyattsville, Md.: National Center for Health Statistics, 2009).
3. Sheela Kennedy and Larry Bumpass, "Cohabitation and Children's Living Arrangements: New Estimates from the United States," *Demographic Research* 19 (2008): 1663–92.
4. Pew Hispanic Center, "From 200 Million to 300 Million: The Numbers behind Population Growth," Pew Research Center Fact Sheet, October 10, 2006 (www.pewhispanic.org/files/factsheets/25.pdf [June 25, 2009]).
5. Pew Hispanic Center, "From 200 Million to 300 Million" (see note 4). These data are also taken from the U.S. Census Bureau website, "Table 1. United States—Race and Hispanic Origin: 1790 to 1990," Internet release date September 13, 2002 (www.census.gov/population/www/documentation/twps0056/tab01.xls [Aug. 20, 2009]).
6. Pew Hispanic Center, "U.S. Population Projections: 2005–2050," Pew Research Center Report, February 11, 2008 (www.pewhispanic.org/files/reports/85.pdf [June 25, 2009]).
7. Sara McLanahan and Christine Percheski, "Family Structure and the Reproduction of Inequalities," *Annual Review of Sociology* 34 (2008): 257–76.
8. Joyce A. Martin and others, *Births: Final Data for 2000,* National Vital Statistics Report 50, no. 5, (Hyattsville, Md.: National Center for Health Statistics, 2002).
9. Stephanie J. Ventura and Christine A. Bachrach, *Nonmarital Childbearing in the United States, 1940–1999,* National Vital Statistics Reports 48, no. 16 (Hyattsville, Md.: National Center for Health Statistics, 2000).
10. Rates are shown for black and white women only because greater racial and ethnic detail is not available in vital statistics data before the early 1990s. Following 1994, the rates and percentages are specifically for non-Hispanic white and non-Hispanic black mothers. Hispanic rates and percentages are not presented in the figure for clarity of presentation. See Ventura and Bachrach, *Nonmarital Childbearing in the United States, 1940–1999* (see note 9).
11. Herbert L. Smith, S. Philip Morgan, and Tanya Koropecky-Cox, "A Decomposition of Trends in the Nonmarital Fertility Ratios of Blacks and Whites in the United States, 1960–1992," *Demography* 33, no. 2 (1996): 141–51.
12. These high fertility rates for Hispanics and Asian Americans also, in part, reflect the relatively young age structures of these two groups.
13. The work of Yolanda Padilla and colleagues, focusing particularly on the Mexican-origin population, was especially helpful in providing descriptive data from the Fragile Families study that we build upon here. See, in particular: Yolanda C. Padilla and others, "The Living Conditions of U.S.-Born Children of Mexican Immigrants in Unmarried Families," *Hispanic Journal of Behavioral Sciences* 28 (2006): 331–49.
14. See the following article for a description of the Fragile Families and Child Well-Being data set: Nancy E. Reichman and others, "Fragile Families: Sample and Design," *Children and Youth Services Review* 23 (2001): 303–26.

15. Sara McLanahan, for example, recently analyzed differences between unmarried and married families at the time of children's birth and summarized that "…married and unmarried parents come from very different worlds." See Sara McLanahan, "Fragile Families and the Reproduction of Poverty," *Annals of the American Academy of Political and Social Science* 621 (2009): 111–31.

16. Kathryn Edin, Laura Tach, and Ronald Mincy, "Claiming Fatherhood: Race and the Dynamics of Paternal Involvement among Unmarried Men," *Annals of the American Academy of Political and Social Science* 621 (2009): 149–77.

17. Erin R. Hamilton and others, "Health Insurance and Health-Care Utilization of U.S.-Born Mexican-American Children," *Social Science Quarterly* 87, no. 5 (2006): 1280–94.

18. Melissa Radey and Karin L. Brewster, "The Influence of Race/Ethnicity on Disadvantaged Mothers' Child Care Arrangements," *Early Childhood Research Quarterly* 22 (2007): 379–93.

19. Frank Furstenberg, "If Moynihan Had Only Known: Race, Class, and Family Change in the Late Twentieth Century," *Annals of the American Academy of Political and Social Science* 621 (2009): 94–110; see also Matthew D. Bramlett and William D. Mosher, *Cohabitation, Marriage, Divorce, and Remarriage,* United States Vital and Health Statistics 23, no. 22 (2002); McLanahan and Percheski, "Family Structure and the Reproduction of Inequalities" (see note 7).

20. S. Phillip Morgan and others, "Racial Differences in Household and Family Structure at the Turn of the Century," *American Journal of Sociology* 98, no. 4 (1993): 798–828.

21. Douglas S. Massey and Robert J. Sampson, "Introduction: Moynihan Redux: Legacies and Lessons," *Annals of the American Academy of Political and Social Science* 621 (2009): 6–27.

22. Ibid.

23. Linda M. Burton and M. Belinda Tucker, "Romantic Unions in an Era of Uncertainty: A Post-Moynihan Perspective on African American Women and Marriage," *Annals of the American Academy of Political and Social Research* 621 (2009): 132–49.

24. Ibid.

25. Kathryn Edin and Maria J. Kefalas, *Promises I Can Keep: Why Poor Women Put Motherhood before Marriage* (University of California Press, 2005).

26. Andrew Cherlin and others, "Promises They Can Keep: Low-Income Women's Attitudes toward Motherhood, Marriage, and Divorce," *Journal of Marriage and the Family* 70 (2008): 919–33.

27. Kristen Harknett and Sara S. McLanahan, "Racial and Ethnic Differences in Marriage after the Birth of a Child," *American Sociological Review* 69 (2004): 790–811.

28. William Julius Wilson, *The Truly Disadvantaged* (University of Chicago Press, 1987).

29. Daniel T. Lichter and others, "Race and the Retreat from Marriage: A Shortage of Marriageable Men?" *American Sociological Review* 57 (1992): 781–99; Harknett and McLanahan, "Racial and Ethnic Differences in Marriage after the Birth of a Child" (see note 27).

30. Harknett and McLanahan, "Racial and Ethnic Differences in Marriage after the Birth of a Child" (see note 27).

31. R. S. Oropesa, Daniel T. Lichter, and Robert N. Anderson, "Marriage Markets and the Paradox of Mexican American Nuptiality," *Journal of Marriage and the Family* 56 (1994): 889–907.

32. Nancy S. Landale and R. S. Oropesa, "Hispanic Families: Stability and Change," *Annual Review of Sociology* 33 (2007): 381–405.

33. Ibid.; R. S. Oropesa, "Normative Beliefs about Marriage and Cohabitation: A Comparison of Non-Latino Whites, Mexican Americans, and Puerto Ricans," *Journal of Marriage and the Family* 58 (1996): 49–62.

34. See, for example, Frank D. Bean and others, "The New U.S. Immigrants; How Do They Affect Our Understanding of the African American Experience?" *Annals of the American Academy of Political and Social Science* 621 (2009): 202–20.

35. Marta Tienda and Faith Mitchell, eds., *Multiple Origins, Uncertain Destinies; Hispanics and the American Future* (Washington: National Academies Press, 2006). See, in particular, pages 77–80 regarding concerns over the generational dilution of familism among Hispanic families. See also R. Kelly Raley, T. Elizabeth Durden, and Elizabeth Wildsmith, "Understanding Mexican-American Marriage Patterns Using a Life-Course Approach," *Social Science Quarterly* 85, no. 4 (2004): 872–90, for an empirical evaluation of the familism argument.

36. An exception is Cubans. The proportion of births to unmarried women is lower among U.S.-born Cubans than it is among immigrant Cubans. This likely reflects changing patterns of Cuban immigration to the United States from highly educated, upper-class immigrants in the first wave of immigration in the 1960s to, more recently, less-educated and low-skilled immigrants arriving after the Mariel Boat Lift in 1980. This case exemplifies why cross-generational comparisons are problematic for understanding processes of assimilation—cross-generational differences may reflect differences in the composition of immigrants arriving at different points in time, and in that case later generations are not an appropriate comparison point.

37. Arland Thornton and Linda Young-DeMarco, "Four Decades of Trends in Attitudes toward Family Issues in the United States: The 1960s through the 1990s," *Journal of Marriage and the Family* 63 (2001): 1009–37.

38. Belinda M. Tucker and Angela D. James, "New Families, New Functions: Postmodern African American Families in Context," in *Emerging Issues in African American Life: Context, Adaptation, and Policy*, edited by Vonnie C. McLoyd, Nancy E. Hill, and Kenneth A. Dodge (New York: Guilford, 2009), pp. 86–108.

39. Kelly Musick, "Planned and Unplanned Childbearing among Unmarried Women," *Journal of Marriage and the Family* 64 (2002): 915–29.

40. Pew Hispanic Center, "From 200 Million to 300 Million" (see note 4).

An Ounce of Prevention: Policy Prescriptions to Reduce the Prevalence of Fragile Families

Isabel Sawhill, Adam Thomas, and Emily Monea

Summary

Isabel Sawhill, Adam Thomas, and Emily Monea believe that given the well-documented costs of nonmarital births to the children and parents in fragile families, as well as to society as a whole, policy makers' primary goal should be to reduce births to unmarried parents. The authors say that the nation's swiftly rising nonmarital birth rate has many explanations—a cultural shift toward acceptance of unwed childbearing; a lack of positive alternatives to motherhood among the less advantaged; a sense of fatalism or ambivalence about pregnancy; a lack of marriageable men; limited access to effective contraception; a lack of knowledge about contraception; and the difficulty of using contraception consistently and correctly.

Noting that these explanations fall generally into three categories—motivation, knowledge, and access—the authors discuss policies designed to motivate individuals to avoid unintended pregnancies, to improve their knowledge about contraception, and to remove barriers to contraceptive access. Some motivational programs, such as media campaigns, have been effective in changing behavior. Some, but not all, sex education programs designed to reduce teen pregnancy have also been effective at reducing sexual activity or increasing contraceptive use, or both. Programs providing access to subsidized contraception have also been effective and would be even more so if they could increase the use not just of contraceptives, but of long-acting, reversible contraceptive methods such as intrauterine devices (IUDs) and implants.

Finally, the authors present simulations of the costs and effects of three policy initiatives—a mass media campaign that encourages men to use condoms, a teen pregnancy prevention program that discourages sexual activity and educates participants about proper contraceptive use, and an expansion in access to Medicaid-subsidized contraception. All three have benefit-cost ratios that are comfortably greater than one, making them excellent social investments that can actually save taxpayer dollars.

www.futureofchildren.org

Isabel Sawhill is senior fellow, Cabot Family Chair, and co-director of the Center on Children and Families at the Brookings Institution. Adam Thomas is a research director with the Brookings Institution's Center on Children and Families. Emily Monea is a research analyst with the Brookings Institution's Center on Children and Families. They thank the William and Flora Hewlett Foundation for generous support and thank Daniel Moskowitz and Audrey Douchefrou for helpful research assistance.

Forty percent of all U.S. births in 2007 were nonmarital.[1] The share of infants born to unmarried women under the age of thirty was even higher (52 percent).[2] Out-of-wedlock childbearing has now surpassed divorce as the primary driver of increases in unmarried-parent families.[3] Devising policies to address the increase in the number of single-parent families in recent years thus requires focusing on nonmarital childbearing or "fragile families"—that is, families in which the parents were unmarried at the time of their child's birth.

In this article, we argue that policy makers should be doing everything possible to reduce the prevalence of fragile families. Authors of other articles in this volume argue in favor of providing essential supports to such families, and we would not want to argue against doing so. But given the costs imposed by fragile families on children, society, and the adults involved, it would be better still to limit the growth of these families.

There is a growing consensus among researchers about the negative effects of unmarried parenthood on the children involved. The evidence, which is reviewed by Jane Waldfogel, Terry-Ann Craigie, and Jeanne Brooks-Gunn in their article in this volume, suggests that the best environment for children is a stable two-parent family. Children in single-parent families are more than four times as likely to be poor as children with married parents (with the children of cohabiting parents falling somewhere in between). Children in fragile families also face a wide range of cognitive, emotional, and social problems as they mature.[4] Some of the differences between children in single- and two-parent families are attributable to the fact that the adults most likely to become single parents have different characteristics, and are generally more disadvantaged to begin with, than parents who are married. But even after controlling for most of these differences, researchers still find that children in single-parent or cohabiting families fare less well than those with married parents.[5]

Taxpayers are also adversely affected by the growth of fragile families. The difficult economic circumstances of single parents make it more likely that they will be dependent on government aid to support their children. Fragile families are far more likely than married families to be on welfare and to receive food stamps, benefits from the Women, Infants, and Children (WIC) nutrition program, Medicaid, housing assistance, the earned income tax credit (EITC), and other forms of assistance.[6] As Ariel Kalil and Rebecca Ryan discuss in their article in this volume, 53 percent of never-married mothers in 2004 were receiving some form of public assistance (excluding the EITC).[7]

The effects on parents of out-of-wedlock childbearing have been much debated. Most studies have focused on teenage mothers rather than on all unwed mothers or cohabiting couples. Some have found no adverse effects on women who gave birth as teenagers while others, using better control groups and more recent data, have shown modest adverse effects.[8] One well-controlled study shows that teenage childbearing reduces the probability of receiving a high school diploma by 5 to 10 percentage points and reduces annual income by $1,000 to $2,400.[9] Keeping in mind that almost 40 percent of unwed childbearing begins during the teenage years, these studies shed some light on the consequences of the formation of a fragile family for the adults involved.[10]

Figure 1. Unintended Pregnancies as a Share of All Pregnancies by Age and Marital Status, 2001

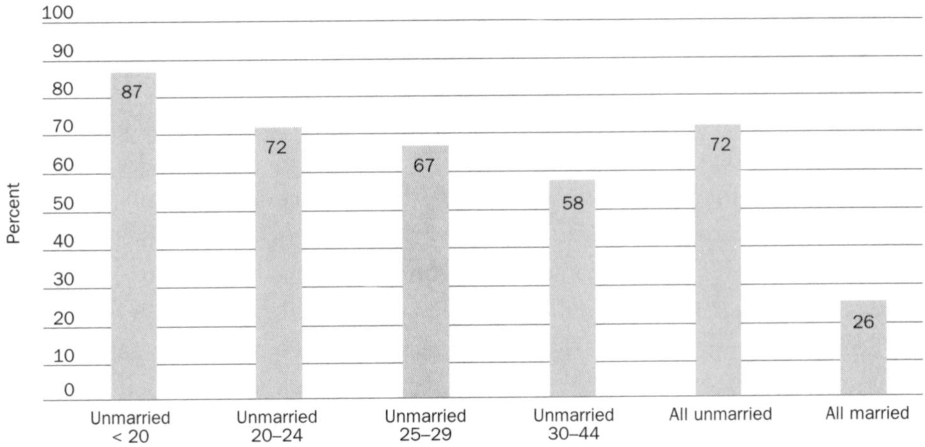

Source: Special tabulations of unpublished data by the Guttmacher Institute for the National Campaign to Prevent Teen and Unplanned Pregnancy. Published data presented in Lawrence B. Finer and Stanley K. Henshaw, "Disparities in Rates of Unintended Pregnancy in the United States, 1994 and 2001," *Perspectives on Sexual and Reproductive Health* 38, no. 2 (2006): 90–96.

The adverse effects on mothers should not be surprising given that the vast majority of pregnancies to young unwed women were not planned at the time of conception. Among all pregnancies to unmarried teens in 2001 (the latest year for which data are available), 87 percent were unintended; for all unmarried women the share was 72 percent. By comparison, only slightly more than a quarter of pregnancies to married women were unintended in that year (see figure 1).

Almost half of these unintended pregnancies to unmarried women (48 percent) are aborted and thus never lead to the formation of a fragile family.[11] The high rate of abortion is a strong indicator that many of the unmarried women who are getting pregnant not only did not intend to get pregnant but feel strongly enough about the inappropriateness of the pregnancy to terminate it. Their access to abortion as one means of resolving an unintended pregnancy raises both practical and moral questions.

At the practical level, access to abortion is constrained by the limited number of providers, high costs, and the very limited availability of public funds to pay these costs.[12] Because private insurance also plays a relatively small role in helping women afford abortions, the result is that a very high proportion of them are paid for out of pocket, making it impractical for many young or low-income women to avail themselves of this option.[13]

Access to abortion also raises a host of moral questions, and the nation's culture war over abortion likely will not end any time soon. While for the first time more Americans identify themselves as pro-life than pro-choice, there is also a strong sentiment in the United States in favor of working toward reducing the need for abortions while at the same time protecting a woman's right to have one.[14] In keeping with this sentiment, and because most women themselves do not relish the prospect of having to undergo an abortion, our focus in the remainder of this article is primarily on preventing unintended pregnancies among young, unmarried women. If such prevention efforts are successful, both pro-life and pro-choice advocates should be pleased. Shifting the focus to the prevention of unplanned pregnancies and in turn reducing the need for abortion is likely to garner much wider support than focusing on abortion alone. As President Barack Obama stated during his 2008 presidential campaign, "We may not agree on abortion, but surely we can agree on reducing the number of unwanted pregnancies." [15]

Why So Many Unintended Pregnancies and Unwed Births?

Before we can address the question of how to reduce the prevalence of fragile families, we must first examine why so many women are having babies on their own. Possible explanations include: a cultural shift toward greater acceptance of unwed childbearing; a lack of positive alternatives to motherhood, especially among the most disadvantaged, or a sense that parenthood confers status or meaning on one's life; fatalism, ambivalence, or lack of planning (as in comments to the effect that "children come from God" or pregnancy "just happens"); a lack of marriageable men, which makes unwed parenting a fallback option for women who want children; the limited availability, high cost, or both, of the most effective forms of contraception; a lack of knowledge about contraception or concerns about its side effects; and, finally, the difficulty of using contraception consistently and correctly, especially in "the heat of the moment."

Research provides some evidence in favor of each of these hypotheses, and probably all play some role, differing in importance from one individual to another. We review each hypothesis in turn, along with the readily available evidence to assess its importance. The review provides a useful context for our later discussion of the specific programs that might reduce unplanned and unwed births and the fragile families they create.

Cultural Norms

Attitudinal data consistently demonstrate that Americans have become increasingly accepting of premarital sex, cohabitation, and having children outside of marriage over the past few decades.[16] The trend largely reflects the more liberal views of younger generations, although attitudes within older generations have shifted as well. Nonetheless, even though the stigma attached to nonmarital childbearing has diminished, most Americans still believe that single women having children is bad for society.[17]

A Lack of Positive Alternatives to Single Motherhood

One reason that many less-advantaged unmarried young women may face an unplanned pregnancy with relative equanimity, or may even choose to have a baby, is that they perceive the adverse consequences for themselves as being small. As already noted, their life prospects are so constrained by their family background and their poor schooling that becoming an unmarried mother may do little to diminish them further.[18]

In fact, for some less-advantaged women, parenthood, even if it is outside of marriage, may be desired for its positive benefits. In-depth interviews conducted by Kathryn Edin and Maria Kefalas with a small sample of lower-income unmarried mothers provide some evidence for this hypothesis, with many of the women crediting their children for "virtually all that they see as positive in their lives." [19] Edin and Kefalas do not claim that these mothers got pregnant because they sought these positive outcomes. But they do argue that childless girls in communities similar to the one they studied are surely influenced to some degree by "the self-proclaimed transformations motherhood has wrought in the lives of so many" of the women around them.[20]

One reason that many less-advantaged unmarried young women may choose to have a baby is that they perceive the adverse consequences for themselves as being small.

Fatalism and Ambivalence

It would be a mistake, based on the foregoing, to conclude that less-advantaged women tally up the benefits and costs of early or out-of-wedlock childbearing and make a rational and considered decision to embark on this lifestyle. As noted, most of the pregnancies that lead to the formation of a fragile family are unintended, and for many women, becoming pregnant involves little decision making.

A nationally representative survey conducted by the Guttmacher Institute for the National Campaign to Prevent Teen and Unplanned Pregnancy (the National Campaign) found a strong sense of fatalism and ambivalence among the young unmarried men and women surveyed. Indeed, the survey found that 38 percent of men and 44 percent of women agree or strongly agree with the statement, "It doesn't matter whether you use birth control or not; when it is your time to get pregnant it will happen." Furthermore, among those who report that it is important for them to avoid pregnancy right now, 32 percent say that they would be pleased if they found out today that they or their partner were pregnant.[21] As the National Campaign writes, ambivalence is "rampant" among these young men and women.[22]

A Lack of Marriageable Men

Perhaps another reason why unintended pregnancy and out-of-wedlock childbearing are on the rise is that women, especially low-income minority women, are unable to find men suitable to marry and raise families with. This view was first posited by William Julius Wilson and Kathryn Neckerman in 1986. They argued that high unemployment, weak connections to mainstream employers, and rising levels of imprisonment created a shortage of marriageable black men, leading to a decline in marriage and a sharp increase in nonmarital childbearing.[23]

Despite some evidence in support of this hypothesis, most recent research has cast doubt on its importance. In their review of the research, David Ellwood and Christopher Jencks conclude that although both men's economic opportunities and the ratio of men to women in a given geographic area or within a demographic group are related to marriage rates, neither men's real wages nor the ratio of men to women has changed enough over the past several decades to explain a substantial fraction of the decline in marriage.[24]

Availability and Cost of Contraception

The high cost and limited availability of contraception may also explain the high rate of unintended pregnancy among unmarried women. Some forms of contraception, such as the male condom, are relatively cheap and readily available in most drugstores or other retail establishments. However, other forms that are more effective or less susceptible to user error—such as the implant or an intrauterine device (IUD)—cost considerably more in terms of both the up-front investment of money and the need to access clinical services to use them.[25] In these cases, cost could prove a formidable barrier to use by lower-income women unless they are covered by Medicaid, have access to a publicly funded clinic, or are fortunate enough to have private insurance.

Substantial federal funding is available to assist those with low incomes or other access problems in obtaining contraception; indeed, in fiscal year 2006, $1.85 billion in public funds went to family planning services.[26] Although Medicaid was the most important source of national funding, Title X of the Public Health Service Act also played a substantial role.[27] Eligibility for Medicaid-subsidized family planning services has traditionally been limited to pregnant women and mothers whose incomes fall below a very low threshold.[28] Over the past decade and a half, however, nearly half of the states have obtained Medicaid family planning waivers that allow them to expand greatly the availability of these services. These states are able to offer family planning services free of cost-sharing to all women of childbearing age—regardless of whether they are pregnant or have children—with incomes generally up to 185 or 200 percent of poverty.[29]

Although the cost and availability of family planning services can be an issue for some, it does not seem to be an insurmountable barrier for the vast majority. For example, the National Campaign found that only 17 percent of men and women aged eighteen to twenty-nine agree with the statement: "I/my partner would use better methods, but they cost too much."[30] And in a 2004 nationally representative survey of women aged eighteen to forty-four, the Guttmacher Institute found that cost and access were not the reasons women most commonly cited for nonuse or inconsistent use of contraceptives.[31]

Many people who are at risk of an unintended pregnancy are ill-informed about various aspects of sex and pregnancy, have concerns or fears about using specific types of contraception, or both.

Lack of Knowledge, Fears, and Myths about Contraception

Evidence suggests that a more important barrier to the use of contraception is that many people who are at risk of an unintended pregnancy lack the knowledge necessary to make the best decisions about their reproductive health. Many are ill-informed about various aspects of sex and pregnancy, have concerns or fears about using specific types of contraception (often those that are the most effective), or both.

In its nationally representative survey of unmarried young adults noted above, the National Campaign found that only about half of this group said that they used contraception regularly. About six in ten said they know "little" or "nothing" about birth control pills, and three in ten said they know "little" or "nothing" about condoms. The survey also found that myths and misinformation about pregnancy and contraception are widespread. For example, 27 percent of women believe it is extremely or quite likely that the pill (or other hormonal methods) leads to serious health problems, like cancer, despite clinical evidence to the contrary. Finally, almost a third of these young adults agreed with the statement: "The government is trying to limit blacks and other minority populations by encouraging the use of birth control."[32] The National Campaign has concluded from these and other data that "confusion about contraception and fertility is overwhelming."[33]

Consistency of Use of Contraception

Another important issue regarding contraception is whether it is used correctly and consistently (every time). Most experts have come to the conclusion that incorrect and inconsistent use is a very important cause of unintended pregnancies. The Guttmacher Institute attributes 52 percent of unintended pregnancies to nonuse of contraception, 43 percent to inconsistent or incorrect use, and only 5 percent to method failure.[34]

Given the role of inconsistent or incorrect contraceptive use in the occurrence of unintended pregnancies, and the reality that careful use—or any use—is difficult in the "heat of the moment," policy makers must give more attention to choice of method among those who do not wish to become parents. Methods that are either permanent or long-acting but reversible, such as implants and IUDs, require little or no work on the part of the contraceptor and have especially low failure rates. Other widely used methods, such as birth control pills and condoms, have relatively low failure rates if used perfectly but require much greater diligence on the part of the user. Inconsistent and incorrect use of these methods is well documented and dramatically reduces their efficacies. So although the pill, when used perfectly, has a failure rate close to zero, its typical-use failure rate is close to 9 percent; for the condom, the perfect-use failure rate is only 2 percent, while the typical-use failure rate is over 17 percent.[35]

Policy Solutions: Reducing the Prevalence of Fragile Families

The seven hypotheses described above are by no means mutually exclusive; each of them is probably at least partially responsible for the increasing prevalence of fragile families. Several of these factors—the evolution of cultural norms, the dearth of positive alternatives to unmarried motherhood, young people's ambivalence or sense of fatalism, and the shortage of marriageable males—curtail individual motivation to avoid childbearing outside of marriage. Others—inadequate knowledge about the efficacy of various contraceptive methods, about how to use them correctly, and about the importance of using them consistently—pertain not to motivation but to the ability of motivated individuals to follow through on their intentions. Yet another factor—the prohibitive cost of and limited access to contraception—can lead to unintended pregnancy even among those armed both with the right information and with the best of intentions. We therefore organize our discussion of policy interventions around these three general considerations: motivation, knowledge, and access.

It is also possible, of course, to limit the number of fragile families by encouraging marriage among single parents and unmarried pregnant women or by encouraging more adoption. The topic of marriage promotion is thoroughly addressed in the article in this volume by Philip and Carolyn Cowan and Virginia Knox. That women with unplanned pregnancies rarely choose to put their children up for adoption makes us pessimistic that promoting adoption can play a significant role.[36] Finally, greater access to affordable abortions could also reduce the number of fragile families, but as argued above, we believe it makes sense to give priority to reducing the need for abortion. We therefore focus specifically on policies that have the potential to limit the number of unintended pregnancies among unmarried women. Because such pregnancies are attributable to a tangle of causes (many of them enumerated in the previous section), we think it unlikely that any single policy will be a "silver-bullet" solution. Indeed, the literature reviewed below collectively suggests that few large-scale interventions, if any, have had big and sustained effects on sexual activity, contraceptive use, pregnancy, or childbearing. But several programs appear to have had modest effects on a large scale, while others have been shown to have had large impacts on a smaller scale. We review this evidence below, beginning with a discussion of programs that address the motivation (or lack thereof) to avoid out-of-wedlock pregnancies.

Programs Addressing Motivation

Of the six different types of programs discussed in this section, four (youth development initiatives, media campaigns, policies to improve educational and economic opportunities, and child support enforcement) have had some success in changing behavior. For the other two (welfare reform and abstinence-only education), the evidence is less encouraging. We discuss first the evidence for programs that have had success and then the evidence for programs that have been less promising.

Youth Development Programs

Programs falling under the "youth development" umbrella focus on improving the life skills and the educational and career opportunities of the target population. Some have been carefully evaluated. In his excellent review of the literature, Douglas Kirby concludes that service-learning programs—in which participants engage in voluntary or unpaid community service—reduce sexual activity or the risk of pregnancy (or both) while youth are enrolled in them.[37] He theorizes that these programs may reduce pregnancy rates by inducing participants to change their outlooks on the future or simply by keeping them too busy to become pregnant.

Media Campaigns and Social Marketing

Because most teenagers attend school, they are generally considered to be especially easily reachable targets for pregnancy prevention messages and services.[38] The mass media, however, represent a potentially powerful vehicle for reaching adults and teens alike. Over the past four decades, "social marketing" has become a popular tool for influencing social behaviors in much the same way that business marketing has been used to influence consumer behavior. A social marketing campaign might seek to curb smoking, promote cancer screenings, or discourage drunk driving. For our purposes, the most relevant campaigns are those that encourage contraceptive use. The effects of such campaigns, however, are difficult to pinpoint, because it is generally not feasible to evaluate them using a random-assignment experimental design.[39]

In their widely cited meta-analysis of the ample (if imperfect) evaluation literature on mass media health campaigns, Leslie Snyder and her co-authors conclude that, on average, campaigns encouraging the adoption of health-enhancing sexual habits (most often, the use of condoms during sex) changed the behavior of about 6 percent of the target population in the desired direction.[40] Seth

Noar argues that the true average effect of media campaigns may be about half that reported by Snyder and her colleagues. Thus, a more conservative estimate is that the average campaign induces about 3 percent of its target population to modify behavior in the desired direction.

Although such effects may seem small, the target audiences of some social marketing campaigns are extremely large and can be reached at a very low cost per person. Moreover, the measured effects of some well-designed campaigns are above average. For example, Rick Zimmerman and his collaborators oversaw and evaluated a saturation media campaign encouraging condom use in Lexington, Kentucky. They compared the change in the frequency of condom use in Lexington before and after the campaign with the equivalent change in Knoxville, Tennessee, which they took to be the study's control city. Their findings imply that the campaign affected the behavior of more than 6 percent of the overall target population.[41]

Programs to Promote Economic Mobility

Out-of-wedlock childbearing is much less common among well-educated women than among their more poorly educated counterparts.[42] Part of this disparity may be attributable to the effect of early and unwed childbearing on one's future educational prospects. But the "causal arrow" may also point in the other direction—as a young woman's long-term economic prospects brighten, she has a greater incentive to avoid having a child outside of marriage, because doing so could pose a threat to her future prospects. Indeed, various studies have found an inverse relationship between educational attainment and subsequent out-of-wedlock childbearing after controlling for a host of other factors.[43] Most recently, Benjamin Cowan, in a well-designed analysis, found that the expectation of facing lower college tuition substantially deters risky sexual behavior among teens.[44] Thus, improving the educational prospects of low-income young women, and enhancing their economic outlook more generally, may help to reduce the incidence of unintended pregnancy and out-of-wedlock childbearing.

Child Support Enforcement

Over the past thirty years, the federal government and many statehouses have taken steps to compel unmarried fathers to contribute to the financial well-being of their children in order to recoup taxpayer costs incurred in their absence.[45] Stricter enforcement of child support obligations raises the cost of unmarried fatherhood (although it also reduces the cost of unmarried motherhood) and may therefore affect men's (or women's) sexual activity and contraceptive use on the margins. Several researchers have examined variation across states and over time in child support enforcement policies and in out-of-wedlock childbearing in an attempt to isolate the effect of the former on the latter. These studies tend to conclude that stricter child support enforcement reduces childbearing by teens and unmarried women.[46] For example, a 2003 paper by Irwin Garfinkel and his coauthors found that increases in child support enforcement during the 1980s and 1990s led to a reduction in nonmarital childbearing of between 6 and 9 percent.[47]

Welfare Policy

A variety of changes were also made to federal and state welfare systems over the past thirty years that should have increased the costs of single motherhood. These changes include a reduction in the real (inflation-adjusted) level of cash assistance for single mothers, a requirement in some states that mothers under the age of eighteen live with a parent or legal guardian and that they enroll in school in order to be able to receive cash assistance, and a requirement that adult welfare recipients work or seek employment.[48] Some studies have found that these changes reduced teenage and out-of-wedlock childbearing, while others have found no such effect.[49] These inconsistencies may have arisen in part because different studies used different measures of welfare policy and focused on different outcomes, or both. On the whole, we conclude that welfare reform likely had a smaller effect on the formation of fragile families than did many of the other policies reviewed here.

Abstinence-Only Education

The Personal Responsibility and Work Opportunity Reconciliation Act of 1996 allocated $50 million annually for programs that encourage abstinence from sex outside of marriage, and this funding has since been expanded.[50] These programs focus exclusively on the avoidance of sexual activity and do not encourage contraceptive use.[51] Evaluations of these programs are of varying quality, but a handful of them have been quite rigorous, relying on random-assignment experimental designs that tracked students in treatment and control groups over several years. Most rigorous evaluations have found that abstinence programs have no statistically significant effect on sexual behavior.[52] However, a few less-rigorous evaluations have found suggestive evidence that some abstinence programs may have at least a moderate effect on some dimensions of sexual behavior. And a newly published evaluation from a random-assignment study shows that one such program reduced the incidence of sexual initiation among young teens and preteens by about a third.[53] Nonetheless, there is only limited evidence that these programs have achieved their stated purpose.

Programs Addressing Knowledge

Sex education programs, broadly defined, are the primary policy mechanism for addressing knowledge gaps in this area. These programs are almost exclusively geared toward adolescents and are often referred to as "teen pregnancy prevention programs," although the lack of knowledge about contraception among young adults suggests a need for similar programs targeted toward that group as well. Programs that fall into this category are enormously diverse. Many, though not all, are conducted in a school setting. Some focus exclusively on sex education, while others also incorporate elements of youth development. Most combine an emphasis on the fail-safe option of sexual abstinence with a "just-in-case" approach to educating participants about contraceptive use, but each program strikes its own balance between these two priorities. Some programs have been carefully evaluated; others, only cursorily or not at all. Some that have been well evaluated have been found to have very large effects on sexual activity, contraceptive use, pregnancy rates, and childbearing. Others appear to have had little if any effect.

The evaluations of most of these programs have focused on their effects either on the incidence of pregnancy or on antecedent behaviors such as contraceptive use and sexual activity. The National Campaign's "What Works" report documents the effects of thirty of the most rigorously evaluated and effective teen pregnancy prevention programs to date.[54] The evaluations of eight of the programs reviewed for the National Campaign's report measured the relevant program's effects on teen pregnancy; about half these evaluations found, using rigorous research designs, that the programs reduced the incidence of pregnancy. These effective programs, however, were generally quite

Table 1. Characteristics of Selected Teen Pregnancy Prevention Programs Found to Have Affected Both Sexual Activity and Contraceptive Use

Among interventions that have been evaluated using random-assignment controlled experimental design

Name of intervention	Details of original study and evaluation	Estimated program cost
Becoming a Responsible Teen	African American youth. Participants were recruited from a low-income community in Jackson, Mississippi. Treatment group: participated in eight sessions in a community-based setting, each one lasting 90 to 120 minutes. Curriculum designed specifically to prevent HIV infection among African American adolescents. Control group: received one-time, two-hour HIV-prevention session. **N* = 246 at baseline; 225 at follow-up one year after completion of the intervention.	Estimated cost per participant: ≈ $70
HIV Prevention for Adolescents in Low-Income Housing Developments	Adolescents aged 12–17. Participants were recruited from 15 low-income housing communities. Primary treatment group: residents of the housing developments that were randomly assigned to receive community treatment. Treatment consisted of distribution of free condoms and brochures, two three-hour workshops on HIV prevention, and a community-wide program with various neighborhood initiatives and workshops for parents. Control group: residents of control developments received free condoms and brochures, watched a videotape about HIV prevention, and discussed the video after viewing. **N* = 1,172 at baseline; 763 at follow-up two months after completion of the intervention.	Cost information not available from team that designed, implemented, and evaluated the intervention.
Safer Choices	Freshmen and sophomores in 20 high schools in California and Texas. Treatment group: students in the schools that were randomly assigned to receive treatment. Intervention was implemented for all students in each treatment school and consisted of 20 sessions focusing on improving students' knowledge about condom use and sexually transmitted infections and on changing their perception of abstinence in order to make it a more appealing option. In addition, clubs and councils were created and speaker series and parenting-education initiatives were implemented in order to change the culture within treatment schools. Control group: students at control schools received standard, five-session sexual-education curriculum and a few other school-wide activities that varied from school to school. **N* = 3,869 at baseline; 3,058 at follow-up about one year after completion of the intervention.	Estimated cost per participant: ≈ $110
Be Proud! Be Responsible!	Urban African American males aged 13–18 in the Philadelphia metropolitan area. Participants were recruited from a local medical clinic, a neighborhood high school, and a local YMCA. Treatment group: participated in five-hour intervention designed to prevent HIV infection. Intervention techniques included small-group discussions, videos, and role-playing. Control group: participated in career-planning intervention of similar length. **N* = 157 at baseline; 150 at follow-up three months after the intervention.	Estimated cost per participant: ≈ $120
Modified Version of "Be Proud!": ¡Cuidate!	Latino youth aged 13–18 in the Philadelphia metropolitan area. Participants were recruited from three local high schools and various community organizations. Treatment and control groups: received interventions similar to the ones described above for "Be Proud" and "Making Proud Choices," although the intervention here was tailored specifically for Latinos and Latinas rather than for African Americans. **N* = 656 at baseline; 553 at follow-up one year after the intervention.	Estimated cost per participant: ≈ $120

expensive and have sometimes been difficult to replicate successfully in settings other than the ones in which they were originally implemented.[55]

There are, however, other programs that are much less expensive and that—although their evaluations did not measure their effects on teen pregnancy—were found to have had substantial effects on sexual activity or contraceptive behavior, or both, using random-assignment research designs. Among the most promising examples of such programs are Becoming a Responsible Teen, HIV

Table 2. Impacts of Selected Teen Pregnancy Prevention Programs Found to Have Affected Both Sexual Activity and Contraceptive Use

Among interventions that have been evaluated using random-assignment controlled experimental design

Name of intervention	**Estimated program effects on sexual abstinence/initiation of sex**	**Estimated program effects on frequency of intercourse**
Becoming a Responsible Teen	One year after the end of the intervention, treatment-group members were about 65% as likely as control-group members to report having had sex during the previous two months.	No results reported for sexual frequency in evaluations of this program.
HIV Prevention for Adolescents in Low-Income Housing Developments	Among participants who were sexually inexperienced at baseline: treatment-group members were about 88% as likely as control-group members to report having initiated sex within two months of the end of the intervention. Among participants who were sexually experienced at baseline: no results for cessation/resumption of sexual activity among sexually experienced participants reported in evaluations of this program.	No results reported for sexual frequency in evaluations of this program.
Safer Choices	Among all members of the analysis sample: no statistically significant difference about one year after completion of the intervention (or at earlier follow-ups) in the self-reported odds of having initiated sex between treatment- and control-group members who were sexually inexperienced at baseline. Among Latino members of the analysis sample: about one year after completion of the intervention, sexually inexperienced treatment-group members were significantly less likely than control-group members to report that they had initiated sex (odds ratio = .57).	About one year after completion of the intervention, no significant differences between treatment- and control-group members in the self-reported frequency of sexual intercourse over the previous three months (nor were such differences observed at earlier follow-ups).
Be Proud! Be Responsible!	No statistically significant difference observed three months after completion of the intervention between treatment- and control-group members in the share of participants who reported having had sex over the previous three months (among boys only).	Three months after the intervention, treatment-group members reported having engaged in about 40% as much sex as control-group members over the previous three months (among boys only).
Modified Version of "Be Proud!": ¡Cuidate!	Using data from follow-ups conducted three months, six months, and one year after the intervention, evaluators concluded that treatment-group members were significantly less likely than control-group members to report having had sexual intercourse in the previous three months. At each of the three follow-ups, treatment-group members were about 85% as likely as control-group members to report having had sex over the previous three months.	No results reported for sexual frequency in evaluations of this program.

continued

Among interventions that have been evaluated using random-assignment controlled experimental design

Estimated program effects on male contraceptive use	Estimated program effects on female contraceptive use	Replication information
Two months after the end of the intervention: about 57% more sexual occasions from the previous two months were reported to have involved the use of a condom among males in the treatment group than among males in the control group. One year after the end of the intervention: no significant difference between treatment-group and control-group males in the proportion of sexual occasions protected by a condom. However, combined-sex analyses showed a significant difference at one year: almost 30% more sexual occasions from the previous two months were reported to have involved the use of a condom among males and females in the treatment group than among males and females in the control group.	Two months after the end of the intervention: about 16% more sexual occasions from the previous two months were reported to have involved the use of a condom among females in the treatment group than among females in the control group. One year after the end of the intervention: about 44% more sexual occasions from the previous two months were reported to have involved the use of a condom among females in the treatment group than among females in the control group.	One successful replication: Curriculum fully implemented in drug-rehabilitation facility; increased abstinence and condom use. One unsuccessful replication: Curriculum shortened by more than half and implemented in a state juvenile reformatory; no observed program effects on sex or contraceptive use.
Self-reports indicate that, as of the follow-up two months after the completion of the intervention, a condom was used at last sexual intercourse about 24% more often among treatment-group members than among control-group members.		No published evaluations of any attempts to replicate program.
About one year after completion of the intervention, males in the treatment group were significantly more likely to report having used contraception at last sexual intercourse (odds ratio = 1.64).	About one year after completion of the intervention, no statistically significant difference between females in the treatment and control groups in the self-reported use of contraception at last sexual intercourse (results for female contraceptive use not reported for earlier follow-ups, but evaluators found a significant difference in the self-reported use of contraception at last intercourse for the combined male and female samples while the intervention was ongoing (odds ratio = 1.76).	No published evaluations of any attempts to replicate program.
Three months after the intervention, a significant difference was observed between average self-reported treatment- and control-group scores (4.4 vs. 3.5, respectively) on condom-use scale where 1 = "never" and 5 = "always" (among boys only).	Intervention was for boys only.	One successful replication: implemented in different communities from original for boys and girls, rather than just for boys; and was evaluated over six months, rather than over just three months. Found to have reduced the incidence of unprotected sex over the evaluation period. One unsuccessful replication: implemented in high-school classrooms during school day. Not found to have any effect on sexual behavior, perhaps because it was mandatory (original version of the program was optional).
Using data from follow-ups conducted three months, six months, and one year after the intervention, evaluators concluded that treatment-group members were significantly more likely to report using condoms consistently. Across the three follow-ups, treatment-group members were between about 50% and about 65% more likely than control-group members to report having used condoms consistently over the previous three months. However, no statistically significant difference observed using data from the three follow-ups between treatment- and control-group members in the share of participants who reported having used condoms at last sexual intercourse.		No published evaluations of any attempts to directly replicate program. However, Making Proud Choices! (MPC), like ¡Cuidate!, was based on the Be Proud! curriculum. MPC: implemented for black boys and girls aged 11–13, found to have reduced self-reported sexual frequency and increased self-reported contraceptive use. See above for information on successful Be Proud! implementations.

Prevention for Adolescents in Low-Income Housing Developments, Safer Choices, Be Proud! Be Responsible!, and ¡Cuidate! Tables 1 and 2 provide an overview of each program's design, target population, costs per participant, key effects, and replicability. Although other programs have produced impressive effects, we focus on these five because they were found by random-assignment evaluations to have affected both sexual frequency and contraceptive use among teens.[56]

Table 2 highlights some of the clearest instances in which these programs are estimated to have had positive effects on sexual activity or contraceptive use, or both. The table also makes plain, however, that no program had a large effect on all of the behavioral dimensions included in this review. Our own analysis of the findings reported in the table (and of additional pieces of data contained in the evaluations of these programs) suggests that, if one were to standardize these effects to the extent possible and to take into account the various findings of no effect, one might conclude that, as a group, these interventions increased the number of teens who were sexually inactive in recent months by about 15 percent on average and that they increased contraceptive use by an average of about 25 percent.[57]

Programs Addressing Access

As noted, the two primary public programs that provide access to subsidized contraception are Medicaid and Title X of the Public Health Service Act. In their study of how expanded eligibility for Medicaid-subsidized family planning services has affected women's contraceptive use, Melissa Kearney and Phillip Levine found that states that were granted family planning waivers reduced by roughly 5 percent the number of all sexually active women aged twenty or older who failed to use contraception at their last intercourse. They also found that the waivers reduced by about 2 percent the number of births to women aged twenty or older.[58]

Programs such as Title X and Medicaid-subsidized family planning would be considerably more effective if they were able to increase not just the use of contraceptives, but the use of long-acting, reversible contraceptive methods (LARCs) such as IUDs and implants. Our tabulations of data from the National Survey of Family Growth suggest that, among recipients of publicly subsidized birth control who are capable of becoming pregnant but are seeking to avoid doing so, only about a third list a LARC as their primary contraceptive method. The remaining two-thirds rely on less-effective methods—such as the pill, condoms, or even withdrawal—that require more diligence on the part of the user and are therefore less likely to be used correctly or consistently. James Trussell and his colleagues show that, even though LARCs tend to cost more than other methods, they are often considerably more cost-effective in the long run.[59] Thus, to the extent that programs providing publicly subsidized contraception are able to encourage more women to take up or switch to longer-acting methods, they may ultimately prevent more pregnancies per dollar spent over the long term.

Policy Simulations

We next present summary findings from a set of benefit-cost simulations of three programs, one to motivate individuals to avoid unintended pregnancies, one to improve their knowledge about contraception, and one to remove barriers to contraceptive access. Specifically, we present findings from simulations of a mass media campaign that encourages men to use condoms, an effective teen

Table 3. Estimated Benefits and Costs of Various Interventions to Prevent Unintended Pregnancy

Percent unless otherwise indicated Benefits and costs	Mass media campaign	Effective teen pregnancy prevention program	Expanded access to subsidized contraception under Medicaid
Percent reduction in pregnancies			
Overall	1.7	0.8	1.9
Among unmarried females	3.4	1.7	2.2
Among teenagers	4.0	7.5	1.4
Percent reduction in births			
Overall	1.0	0.6	1.5
Among unmarried females	2.5	1.6	1.6
Among teenagers	3.4	6.2	1.3
Percent reduction in the number of children born into poverty	2.2	1.4	1.9
Program cost			
Total program cost	$100,000,000	$145,000,000	$265,000,000
Cost per pregnancy avoided	$913	$2,683	$2,165
Cost per birth avoided	$2,512	$5,709	$4,658
Benefit-cost analysis Public savings: based on pregnancy care, infant medical care, and children's benefits			
Public cost savings from prevented pregnancies	$360,460,819	$300,798,840	$1,129,790,608
Benefit-cost ratio	$3.60	$2.07	$4.26

pregnancy prevention program that discourages sexual activity and educates participants about proper contraceptive use, and an expansion in access to Medicaid-subsidized contraception. Our simulations draw on the information contained in this article and in a longer paper.[60]

We conduct these analyses using FamilyScape, a sophisticated simulation tool developed at the Brookings Institution to simulate the effect of policy changes on family formation. FamilyScape simulates the key antecedents of pregnancy (for example, sexual activity, contraceptive use, and female fecundity) and many of its most important outcomes (for example, childbearing within and outside of marriage and among teenaged and non-teenaged mothers, children's chances of being born into poverty, and abortion).[61] Behaviors and outcomes of interest are simulated at the individual level and are allowed to vary according to certain demographic characteristics. With few adjustments to these individually specified behaviors, FamilyScape tracks real-world outcomes relatively well. That is, it can generally replicate such aggregate outcomes as pregnancy or birth rates based on a set of empirically derived assumptions about how often people have sex, do or do not use contraception of a particular type, do or do not have an abortion, do or do not marry, and so forth.

For the simulated expansion of Medicaid-subsidized family planning services, we assume that contraceptive use would increase by about 2.5 percentage points in all states that have not yet been granted an income waiver.[62] We also assume that this increase would be concentrated among low-income women, most of whom are unmarried. We assume that the simulated mass media campaign would be ongoing, that its target population would be unmarried men between the ages of fifteen and forty-four, and that 3 percent of that group would switch from using no contraception to using condoms as a result of the campaign.[63] For the simulated teen pregnancy prevention program, we assume that a well-designed and effective campaign that is taken to scale nationally would have about half of the impact of the small-scale campaigns whose effects are summarized in table 2. (Previous research suggests that maintaining the effectiveness of high-quality programs is difficult when they are replicated in new settings.) Because most findings described in table 2 are for low-income adolescents, we also make the simplifying assumption that the program would be targeted on teens of low socioeconomic status.[64]

Table 3 shows the findings of our policy simulations. It is important, when examining these findings, to bear in mind that a program might appear to be relatively more or less efficacious depending simply on the target group chosen. For example, the teen pregnancy prevention program has a smaller effect (0.8 percent) on the overall pregnancy rate than on the rate of teenage pregnancy (7.5 percent).

The bottom panel of the table shows the results of our benefit-cost analysis.[65] We estimate these programs' costs using data described in endnote 66, and we estimate their benefits by measuring the taxpayer savings associated with the pregnancies that they would prevent. We measure these savings by focusing specifically on the costs to taxpayers of providing publicly subsidized medical care for pregnant women, publicly subsidized medical care for infants, and means-tested government benefits for young children.[66] We chose this definition of cost savings because it is measurable using available data and is broadly consistent with the approaches taken by other researchers who have conducted related exercises.

All three policies have benefit-cost ratios that are comfortably greater than one. Some policies, however, are more cost-effective than others. For example, even though the Medicaid expansion is by far the most expensive of the three policies, its benefit-cost ratio is also the largest. This finding partially reflects the Medicaid expansion's focus on lower-income women who are likely to qualify for the government benefits and services on which our cost-savings estimates are based. It also reflects the efficient targeting of the Medicaid expansion: when money is spent on improving access to Medicaid-funded contraceptive services, a relatively large share of that money provides contraception to women who are likely to use it. By contrast, our simulated sex education program serves large swaths of teens whose behaviors remain unchanged by the intervention. Similarly, although the media campaign reaches many people relatively cheaply—we estimate its annual cost per member of the target population to be about $2.70—it changes the behavior of only a small share of these individuals. Thus, the campaign's benefit-cost ratio is higher than that of the teen pregnancy program but lower than that of the Medicaid expansion.

Many of these conclusions are relatively insensitive to large changes in the assumptions underlying the analysis. For example, even if these programs were half as effective —or twice as expensive—as we assume them to be, all three would have benefit-cost ratios greater than one. Moreover, even if the cost of the Medicaid expansion were twice what we assume—or if the benefits of teen pregnancy prevention programs were twice as large as is implied by our analysis—the former program would still be modestly more cost-effective than the latter. As we show in a separate paper, however, none of these policies is estimated to be cost-effective if one's measure of taxpayer savings excludes the public cost of benefits provided to children after they are born. We would argue, though, that these savings should be included. Indeed, if we were to extend even further the window of time over which we measure the public cost of providing children's benefits and services, our estimates would show that these policies are still more cost-effective.

Our bottom-line assessment is that all three programs are sound investments worthy of consideration by policy makers. We further conclude that, for policy makers most interested in reducing teen pregnancy, a well-designed curricular program focusing specifically on teens would be the most sensible option to pursue. For policy makers intent instead on implementing a program that is cost-effective but comparatively inexpensive, a media campaign might make the most sense. And for those interested in preventing unintended pregnancy and childbearing more generally, expanding Medicaid-subsidized family planning services might be most appropriate option. More to the point, these findings suggest that expanding contraceptive access is likely to be more cost-effective than many of the competing alternatives that have the same basic objective.

Looking Ahead

We began by describing seven hypotheses about why unwed pregnancies are a growing social problem in the United States. We then grouped them into three broad categories: a lack of motivation to avoid unwed pregnancy, a lack of knowledge about how to avoid pregnancy, and a lack of access to the contraception that makes it possible to avoid pregnancy. Our benefit-cost analyses of policies designed to address each of these problems yield two key insights. One is that several different policy options are likely to reduce the incidence of unintended pregnancy and childbearing in a cost-effective manner. The other is that not all contraceptives are created equal. Some are far more effective in practice than others, once the likelihood of incorrect or inconsistent use is factored into the equation. Our findings suggest that policy makers should consider "going to scale" with programs designed to encourage safer sexual behavior and should expand access to effective contraception among individuals who might not otherwise be able to afford it. Given the high personal and public costs of unintended pregnancy, the need for bold policy interventions in this arena is now greater than ever.

Endnotes

1. Brady E. Hamilton, Joyce A. Martin, and Stephanie J. Ventura, "Births: Preliminary Data for 2007," *National Vital Statistics Reports* 57, no. 12 (2009).

2. Ibid.

3. Adam Thomas and Isabel Sawhill, "For Love *and* Money? The Impact of Family Structure on Family Income," *Future of Children* 15, no. 2 (2005): 57–74.

4. Paul R. Amato, "The Impact of Family Formation Change on the Cognitive, Social, and Emotional Well-Being of the Next Generation," *Future of Children* 15, no. 2 (2005): 75–96.

5. Ibid.; Thomas and Sawhill, "For Love *and* Money?" (see note 3).

6. Jane Lawler Dye, "Participation of Mothers in Government Assistance Programs: 2004," Current Population Reports (Washington: U.S. Census Bureau, May 2008); Tax Policy Center, "EITC Distribution 2000 and 2003" (www.taxpolicycenter.org/taxfacts/displayafact.cfm?DocID=329&Topic2id=20&Topic3id=22 [Jan. 28, 2010]).

7. Dye, "Participation of Mothers in Government Assistance Programs" (see note 6).

8. See, for example, Saul D. Hoffman, "Teenage Childbearing Is Not So Bad After All… Or Is It? A Review of the New Literature," *Family Planning Perspectives* 30, no. 5 (1998): 236–39, 243; V. Joseph Hotz, Susan Williams McElroy, and Seth G. Sanders, "Consequences of Teen Childbearing for Mothers through 1993," in *Kids Having Kids: Economic Costs and Social Consequences of Teen Pregnancy*, edited by Saul D. Hoffman and Rebecca A. Maynard (Washington: Urban Institute Press, 2008).

9. Jason H. Fletcher and Barbara L. Wolfe, "Education and Labor Market Consequences of Teenage Childbearing: Evidence Using the Timing of Pregnancy Outcomes and Community Fixed Effects," *Journal of Human Resources* 44, no. 2 (2009): 303–25.

10. Authors' calculations from the National Center for Health Statistics' National Vital Statistics System birth data files.

11. Special tabulations of unpublished data by the Guttmacher Institute for the National Campaign to Prevent Teen and Unplanned Pregnancy. Published data presented in Lawrence B. Finer and Stanley K. Henshaw, "Disparities in Rates of Unintended Pregnancy in the United States, 1994 and 2001," *Perspectives on Sexual and Reproductive Health* 38, no. 2 (2006): 90–96.

12. Rachel K. Jones and others, "Abortion in the United States: Incidence and Access to Services, 2005," *Perspectives on Sexual and Reproductive Health* 40, no. 1 (2008): 6–16.

13. Stanley K. Henshaw and Lawrence B. Finer, "The Accessibility of Abortion Services in the United States, 2001," *Perspectives on Sexual and Reproductive Health* 35, no. 1 (2003): 16–24.

14. Lydia Saad, "More Americans 'Pro-Life' than 'Pro-Choice' for First Time" (Gallup, May 15, 2009), (www.gallup.com/poll/118399/more-americans-pro-life-than-pro-choice-first-time.aspx [Jan. 28, 2010]); Rachel Laser and Jim Kessler, "A Consensus on the Abortion Debate" (Washington: Third Way, April 2008).

15. Huffington Post, "Barack Obama Democratic Convention Speech" (www.huffingtonpost.com/2008/08/28/barack-obama-democratic-c_n_122224.html [Jan. 28, 2010]).

16. Paul Taylor, Cary Funk, and April Clark, "Generation Gap in Values, Behaviors: As Marriage and Parenthood Drift Apart, Public Is Concerned about Social Impact" (Washington: Pew Research Center, July 2007); David J. Harding and Christopher Jencks, "Changing Attitudes toward Premarital Sex: Cohort, Period, and Aging Effects," *Public Opinion Quarterly* 67, no. 2 (2003): 211–26; Arland Thornton and Linda Young-DeMarco, "Four Decades of Trends in Attitudes toward Family Issues in the United States: The 1960s through the 1990s," *Journal of Marriage and Family* 63, no. 4 (November 2001): 1009–37.

17. Taylor, Funk, and Clark, "Generation Gap in Values, Behaviors" (see note 16).

18. For a review of this literature, see Barbara Wolfe and others, "Do Youth Nonmarital Childbearing Choices Reflect Income and Relationship Expectations?" *Journal of Population Economics* 20, no. 1 (2007): 73–100.

19. Kathryn Edin and Maria Kefalas, *Promises I Can Keep: Why Poor Women Put Motherhood before Marriage* (University of California Press, 2005), p. 171.

20. Ibid., p. 262.

21. Kathleen Kaye, Katherine Suellentrop, and Corinna Sloup, "The Fog Zone: How Misperceptions, Magical Thinking, and Ambivalence Put Young Adults at Risk for Unplanned Pregnancy" (Washington: National Campaign to Prevent Teen and Unplanned Pregnancy, December 2009).

22. National Campaign to Prevent Teen Pregnancy, "What 20-Somethings Are Saying about Pregnancy, Sex, and Childbearing: Findings from Focus Groups" (Washington, June 2007).

23. William Julius Wilson and Kathryn M. Neckerman, "Poverty and Family Structure: The Widening Gap between Evidence and Public Policy Issues," in *Fighting Poverty,* edited by Sheldon H. Danziger and Daniel H. Weinberg (Harvard University Press, 1986).

24. David T. Ellwood and Christopher Jencks, "The Spread of Single-Parent Families in the United States since 1960," in *The Future of the Family,* edited by Daniel P. Moynihan, Timothy M. Smeeding, and Lee Rainwater (New York: Russell Sage Foundation, 2004).

25. See James Trussell and others, "Cost Effectiveness of Contraceptives in the United States," *Contraception* 79, no. 1 (2009): 5–14.

26. Adam Sonfield, Casey Alrich, and Rachel Benson Gold, "Public Funding for Family Planning, Sterilization and Abortion Services, FY 1980–2006," Occasional Report 38 (New York: Guttmacher Institute, 2008).

27. Rachel Benson Gold and others, "Next Steps for America's Family Planning Program: Leveraging the Potential of Medicaid and Title X in an Evolving Health Care System" (New York: Guttmacher Institute, 2009).

28. Adam Thomas and Isabel V. Sawhill, "Keep Politics Away from the Promise of Family Planning" (Washington: Brookings Institution, February 2009).

29. Guttmacher Institute, "State Policies in Brief: State Medicaid Family Planning Eligibility Expansions" (New York: Guttmacher Institute, March 2010); Jennifer J. Frost, Adam Sonfield, and Rachel Benson Gold, "Estimating the Impact of Expanding Medicaid Eligibility for Family Planning Services," Occasional Report 28 (New York: Guttmacher Institute, August 2006).

30. National Campaign to Prevent Teen and Unplanned Pregnancy, "Magical Thinking: Young Adults' Attitudes and Beliefs about Sex, Contraception, and Unplanned Pregnancy" (Washington, 2008).

31. Jennifer J. Frost, Jacqueline E. Darroch, and Lisa Remez, "Improving Contraceptive Use in the United States," *In Brief*, no. 1 (New York: Guttmacher Institute, 2008); Guttmacher Institute, "Improving Contraceptive Use in the United States" (www.guttmacher.org/presentations/2009/01/06/ICU_ARHP-CORE.pdf [Jan. 28, 2010]).

32. Kaye, Suellentrop, and Sloup, "The Fog Zone" (see note 21).

33. National Campaign to Prevent Teen and Unplanned Pregnancy, "What 20-Somethings Are Saying" (see note 22).

34. Frost, Darroch, and Remez, "Improving Contraceptive Use" (see note 31).

35. Kathryn Kost and others, "Estimates of Contraceptive Failure from the 2002 National Survey of Family Growth," *Contraception* 77, no. 1 (2008): 10–21.

36. Since 1987, the number of adoptions annually has remained relatively constant, ranging from 118,000 to 127,000 a year. In comparison, there were more than 1.3 million unintended births in 2001. Sources: Child Welfare Information Gateway, "How Many Children Were Adopted in 2000 and 2001?" (Washington, August 2004); special tabulations of unpublished data by the Guttmacher Institute for the National Campaign to Prevent Teen and Unplanned Pregnancy (see note 11).

37. Douglas Kirby, "Emerging Answers 2007: Research Findings on Programs to Reduce Teen Pregnancy and Sexually Transmitted Diseases" (Washington: National Campaign to Prevent Teen and Unplanned Pregnancy, November 2007).

38. Mark W. Nowak, Michael E. Fishman, and Mary E. Farrell, "State Experience and Perspectives on Out-of-Wedlock Births" (Falls Church, Va.: Lewin Group, February 2003).

39. Seth Noar, "Challenges in Evaluating Health Communication Campaigns: Defining the Issues," *Communication Methods and Measures* 3, no. 1 (2009): 1–11.

40. Leslie B. Snyder and others, "A Meta-Analysis of the Effect of Mediated Health Communication Campaigns on Behavior Change in the United States," *Journal of Health Communication* 9, Supplement 1 (2004): 71–96.

41. Rick S. Zimmerman and others, "Effects of a Televised Two-City Safer Sex Mass Media Campaign Targeting High-Sensation-Seeking and Impulsive-Decision-Making Young Adults," *Health Education & Behavior* 34, no. 5 (2007): 810–26.

42. For example, in our own tabulations of 2006 birth data from the National Vital Statistics System, we find that about 60 percent of births to women with less than a high school degree are out of wedlock. Among women with a high school degree, some college, a college degree, and more than a college degree, the corresponding percentages are about 50 percent, 38 percent, 12 percent, and 4 percent, respectively.

43. Sandra E. Black, Paul J. Devereaux, and Kjell G. Salvanes, "*Fast Times at Ridgemont High?* The Effect of Compulsory Schooling Laws on Teenage Births" (Cambridge, Mass.: National Bureau of Economic Research, November 2004); Janet Currie and Enrico Moretti, "Mother's Education and the Intergenerational Transmission of Human Capital: Evidence from College Openings," *Quarterly Journal of Economics* 118, no. 4 (2003): 1495–1532; David Ellwood, Ty Wilde, and Lily Batchelder, "The Mommy Track Divides: The Impact of Childbearing on Wages of Women of Differing Skill Levels" (Harvard University, March 2004);

Robert Haveman and Barbara Wolfe, "The Determinants of Children's Attainments: A Review of Methods and Findings," *Journal of Economic Literature* 33, no. 4 (1995): 1829–78; Jennifer Manlove, "The Influence of High School Dropout and School Disengagement on the Risk of School-Age Pregnancy," *Journal of Research on Adolescence* 8, no. 2 (1998): 187–220; Justin McCrary and Heather Royer, "The Effect of Female Education on Fertility and Infant Health: Evidence from School Entry Policies Using Exact Date of Birth" (Cambridge, Mass.: National Bureau of Economic Research, June 2006).

44. Benjamin W. Cowan, "Forward-Thinking Teens: The Effects of College Costs on Adolescent Risky Behavior," unpublished dissertation paper (Madison, Wis.: University of Wisconsin at Madison, November 2009).

45. Robert D. Plotnick and others, "The Impact of Child Support Enforcement Policy on Nonmarital Childbearing" (Seattle: University of Washington, 2005).

46. Irwin Garfinkel and others, "The Roles of Child Support Enforcement and Welfare in Non-Marital Childbearing," *Journal of Population Economics* 16, no. 1 (2003): 55–70; Lingxin Hao, Nam M. Astone, and Andrew J. Cherlin, "Effects of Child Support and Welfare Policies on Nonmarital Teenage Childbearing and Motherhood," *Population Research and Policy Review* 25, no. 3 (2007): 235–57; Chien-Chung Huang and Wen-Jui Han, "Child Support Enforcement and Sexual Activity of Male Adolescents," *Journal of Marriage and Family* 69, no. 3 (2007): 763–77; Plotnick and others, "The Impact of Child Support Enforcement Policy on Nonmarital Childbearing" (see note 45).

47. Garfinkel and others, "The Roles of Child Support Enforcement and Welfare in Non-Marital Childbearing" (see note 46).

48. Lisa A. Gennetian and others, "How Welfare and Work Policies for Parents Affect Adolescents: A Synthesis of Research" (New York: MDRC, May 2002); Leonard M. Lopoo and Thomas DeLeire, "Did Welfare Reform Influence the Fertility of Young Teens?" *Journal of Policy Analysis and Management* 25, no. 2 (2006): 275–98.

49. For examples of studies concluding that welfare reform reduced teen or out-of-wedlock childbearing, see Lopoo and DeLeire, "Did Welfare Reform Influence the Fertility of Young Teens?" (see note 48), and Garfinkel and others, "The Roles of Child Support Enforcement and Welfare in Non-Marital Childbearing" (see note 46). For the results of a relatively comprehensive meta-analysis showing that welfare reform had few such effects, if any, see Gennetian and others, "How Welfare and Work Policies for Parents Affect Adolescents" (see note 48).

50. Christopher Trenholm and others, "Impacts of Four Title V, Section 510 Abstinence Education Programs: Final Report" (Princeton, N.J.: Mathematica Policy Research, Inc., April 2007).

51. On these programs' curricula, see Kirby, "Emerging Answers 2007" (see note 37). On the evaluations of these programs, see Trenholm and others, "Impacts of Four Title V, Section 510 Abstinence Education Programs" (see note 50).

52. Kirby, "Emerging Answers 2007" (see note 37).

53. On the suggestive evidence reported in certain less-rigorous studies, see Kirby, "Emerging Answers 2007" (see note 37). On the recently published randomized evaluation of an abstinence-only intervention, see John B. Jemmott, Loretta S. Jemmott, and Geoffrey T. Fong, "Efficacy of a Theory-Based Abstinence-Only Intervention over 24 Months: A Randomized Controlled Trial with Young Adolescents," *Archives of Pediatrics & Adolescent Medicine* 164, no. 2 (2010): 152–59.

54. Katherine Suellentrop, "What Works 2009: Curriculum-Based Programs That Prevent Teen Pregnancy" (Washington: National Campaign to Prevent Teen and Unplanned Pregnancy, 2009).

55. We refer here to the interventions known as the Teen Outreach Program, Children's Aid Society-Carrera, and Focus on Kids Plus Impact. For more information on these programs, see Advocates for Youth, "Science and Success, Second Edition: Sex Education and Other Programs That Work to Prevent Teen Pregnancy, HIV, & Sexually Transmitted Infections" (Washington: 2008). For additional information on CAS-Carrera, see Kirby, "Emerging Answers 2007" (see note 37).

56. For a description of how the costs of these programs were estimated, see Adam Thomas, "'Plans Are Useless, but Planning Is Indispensable': A Benefit-Cost Assessment of Three Pregnancy-Prevention Strategies" (Washington: Brookings Institution, May 2010). For more information on Becoming a Responsible Teen, see Janet S. St. Lawrence and others, "Cognitive-Behavioral Intervention to Reduce African American Adolescents' Risk for HIV Infection," *Journal of Consulting and Clinical Psychology* 63, no. 2 (1995): 221–37; and Janet S. St. Lawrence and others, "Reducing STD and HIV Risk Behavior of Substance-Dependent Adolescents: A Randomized Controlled Trial," *Journal of Consulting and Clinical Psychology* 70, no. 4 (2002): 1010–21. For more information on HIV Prevention for Adolescents in Low-Income Communities, see Kathleen J. Sikkema and others, "Outcomes of a Randomized, Controlled Community-Level HIV Prevention Intervention for Adolescents in Low-Income Housing Developments," *AIDS* 19, no. 14 (2005): 1509–16. For more information on Safer Choices, see Karin Coyle and others, "Safer Choices: Reducing Teen Pregnancy, HIV, and STDs," *Public Health Reports* 116, Supplement 1 (2001): 82–93, and Douglas Kirby and others, "The 'Safer Choices' Intervention: Its Impact on the Sexual Behaviors of Different Subgroups of High School Students," *Journal of Adolescent Health* 35, no. 6 (2004): 442–52. For more information on the Jemmott curricula, see John B. Jemmott and others, "Reductions in HIV Risk-Associated Sexual Behaviors among Black Male Adolescents: Effects of an AIDS Prevention Intervention," *American Journal of Public Health* 82, no. 3 (1992): 372–77; John B. Jemmott and others, "Abstinence and Safer Sex HIV Risk-Reduction Interventions for African American Adolescents: A Randomized Controlled Trial," *Journal of the American Medical Association* 279, no. 19 (1998): 1529–36; Antonia H. Villarruel, John B. Jemmott, and Loretta S. Jemmott, "A Randomized Controlled Trial Testing an HIV Prevention Intervention for Latino Youth," *Archives of Pediatrics & Adolescent Medicine* 160, no. 11 (2006): 772–77. See also Suellentrop, "What Works 2009" (see note 54); Advocates for Youth, "Science and Success, Second Edition" (see note 55); Kirby, "Emerging Answers 2007" (see note 37), for additional information on these programs.

57. For a description of how these average effects were estimated, see Thomas, "'Plans Are Useless, but Planning Is Indispensable'" (see note 56).

58. Melissa S. Kearney and Phillip B. Levine, "Subsidized Contraception, Fertility, and Sexual Behavior," *Review of Economics and Statistics* 91, no. 1 (2009): 137–51.

59. Trussell and others, "Cost Effectiveness of Contraceptives in the United States" (see note 25).

60. See Thomas, "Plans Are Useless, but Planning Is Indispensable" (see note 56), for a thorough discussion of how the parameters for these benefit-cost simulations were developed and for a presentation of results from a range of sensitivity analyses that, in the interest of brevity, we do not discuss here.

61. For more information on FamilyScape, see Adam Thomas and Emily Monea, "FamilyScape: A Simulation Model of Family Formation" (Washington: Brookings Institution, May 2009).

62. In early simulations, we assumed—based on Kearney and Levine's finding cited above—that implementation of these waivers would increase contraceptive use by about 5 percent. However, the effect of this increase on the rate of childbearing within our simulation was greater than the equivalent effect that Kearney and Levine estimate the policy to have had among states that have already expanded their eligibility limits. Thus, we simulate a smaller increase in contraceptive use by relying on an alternative estimate that is contained within the confidence intervals reported in Kearney and Levine's paper and produces a reduction in childbearing that is closer to the effect that they estimate the policy to have had. Since the average income-eligibility threshold for these services in waiver states is a little less than twice the federal poverty threshold, we assume that this behavioral change would be concentrated among females who are below 200 percent of the poverty line. We assume the cost of the expansion to be $188 per woman served, and we assume that a little more than 5 percent of women in new waiver states would be served by the program as a result of these expansions. These assumptions are based on estimates reported in Kearney and Levine, "Subsidized Contraception, Fertility, and Sexual Behavior" (see note 58).

63. In fact, we assume that a smaller share of teens (1.5 percent) would alter their behavior, given that they have a higher baseline condom-usage rate prior to the simulation of the new policy. We estimate that the cost of such a campaign would be $100 million a year. We make this assumption based on our analysis of cost data from other national, health-related media campaigns such as the Truth and VERB campaigns.

64. More specifically, we assume that, within the simulation's target population, there would be a 7.5 percent increase in sexual inactivity among teens; a comparable decrease in the average frequency of sex among those who remain sexually active; and a 12.5 percent increase in the number of male and female contraceptors. We assume further that the program would cost $50 a year for each member of the target population. Regarding the difficulty of replicating well-designed and well-executed programs with a high degree of fidelity, see Kirby, "Emerging Answers 2007" (see note 37).

65. Our simulations account for the fact that the prevention of unintended pregnancies sometimes causes them simply to be postponed rather than avoided altogether and that the government saves substantially less money on the prevention of pregnancies in the former category than on the prevention of pregnancies in the latter category.

66. We estimate the average public cost savings associated with the prevention of an unintended fetal loss to a low-income mother to be $750. We estimate the public cost savings associated with the prevention of a live birth to a low-income mother separately for teens and non-teens. We estimate the average public cost savings associated with the prevention of a teen and a non-teen birth to a low-income mother to be $19,000 and $24,000, respectively. Because public subsidies for abortions are—relative to the level of subsidies for births, in particular—quite small, we opt for the sake of simplicity not to account for cost savings associated with the prevention of an abortion.

Incarceration in Fragile Families

Christopher Wildeman and Bruce Western

Summary

Since the mid-1970s the U.S. imprisonment rate has increased roughly fivefold. As Christopher Wildeman and Bruce Western explain, the effects of this sea change in the imprisonment rate—commonly called mass imprisonment or the prison boom—have been concentrated among those most likely to form fragile families: poor and minority men with little schooling.

Imprisonment diminishes the earnings of adult men, compromises their health, reduces familial resources, and contributes to family breakup. It also adds to the deficits of poor children, thus ensuring that the effects of imprisonment on inequality are transferred intergenerationally. Perversely, incarceration has its most corrosive effects on families whose fathers were involved in neither domestic violence nor violent crime before being imprisoned. Because having a parent go to prison is now so common for poor, minority children and so negatively affects them, the authors argue that mass imprisonment may increase future racial and class inequality—and may even lead to more crime in the long term, thereby undoing any benefits of the prison boom.

U.S. crime policy has thus, in the name of public safety, produced more vulnerable families and reduced the life chances of their children. Wildeman and Western advocate several policy reforms, such as limiting prison time for drug offenders and for parolees who violate the technical conditions of their parole, reconsidering sentence enhancements for repeat offenders, and expanding supports for prisoners and ex-prisoners.

But Wildeman and Western argue that criminal justice reform alone will not solve the problems of school failure, joblessness, untreated addiction, and mental illness that pave the way to prison. In fact, focusing solely on criminal justice reforms would repeat the mistakes the nation made during the prison boom: trying to solve deep social problems with criminal justice policies. Addressing those broad problems, they say, requires a greater social commitment to education, public health, and the employment opportunities of low-skilled men and women. The primary sources of order and stability—public safety in its wide sense—are the informal social controls of family and work. Thus, broad social policies hold the promise not only of improving the well-being of fragile families, but also, by strengthening families and providing jobs, of contributing to public safety.

www.futureofchildren.org

Christopher Wildeman is an assistant professor of sociology and faculty affiliate of the Center for Research on Inequalities and the Life Course at Yale University. Bruce Western is a professor of sociology and director of the Multidisciplinary Program in Inequality and Social Policy at the John F. Kennedy School of Government at Harvard University.

Over the past thirty-five years, the U.S. incarceration rate has risen fivefold, from around 100 to around 500 prisoners for every 100,000 people. In just the past decade, imprisonment has become commonplace for young men living in poor and minority communities, and life in fragile families has been significantly altered. As incarceration rates have soared, poor women and children have been left to deal with the separation, visitation, and return of their progeny, partners, and parents. A burgeoning research literature shows that incarceration, on average, impairs health and diminishes the earnings of adult men, many of whom are fathers. Incarceration also elevates the risk of divorce and separation, diminishes the financial resources and well-being of wives and girlfriends left behind, and is linked to increases in children's aggression, behavioral problems, and social marginalization. By further reducing the well-being of fragile families, mass imprisonment lays the groundwork for a vicious cycle in which the criminal justice system does not diminish—and may even increase—addiction, abuse, and crime.

We first describe the concentration of incarceration in, and negative effects on, fragile families and then discuss the implications of these findings and suggest some future directions for policy. Sentencing policies that would shrink the penal population while preserving public safety offer one key direction for reform. But criminal justice reform will go only so far in reducing the negative effects of crime and incarceration on fragile families. Because many of the men who come into contact with the criminal justice system struggle with chronic unemployment, untreated addiction, poor health, and mental illness, protecting fragile families from the effects of violence and antisocial behavior will ultimately depend on social policy as much as criminal justice reform. Social policies that provide the structure and stakes in conformity known to control crime hold real promise for buffering fragile families from the negative effects of both crime and incarceration. Such policies will enable the nation to begin to move away from the formal sanctions of prison and jail sentences to the informal social controls of stable work and family life.

Most of the chapters in this volume rely primarily on research that uses data from the Fragile Families and Child Wellbeing Study. Because most of the research they review uses these unique data, the authors of these chapters can use the term "fragile families" in the strict sense—families in which the parents were unmarried when the child was born. For better or for worse, much of the research we rely on did not use data from the Fragile Families and Child Wellbeing Study. But, as we show, most of the families who experience incarceration were probably unmarried—and almost certainly were vulnerable in other ways—at the time of the child's birth. Thus, we use the term "fragile families" in this chapter to describe families who experience incarceration, even though not all of the families we consider were "fragile families" in the strict sense.

The Demography of Punishment in America

In order to understand why incarceration may be so consequential for children in fragile families, we first must determine what is unique about American imprisonment. In this section, we document the novelty of American imprisonment, discuss the causes of the prison boom, and outline how common imprisonment is for adult men and parental imprisonment is for children.

Mass Imprisonment in Comparative-Historical Perspective

For most of the twentieth century, researchers studying U.S. child well-being were unlikely to see prisons as a source of social inequality. As late as the mid-1970s, only 100 out of every 100,000 Americans were incarcerated in a state or federal prison; only 2 percent of the population went to prison at any point in their lives.[1] The nation's penal system would have seemed unlikely to weigh heavily on citizens' life chances, not just because the incarceration rate was low in an absolute sense, but also because of its historic stability. For the first three-quarters of the twentieth century, the American imprisonment rate per 100,000 rarely exceeded 125 or fell below 75.[2]

Today the U.S. incarceration rate is about seven times higher than the West European average and is approached only by rates in the penal systems of some former Soviet republics and South Africa.[3] This is a drastic change from the early 1970s, when the American incarceration rate was only about twice the rate of most other wealthy democracies. Although the U.S. rate has been rising more slowly in recent years, it has continued to climb even through a recession that has caused deep cuts in state budgets. The American incarceration rate has been much higher than that of other long-standing democracies since at least the late 1980s, but American men have been at extremely high lifetime risk of imprisonment beginning only in the past decade, further setting the American penal system apart from those of other democracies. As of the early 2000s, 6.6 percent of Americans, and more than 11 percent of American men, could expect to go to prison at some point.[4] These figures show that mass imprisonment[5] is historically novel within America and that imprisonment is now a common experience for adult men.

The Causes of Mass Imprisonment

What caused the U.S. imprisonment rate to increase so sharply? Rising crime would seem an obvious suspect. But because crime rates have risen and fallen significantly since the mid-1970s while the imprisonment rate has been climbing without interruption, the year-to-year fluctuations in crime are unlikely to have directly produced the steady decades-long increase in the imprisonment rate. Though a variety of explanations have been proposed, researchers agree on two main causes for rising imprisonment: changes in the economic and social life of urban men with little schooling, and a punitive turn in criminal justice policy. It is helpful to think of the first as providing the raw material for the prison boom and the second as transforming this raw material into a greatly enlarged penal population.

Before the late 1960s, urban manufacturing industries helped guarantee the livelihoods of low-skilled men in American cities. Unemployment rates of these men were relatively high compared with those of men with more schooling, but most prime-age men with only a high school education were working at wages that could support a family. Their jobs provided stakes in conformity[6] not only through their stability, but also through the family ties that a steady paycheck helped support. Urban manufacturing thus provided not just a decent standard of living, but also a daily routine and an attachment to mainstream social institutions. In this setting, deindustrialization was catastrophic. Widespread joblessness in poor urban neighborhoods coupled with the emergence of a gray economy and a booming drug trade to foster addiction and careers in crime, leaving young men in inner cities vulnerable to arrest and prosecution.[7]

Table 1. Cumulative Risk of Imprisonment by Age 30–34 for Men Born between 1945–49 and 1975–79, by Race and Education

Percent	Birth cohort 1945–49	1950–54	1955–59	1960–64	1965–69	1970–74	1975–79
White men							
High school dropouts	4.2	7.2	8.0	8.0	10.5	14.8	15.3
High school only	0.7	2.0	2.1	2.5	4.0	3.8	4.1
All noncollege	1.8	2.9	3.2	3.7	5.1	5.1	6.3
Some college	0.7	0.7	0.6	0.8	0.7	0.9	1.2
All men	1.2	1.9	2.0	2.2	2.8	2.8	3.3
African American men							
High school dropouts	14.7	19.6	27.6	41.6	57.0	62.5	69.0
High school only	10.2	11.3	9.4	12.4	16.8	20.3	18.0
All noncollege	12.1	14.1	14.7	19.9	26.7	30.9	35.7
Some college	4.9	3.5	4.3	5.5	6.8	8.5	7.6
All men	9.0	10.6	11.5	15.2	20.3	22.8	20.7

Source: Bruce Western and Christopher Wildeman, "The Black Family and Mass Incarceration," *Annals of the American Academy of Political and Social Science* 621, no. 1 (2009): 231.

At this point, changes in the criminal justice system became important. As late as the mid-1970s, many arrests—most significantly, for public order and drug offenses—would have drawn no more than a small fine or a short spell of community supervision. From the mid-1970s, a punitive shift in criminal justice policy turned imprisonment into the primary penalty for a felony conviction. Tougher drug sentences, together with limits on parole and sentence enhancements for repeat and violent offenders, increased prison admission rates and time served in prison.[8] Policing also intensified, and drug arrest rates, particularly among African Americans, increased sharply through the 1980s. In this way, the combination of a declining labor market for low-skill men and a punitive shift in criminal justice policies produced a sharp increase in incarceration rates.

Disparities in the Cumulative Risk of (Parental) Imprisonment

Were imprisonment evenly distributed throughout the population, it would be of no greater consequence for fragile families than for any other demographic group. But large racial and class disparities in imprisonment have produced extremely high lifetime risks of imprisonment for minority men with little schooling, and small but rapidly growing risks of imprisonment for similar women. Because these men and women are unlikely to marry but no less likely than those outside of prison to have children, they are likely to form fragile families.

Table 1 shows changes in the risk of imprisonment by age thirty to thirty-four for cohorts of men born between 1945–49 and 1975–79.[9] The risk nearly tripled for white men and more than doubled for African American men. Although both groups experienced large relative increases in the risk of imprisonment, the absolute change in this risk was much larger for African American men. In the youngest cohort, born between 1975 and 1979, around one in five African American men experienced imprisonment; for comparable white men, the risk was around one in thirty.

When risks are further broken down by level of education within racial groups, differences

Figure 1. Percentage of Men Aged 22–30 Who Were Married in 2000 and Men Aged 33–40 Who Were Fathers in 1997–98

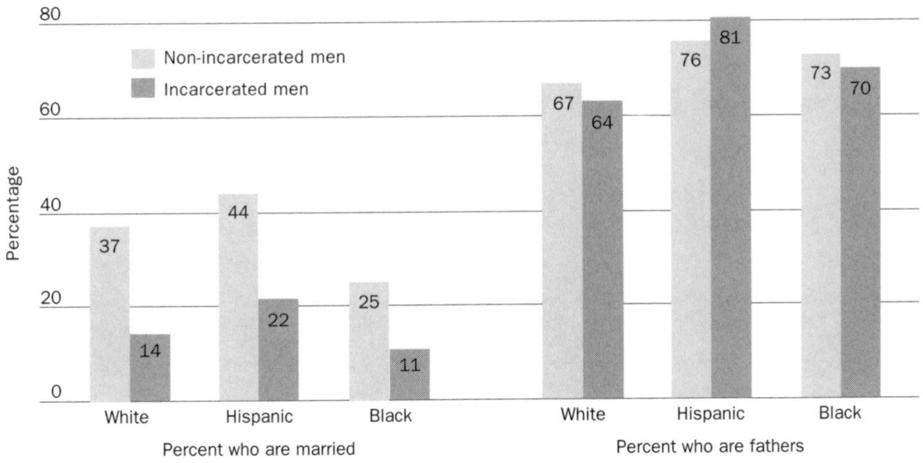

Source: Bruce Western, *Punishment and Inequality in America* (New York: Russell Sage, 2006), p. 137.

in the risk of imprisonment become even more pronounced. Most notably, African American men in recent cohorts who did not complete some college had around a one in three chance of going to prison at some point, while African American men in the same cohort who dropped out of high school had a two in three chance of being incarcerated. Imprisonment among white men is significantly lower. Even for the most marginal group of white men—those who did not complete high school—only 15.3 percent went to prison. Thus the consequences of mass imprisonment are concentrated among those already most on the periphery of society—African American and (to a lesser degree) white men with little schooling—the same segments of society in which fragile families are most likely to be formed.

Incarceration and single parenthood, concentrated among minority men and women with little schooling, combined to produce high rates of imprisonment among fathers in disadvantaged families. The combination of incarceration and single parenthood is reflected in marriage rates of men in prison. While about 25 percent of African American men aged twenty-two to thirty who are not incarcerated are married, the marriage rate is only 11 percent among incarcerated men (figure 1). Surveys of men in prison find that though they are less likely to be married than men who are not in prison, they are just as likely to have children. As a result, African American children growing up in fragile families are likely to have fathers who have been incarcerated at some point.

While children growing up in fragile families are likely to have a father who has been incarcerated, how likely is it that children overall will have a parent, either a father or a mother, who is imprisoned during their childhood? Table 2 reports estimates of a child's risk of paternal and maternal imprisonment by age fourteen. The table compares two cohorts, one born in 1978 and reaching age fourteen in 1992, at the beginning of the era of mass incarceration, and a younger cohort born in 1990 and reaching age fourteen in 2004, at

Table 2. Cumulative Risk of Paternal and Maternal Imprisonment by Age Fourteen for Children Born in 1978 and 1990, by Race and Parental Education

	White children				African American children			
Percent	Paternal		Maternal		Paternal		Maternal	
	1978	**1990**	**1978**	**1990**	**1978**	**1990**	**1978**	**1990**
All children	2.2	3.6	0.2	0.6	13.8	25.1	1.4	3.3
By parental education								
All noncollege	2.9	5.6	0.2	0.8	15.6	30.2	1.5	3.6
High school dropout	4.1	7.2	0.2	1.0	22.0	50.5	1.9	5.0
High school only	2.0	4.8	0.2	0.7	10.2	20.4	0.9	2.6
Some college	1.4	1.7	0.2	0.3	7.1	13.4	1.2	2.6

Source: Christopher Wildeman, "Parental Imprisonment, the Prison Boom, and the Concentration of Childhood Disadvantage," *Demography* 46, no. 2 (2009): 271, 273.

the height of the American prison boom.[10] The table indicates that parental, especially paternal, imprisonment has become quite common for children in fragile families in the past decade. One of every four African American children born in 1990 had a father go to prison. For children of high school dropouts, the share was one-half. For whites, by contrast, only seven of every one hundred children born in 1990 whose fathers were high school dropouts experienced paternal imprisonment. Estimates using data from the Fragile Families and Child Wellbeing Study confirm that many children in fragile families experience paternal imprisonment.[11]

In light of rapid growth in the risk of imprisonment for women over this period, the risk of maternal imprisonment might also be expected to have grown.[12] Table 2 also presents estimates of the risk of maternal imprisonment, by maternal education and the child's race and birth cohort, and suggests two conclusions. First, the risk of maternal imprisonment for white children is tiny. Even white children whose mothers did not finish high school had only a 1 percent chance of experiencing maternal imprisonment. Second, for African American children, especially those with low-education mothers, maternal imprisonment has become somewhat common. Fully 5 percent of African American children born in 1990 to mothers who did not complete high school had their mother imprisoned. Even more striking, the risk of paternal imprisonment for white children born in 1990 (3.6 percent) is comparable to the risk of maternal imprisonment for African American children born that same year (3.3 percent).

The focus in this section has been on racial disparities in the risk of parental imprisonment during childhood. But point-in-time disparities are important too. By the year 2000, nearly 10 percent of all African American children but only 1 percent of all white children had a parent incarcerated on any given day.[13] This statistic emphasizes the potentially substantial racial disparities in the total amount of time children spend with a parent incarcerated.

Research Findings on the Consequences of Imprisonment for Fragile Families

Ubiquitous imprisonment associated with mass incarceration is concentrated among the parents of fragile families. Even if it has no negative consequences for children, the concentration of imprisonment in this already-marginal group suggests a fundamental change in the social experience of childhood. More fundamentally, however, rising rates of incarceration in fragile families may further diminish the life chances of poor children.

Research on the social and family life of men with a history of incarceration dates to the beginning of the twentieth century.[14] Three areas of research—on adult men, their partners, and their children—foreshadow the contemporary focus. Field studies, mostly in prison, described behavioral changes produced by prolonged institutionalization and concluded that imprisonment undermined the social life of inmates by exacerbating criminality or impairing their capacity for normal social interaction.[15] A handful of studies that examined the partners of incarcerated men attempted to distinguish the effects of incarceration from the pre-existing vulnerability of the family relationships of crime-involved men.[16] And clinical studies under the guidance of William Sack tended to find that paternal incarceration exacerbated pre-existing behavioral and psychological problems in children.[17]

Though contemporary research replays several of these themes, older research is limited in at least three ways. First, because it was conducted before the prison boom, when the imprisonment rate was lower, it may have been reasonable for researchers to assume that the men and women in prison were so highly involved in crime that their social and family contribution may have been small even had they not been in prison. But as the imprisonment rate has grown, prisoners have come to resemble more closely the general population. Thus, although the current generation of prisoners is still more likely to engage in behaviors harmful to family life than the average free person in the population, their absence is more likely to harm the fragile families from which many of them come today than it would have been in the past.

Second, most of the earlier work on the consequences of imprisonment for adult men and families used small, nonrepresentative samples and tended to observe the adult men or their families only after they had come into contact with the penal system. Because small, nonrepresentative samples are unlikely to represent the experiences of the population, these earlier studies yield limited insight into how imprisonment affects the average family experiencing that event. Nor did most of these studies consider changes in family life that could have resulted from the period of incarceration. Because prisoners tend to differ from the average free member of society in a number of ways, their family lives may have been different from the norm even had they not gone to prison. Looking at changes in family life is thus vital for research in this area.

And, third, earlier research did not address the broader spillover effects of incarceration. Recent research has shown that imprisonment is concentrated in poor and minority communities. Though little of this research specifically tests the effects of living in a high-incarceration community, most researchers speculate that the effects are negative.[18] The mechanisms through which high incarceration rates affect communities remain virtually untested empirically, though many have been hypothesized. These potential spillover effects of imprisonment could not have been anticipated by the first wave of research on prisoners and their families because imprisonment was so uncommon in that era, even

Table 3. Father Characteristics by Incarceration History and Relationship Type Five Years after the Birth of a Child

Percent unless otherwise indicated	Ever-incarcerated fathers			Never-incarcerated fathers		
	Married	Cohabiting	Nonresident	Married	Cohabiting	Nonresident
Ever abusive*	8.5	9.9	22.5	1.3	2.3	9.0
Ever abused drugs or alcohol**	16.0	22.0	41.6	6.3	10.7	14.5
Self-control***	3.5	3.5	2.7	3.8	3.7	3.3
High school dropout	39.0	52.9	47.6	19.5	38.4	32.5
N	187	191	1,202	1,032	307	923

* The father is considered to have ever been abusive if the mother reported at any follow-up interview that she had ever been cut, bruised, or seriously hurt in a fight by the father.
** The father is considered to have ever had a drug or alcohol problem if either he or the mother reported at any follow-up interview that drugs or alcohol had interfered with his personal relationships or work.
*** Paternal self-control is based on questions answered by the mother about how often the father engaged in a number of behaviors showing high or low self-control. (Higher scores indicate greater self-control.)
Source: Authors' calculations using data from the Fragile Families and Child Wellbeing Study.

in the poorest neighborhoods. Our focus here is on how going to prison, having a partner go to prison, or having a parent go to prison affects subsequent life chances, but one focus for future research would be to consider how living in a high-incarceration neighborhood affects families who do not directly experience incarceration.

Recent studies are better able than older research to assess the effects of incarceration on contemporary fragile families, but these studies still face acute challenges. The most serious is causal inference: does imprisonment cause negative outcomes for families or are the two simply linked? The factors influencing incarceration—men's criminality, poor social environment, and human capital deficits—are strongly correlated with poor family outcomes. To illustrate why the pre-existing differences between individuals who are incarcerated and those who are not are a concern, table 3 presents estimates based on the Fragile Families and Child Wellbeing Study of domestic abuse, drug and alcohol abuse, self-control, and high school completion for ever- and never-incarcerated fathers five years after the birth of a child. Given the large differences between fathers who were and were not incarcerated, it may be that it is the characteristics of fathers who go to prison rather than the experience of imprisonment that accounts for the poor outcomes in their families.

Improvements in research data and methods strengthen causal inferences a little, but episodes of antisocial behavior that cause incarceration and family disruption are very difficult to separate from the disruptive effects of incarceration itself. Because researchers rarely have accurate measures of changes in the level of drug (or alcohol) use, say, it is difficult to know if changes in these behaviors may have caused both incarceration and the attendant negative outcomes. Stronger causal conclusions require more controlled experiments (with study subjects being divided randomly into control and treatment groups)[19] or studies of natural experiments exploiting policy variation.[20] But conducting controlled experiments is often impractical in criminal justice settings, and natural experiments are rare and tend not to be population-representative. Thus the research reviewed here uses nationally representative, longitudinal data; the studies' subjects are not, of course, randomly assigned into prison, but the studies do control for fixed traits of individuals.

In the next three sections we review evidence on the effects of incarceration on adult men, their romantic partners, and their children. The "effect of incarceration" in this research contrasts outcomes for those who go to prison with outcomes for those who do not. In most cases, the control group receives no alternative programming or criminal justice punishment. Although we address this issue explicitly when considering the effects of parental incarceration on children (and also in our policy prescriptions later), we think it merits mentioning now as well because the high levels of antisocial behavior and addiction exhibited by the men (and women) who experience incarceration at some point suggest that "nothing" is not a good alternative. So though incarceration is likely not the best solution to the problems faced in fragile families, different interventions in the lives of these families may foster their well-being.

Effects on Adult Men

To see how parental incarceration may affect children, we begin by reviewing research on the socioeconomic consequences of imprisonment, much of which focuses on the destabilizing effects of prison time on the life course of men. A key outcome for the economic well-being of children is the post-incarceration earnings and employment of fathers. Although much research considers the effects of imprisonment on men's economic prospects generally, we focus here only on its effects on earnings.[21] Survey-based estimates from analyses of the National Longitudinal Survey of Youth (1979) indicate that incarceration diminishes men's earnings by up to 30 percent even long after leaving prison.[22] Less research exists on the effects of imprisonment on the earnings of adult women, but the little existing research suggests that effects may be smaller for women than they are for men.[23] Although it remains unclear what share of diminished earnings is due to changes in human capital during imprisonment, research using an experimental audit design shows that a substantial share is likely attributable to employers' strong negative reaction to job applicants with criminal records.[24]

Research also suggests that the experience of imprisonment harms both mental and physical health. The often brutal prison environment can impair mental health, which has consequences for labor market success, relationship stability, and parenting quality. Effects on mental health can thus spill over into a host of other domains.[25] Imprisonment affects physical health in two main areas. First, formerly incarcerated men are more likely than otherwise comparable men to suffer from various infectious and stress-related diseases.[26] In probably the most sophisticated analysis to date, Rucker Johnson and Steven Raphael show that state-level imprisonment rates play an important role in increasing racial disparities in AIDS for both men and women.[27] Second, men are at high risk of death in the first two weeks after they are released from prison, although it is unclear whether it is imprisonment or the characteristics of the men that lead to this high risk.[28]

Effects on Partners

By removing men from the labor market, marking them as criminals, and making it difficult for them to acquire more skills, incarceration diminishes their earnings. By exposing them to infectious disease, stress, and the stigma of a criminal record, incarceration compromises their health. If men who are likely to go to prison have little to do with their children and the mothers of their children, then the effects of incarceration end with the offender. But although formerly incarcerated men are often seen as being disconnected from their families, ethnographers suggest that many such men are involved in family life.[29] Moreover, even the families of men who sometimes engage in behaviors damaging to family life tend to see their incarceration as a net loss in both the short term and the long term.[30]

At the very least, incarceration may take a toll on familial resources. In the short term—while a man is in prison—it both diminishes family income and increases family expenses. Incarcerated men have no meaningful income and cannot pass on even their meager income to their families on the outside. Keeping in contact with an incarcerated family member is also expensive. In addition to paying for costly collect phone calls and contributing to commissary accounts, families can incur large expenses making visits.[31] Because many of the families of the incarcerated are already poor, the costs of having a family member in prison are extremely high.

When men are released, the long-term effects of a prison record on earnings and employment also diminish familial financial resources, though until recently the size of these effects was unknown. A recent analysis of data from the Fragile Families and Child Wellbeing Study, however, indicates that men with incarceration histories are 14 percent less likely than otherwise comparable men who have not been incarcerated to contribute financially to their families with small children. Furthermore, those who do contribute give, on average, $1,400 less a year than similar men.[32] Because many of these families are poor, they thus face increased material hardship.[33]

Economic costs are not the only costs associated with the imprisonment of a family member. Incarceration also contributes to the dissolution of romantic unions.[34] Although researchers generally agree that incarceration has negative effects on relationship stability, they differ in their views on how it affects the formation of new unions. On the one hand, quantitative evidence suggests that incarceration does not prevent the formation of marital bonds.[35] On the other hand, qualitative data suggest that poor women are unlikely to tie themselves to men who have been incarcerated, not solely because incarceration is a marker of criminality, but also because marriage to a man with a criminal record endows them with his low social status.[36] It is thus unclear whether incarceration itself diminishes men's marriage prospects. Even if incarceration does not hinder the formation of stable unions, however, its substantial effects on the risk of divorce and separation likely increase the number of children growing up in fragile families.

Not all couples with an incarcerated partner break up, however. Few quantitative studies consider the effects of imprisonment on a partner, but ethnographic research suggests that the emotional and social costs of a partner's incarceration are substantial. On the most basic level, it is, for many women, a heart-wrenching experience that can lead to depression.[37] Some ethnographic research also suggests that women keep their partner's incarceration a secret to try to avoid the stigma,[38] although this claim is contested by other ethnographers.[39] Women who keep their partner's incarceration a secret may withdraw from social networks, potentially leading to social isolation. When isolation and depression couple with poverty, it seems likely that, on average, having a partner incarcerated compromises women's well-being.

Although qualitative researchers have produced excellent research on this topic, there are few large-scale quantitative studies. Of the many gaps in current research, the lack of quantitative evidence in this area may be the most pressing.

Having a partner incarcerated could also influence the long-term well-being of other family members by changing men's behaviors in ways that alter relationship dynamics. Some research suggests that imprisonment can change men's behavior for the better. Ethnographers report, for instance, that prison time gives some men time to consider how and why they might "go straight."[40] Prisons might also positively affect health by limiting drug use and treating addiction and chronic disease. In this context, Megan Comfort has described prisons as "social service providers of first resort" for poor men.[41]

Other research, however, points to negative behavioral effects of prison. Anne Nurse argues that prison socializes men who had not previously been violent to solve problems with violence.[42] As prisons have become more crowded and as public funding for educational and other programs has fallen, these negative behavioral effects of incarceration have likely become more acute.[43] By making men more violent, it is likely that imprisonment, on average, changes men's behavior for the worse, making them worse fathers and partners. Even among women who were relieved to see a partner incarcerated because he might get needed drug treatment in prison, almost all recognized that imprisonment had negative consequences in the long run.[44]

In sum, research suggests that men's incarceration harms their romantic partners, on average, though some women are relieved at having a partner who was abusive or struggling with addiction removed from the house. These average negative effects are especially intriguing in light of table 3. Having a partner incarcerated appears to harm women, and as we will show, having a father incarcerated has negative effects on children. Yet, formerly incarcerated men are more likely to be abusive, have higher rates of addiction, and poorer self-control than other fathers. This is a pressing issue for policy makers, because though the average effects of incarceration on family life are negative, some of these men periodically engage in behaviors damaging to family life even before going to prison. As we discuss in detail later, we think that these findings call out for criminal justice interventions that not only do not incarcerate men who have been involved in relatively minor crimes, but also attempt to curb the antisocial behaviors (including crime, addiction, and abuse) that they engage in that harm family life.

Effects on Children

Research on adult men suggests that imprisonment diminishes their earnings, disrupts their romantic unions, and compromises their health. Likewise, the imprisonment of a partner, on average, compromises the well-being of those who are left behind. Because incarceration harms adult men and women, it may also diminish the life chances of children. If it does so, then the effects of imprisonment on inequality are transferred intergenerationally. The potential intergenerational effects of imprisonment on inequality have not been lost on researchers, who have shown much interest in this area.[45]

Given the negative effects of incarceration on familial resources,[46] paternal involvement,[47] and family structure,[48] we might expect these changes to link having a parent imprisoned with poor child outcomes. Yet recent research has found little evidence in support of any of these links. In fact, some research suggests that it is the cycle of having a parent imprisoned and released or the stigma of incarceration rather than these other changes that most harms child well-being.[49]

Researchers have long been fascinated by the intergenerational transmission of crime. Until recently, most of this research focused on the effects of parental criminality, rather than incarceration, on children, but research in this area increasingly suggests that both parental criminality and incarceration influence children's criminality. Isolating a causal relationship is difficult, but a number of studies show an association between parental incarceration and the criminality of children. Using data from the Cambridge Study in Delinquent Development, Joseph Murray and David Farrington demonstrate a link between parental incarceration and boys' criminality and delinquency throughout the life course.[50] Other work using data from the Add Health Study, which is more broadly representative of the children of the prison boom, shows a similar relationship for contemporary young adults.[51] Neither of these datasets makes it possible to consider the effects of a change in parental incarceration status on children's delinquency and criminality, but other research does. One analysis of data from the Fragile Families and Child Wellbeing Study indicates that recent experiences of paternal incarceration are associated with substantial increases in the physical aggression of boys, but not girls.[52] Although this study considers effects only on children while they are still young (rather than following them as they become adults), the repeated measures of paternal incarceration and a child behavioral problem that may be associated with future criminality suggests the robustness of the relationship between having a father incarcerated and engaging in criminal activity.

Many studies have considered the consequences of parental incarceration for children's behavioral problems more broadly. One uses the Fragile Families data to show that having parents with a history of incarceration is associated, for three-year-old children, with externalizing behaviors such as having temper tantrums or "acting out" in other ways, but not with internalizing behaviors such as being anxious, depressed, or withdrawn.[53] Another study using data from school-aged children in Chicago finds that parental incarceration is associated with change in both externalizing and internalizing behaviors.[54] A final study using data from the Cambridge Study in Delinquency Development suggests that parental imprisonment contributes to higher levels of internalizing behaviors in a sample of boys and that these effects linger throughout the adult years.[55] In studies considering behavioral problems, therefore, the relationship with children's externalizing behaviors is robust across the life course, while the relationship with internalizing behaviors holds only for older children.

Although most research on the consequences of parental incarceration for children focuses on behavioral problems or aggression, other outcomes that are proxies for severe social marginalization merit attention as well. To date, research in this area focuses on three outcomes: homelessness, foster care placement, and infant mortality. In general, research in this area finds that children of incarcerated parents are at elevated risk of all three.[56] It also suggests that at least for foster care placement, maternal incarceration may have more substantial effects than paternal incarceration does, underlining the importance of the increase in the risk of maternal imprisonment for African American children—at least for children's risk of experiencing severe forms of disadvantage like this.[57] In fact, one study shows that the change in the female imprisonment rate explains fully 30 percent of the increase in foster care caseloads between 1985 and 2000.[58] Thus, these studies suggest that parental incarceration may increase not only criminality and behavioral problems more broadly, but also the risk of being severely marginalized in childhood and adolescence.

By further reducing the well-being of fragile families, mass imprisonment lays the groundwork for a vicious cycle in which the criminal justice system does not diminish—and may even increase—addiction, abuse, and crime.

Although the average effects of parental incarceration on children are of keen interest, those effects are likely to vary depending on the characteristics of fathers. Despite the importance of considering variations in the effects of paternal incarceration on children, researchers as yet know little about how effects vary with paternal characteristics and behaviors.[59] Two studies, however, consider how they vary by whether the father was reported by the mother to have been abusive. The first, which uses data from the Fragile Families and Child Wellbeing Study, finds that although paternal incarceration decreases the physical aggression of boys whose fathers had abused their mothers, it was associated with increases in aggression for boys whose fathers were not known to have abused their mothers. For boys whose fathers were incarcerated for a violent crime, aggression did not change significantly.[60] Another study finds that parental incarceration increases infant mortality risk only among children whose mothers had not been abused by the father.[61] Though a thin reed, this research suggests that incarceration likely has more negative effects for children if the father was not violent or abusive.

What are we to make of these findings? First, it may be wrong to talk about a single "effect of incarceration," because the consequences depend on an offender's history of violent behavior. Changes in penal policy have increased the number of incarcerations for nonviolent offenses, by mandating prison time for drug crimes and by re-imprisoning parolees not for new crimes but for technical parole violations. If the negative effects of incarceration on families are particularly large for nonviolent men, penal policy has harmed families by increasing the share of nonviolent offenders in prison. Second, the distinction between "violent" and "nonviolent" offenders offers convenient rhetoric but may be a poor description of real people. Violence is partly dispositional. Some people are quick to anger and prone to aggression. But violence is also situational, promoted by environments characterized by conflict with weak social controls. It is very hard as a matter of public policy to identify just those with a violent disposition. A public safety policy that weighs the interests of children must thus work to eliminate the environments in which family violence is likely to arise.

Implications of the Research

Research has shown that imprisonment negatively affects formerly incarcerated men and their romantic partners and children. Perversely, the corrosive effects of incarceration on family life are especially pronounced when the fathers were involved in neither domestic violence nor violent crime before being imprisoned. What are the implications of these findings for crime control and for American inequality?

The concentration of the risk of imprisonment among America's most marginal men and the harm thereby inflicted on the lives of their romantic partners and children have profound implications for the nation's crime control policy. Whereas stable employment and family ties discourage crime, incarceration limits labor market opportunities and breaks tenuous family ties. Having stably married parents and positive role models discourages boys from engaging in delinquency, yet parental incarceration often leads to union dissolution, thereby pushing fathers away from children. It also promotes further antisocial behavior among fathers. In so doing, mass incarceration may cause crime in both the short and long term.

Important as the unanticipated criminogenic effects of mass imprisonment may be, the effects on racial and class inequality may be even more consequential. As parental imprisonment has changed from an extremely rare to a common experience in the life course of the children who grow up in fragile families, America has become more unequal. To the degree that the experience of parental imprisonment has long-lasting negative effects on the children of the prison boom, effects of mass imprisonment on inequality will persist well into the future. By further diminishing the life chances of the children who grow up in fragile families, mass imprisonment may entrench a vicious circle in which the disadvantages wrought by being born into a fragile family are further compounded by the criminal justice system, thereby generating greater future inequality.

Policy Prescriptions

The research that we have reviewed shows that incarceration contributes to family breakup and adds to the deficits of poor children. Despite almost universal agreement that strong families are a powerful source of social order and public safety, U.S. crime policy has, in the name of public safety, produced more vulnerable families and probably reduced the life chances of their children.

To avoid contradictions like this, policy makers must ask of any proposed reform: what will it do to families? Changes in criminal sentencing over the past thirty years offer a prime example. In at least two areas, punitive sentencing has had substantially negative effects on families. First, the widespread adoption of mandatory minimum prison sentences for drug crimes has incarcerated many men without significant histories of violence. Ironically, the families of these previously nonviolent men appear to have suffered the largest negative effects. Policy reform in this area would thus significantly limit prison time for drug offenders. Second, re-imprisoning parolees for violating the technical conditions of their parole has also incarcerated great numbers of men who pose relatively little risk to public safety. Technical parole violators have not necessarily committed new offenses, but have been sent back to prison for missing appointments, failing drug tests, or violating other conditions of parole.

For both drug offenders and parole violators, inexpensive and effective alternatives to incarceration are available. They include intensive community supervision, drug treatment where necessary, and a system of graduated sanctions that allows parole and probation officers to respond quickly to violations without sentencing offenders to disproportionately severe prison time. In Project HOPE in Hawaii, for example, probation violators who received swift, certain, but very short jail stays significantly reduced violations and drug use.[62]

Drug offenders and technical parole violators are the low-hanging fruit for sentencing reform. More ambitious reform would also review sentencing enhancements for repeat offenders, such as three-strikes statutes and truth-in-sentencing measures that require long stays in prison before eligibility for release. Three-strikes, truth-in-sentencing, and related measures have increased time served in prison, severely straining family ties and multiplying the costs to families of visitation.

Policies to support men and women returning home from prison could further reduce the costs to fragile families of high rates of incarceration. Though such programs exist, we suggest strengthening existing programs and making them more widely available. So-called prisoner reentry policies begin while men and women are still in prison. Substance abuse, education, training, and work programs are aimed at reducing recidivism and preparing incarcerated men and women for life in free society. Because prisoners average less than a twelfth-grade education, expanded educational programming in prison seems an urgent priority. The federal prison system, which houses about 10 percent of all prisoners, provides a good model for the states by mandating 240 hours of school programming for all prisoners without high school degrees. Improved literacy and more schooling would likely benefit fragile families by enhancing formerly incarcerated fathers' economic opportunities and, perhaps, the quality of their parenting. Vocational and work programs in prison are also associated with significant reductions in recidivism, as long as ten years after prison release.[63]

After release, prisoner reentry efforts often help men and women connect to services and job opportunities. Reentry programs provide transitional services for housing, treatment, education and training, and job placement. Recent evaluations suggest that when such services are offered immediately after prison release, they can reduce recidivism and improve employment among ex-prisoners. In particular, transitional employment programs that place former inmates in small crews to work on construction and community service projects have been found to reduce recidivism significantly several years after entry into the program.[64] A few programs, such as Family Justice (formerly La Bodega de la Familia) in New York, involve family members and friends directly, enlisting them to support former prisoners in readjusting to the routines of free society and in participating in drug treatment programs.[65]

Though sentencing reform and prisoner reentry policy can help reduce the negative effects of incarceration on fragile families, perhaps the most effective proposals lie outside the sphere of criminal justice. Criminal justice reform, by itself, will not solve the problems of school failure, joblessness, untreated addiction, and mental illness that pave the pathway to prison in the first place. Chronically idle young men (and increasingly women) with few resources for self-improvement still present a social problem even if they are not incarcerated at high rates. Ultimately, addressing that problem will require a greater social commitment to education, public health, and the employment opportunities of low-skill men and women.

The great mistake of the prison boom was trying to solve hard social problems through crime policy. Punitive criminal justice not only failed to ameliorate those problems, but achieved only questionable success even as a strategy for enhancing public safety. Taking full account of the negative social effects of incarceration shows that the costs of mass imprisonment are far higher than correctional budgets suggest. More fundamentally, criminal justice agencies are only residual sources of social order. The primary sources of order and stability—public safety in its wide sense—are the informal social controls of family and work. The disruptive effects of mass incarceration that are concentrated in America's fragile families have weakened these sources of public safety. From this perspective, social policy holds the promise not only of improving the well-being of fragile families, but also, by strengthening families and providing jobs, of contributing to public safety.

Endnotes

1. Thomas P. Bonczar, *Prevalence of Imprisonment in the U.S. Population, 1974–2001* (Washington: Bureau of Justice Statistics Special Report, 2003).

2. Alfred Blumstein and Jacqueline Cohen, "A Theory of the Stability of Punishment," *Journal of Criminal Law and Criminology* 64, no. 2 (1973): 198–207.

3. Bruce Western, *Punishment and Inequality in America* (New York: Russell Sage, 2006), p. 14.

4. Bonczar, *Prevalence of Imprisonment in the U.S. Population, 1974–2001* (see note 1).

5. David Garland, "Introduction: The Meaning of Mass Imprisonment," in *Mass Imprisonment: Social Causes and Consequences,* edited by David Garland (Thousand Oaks, Calif.: Sage, 2001), pp. 1–3.

6. Jackson Toby, "Social Disorganization and Stake in Conformity: Complementary Factors in the Predatory Behavior of Hoodlums," *Journal of Criminology, Criminal Law, and Police Science* 48, no. 1 (1957): 12–17. See also the contemporary classic on the subject: Robert J. Sampson and John H. Laub, "Crime and Deviance over the Life Course: The Salience of Adult Social Bonds," *American Sociological Review* 55, no. 5 (1990): 609–27.

7. William Julius Wilson, *The Truly Disadvantaged* (University of Chicago Press, 1987).

8. Western, *Punishment and Inequality in America* (see note 3), p. 70.

9. Bruce Western and Christopher Wildeman, "The Black Family and Mass Incarceration," *Annals of the American Academy of Political and Social Science* 621, no. 1 (2009): 221–42. See also Becky Pettit and Bruce Western, "Mass Imprisonment and the Life Course: Race and Class Inequality in U.S. Incarceration," *American Sociological Review* 69, no. 2 (2004): 151–69.

10. Christopher Wildeman, "Parental Imprisonment, the Prison Boom, and the Concentration of Childhood Disadvantage," *Demography* 46, no. 2 (2009): 265–80.

11. Ibid.

12. Alfred Blumstein and Allen J. Beck, "Population Growth in U.S. Prisons, 1980–1996," *Crime and Justice* 26 (1999): 17–62.

13. Western, *Punishment and Inequality in America* (see note 3), p. 138.

14. Megan Comfort, *Doing Time Together: Love and Family in the Shadow of the Prison* (University of Chicago Press, 2008), pp. 214–22; John Hagan and Ronit Dinovitzer, "Collateral Consequences of Incarceration for Children, Communities, and Prisoners," *Crime and Justice* 26 (1999): 121–62; and Joseph Murray and David Farrington, "Effects of Parental Imprisonment on Children," *Crime and Justice* 37 (2008): 133–206.

15. Donald Clemmer, *The Prison Community* (Boston: Christopher Publishing House, 1940); Gresham M. Sykes, *The Society of Captives: A Study of a Maximum Security Prison* (Princeton University Press, 1958).

16. Pauline Morris, *Prisoners and Their Families* (London: George Allen & Unwin, 1965); P. Thompson and Pauline Morris, *Report on the Work of the Prisoners' Wives Service* (London, 1972); and Laura T. Fishman, *Women at the Wall: A Study of Prisoner's Wives Doing Time on the Outside* (State University of New York Press, 1990). For a review, see Comfort, *Doing Time Together* (see note 14), pp. 214–22.

17. See especially William H. Sack, "Children of Imprisoned Fathers," *Psychiatry* 40 (1977).

18. One of the few studies of the effects of the spatial concentration of incarceration is provided by Todd Clear, *Imprisoning Communities: How Mass Incarceration Makes Disadvantaged Neighborhoods Worse* (Oxford University Press, 2007).

19. Devah Pager, "The Mark of a Criminal Record," *American Journal of Sociology* 108, no. 3 (2003): 937–75.

20. Jeffrey A. Fagan, "The Comparative Impacts of Juvenile and Criminal Court Sanctions on Adolescents Felony Offenders," *Law and Policy* 18, no. 1 (1996): 77–119.

21. Harry Holzer, "Collateral Costs: Effects of Incarceration on Employment and Earnings among Young Workers," in *Do Prisons Make Us Safer? The Benefits and Costs of the Prison Boom,* edited by Steven Raphael and Michael A. Stoll (New York: Russell Sage, 2009), pp. 239–65.

22. For three examples, see Western, *Punishment and Inequality in America* (see note 3), p. 119; Richard B. Freeman, "Crime and the Employment of Disadvantaged Youth," in *Urban Labor Markets and Job Opportunity,* edited by George Peterson and Wayne Vroman (Washington: Urban Institute, 1992), pp. 201–37; Steven Raphael, "Early Incarceration Spells and the Transition to Adulthood," in *The Price of Independence: The Economics of Early Adulthood,* edited by Sheldon Danziger and Cecilia Elena Rouse (New York: Russell Sage, 2007), pp. 278–305. See also Charles E. Lewis Jr., Irwin Garfinkel, and Qin Gao, "Incarceration and Unwed Fathers in Fragile Families," *Journal of Sociology & Social Welfare* 34, no. 3 (2007): 77–94.

23. Rosa Minhyo Cho and Robert LaLonde, "The Impact of Incarceration in State Prison on the Employment Prospects of Women," *Journal of Quantitative Criminology* 24, no. 3 (2008): 243–65.

24. Pager, "The Mark of a Criminal Record" (see note 19).

25. Craig Haney, *Reforming Punishment: Psychological Limits to the Pains of Imprisonment* (Washington: American Psychological Association, 2005).

26. Michael Massoglia, "Incarceration as Exposure: The Prison, Infectious Disease, and Other Stress-Related Illnesses," *Journal of Health and Social Behavior* 49, no. 1 (2008): 56–71. See also Jason Schnittker and Andrea John, "Enduring Stigma: The Long-Term Effects of Incarceration on Health," *Journal of Health and Social Behavior* 48, no. 1 (2007): 115–30.

27. Rucker Johnson and Steven Raphael, "The Effects of Male Incarceration Dynamics on Acquired Immune Deficiency Syndrome Infection Rates among African American Women and Men," *Journal of Law and Economics* 52, no. 2 (2009): 251–94.

28. Ingrid A. Binswanger and others, "Release from Prison—A High Risk of Death for Former Inmates," *New England Journal of Medicine* 356, no. 2 (2007): 157–65.

29. Donald Braman, *Doing Time on the Outside: Incarceration and Family Life in Urban America* (University of Michigan Press, 2004).

30. Comfort, *Doing Time Together* (see note 14).

31. Ibid.

32. Amanda Geller, Irwin Garfinkel, and Bruce Western, "Incarceration and Support for Children in Fragile Families," *Demography* (forthcoming).

33. Ofira Schwartz-Soicher, Amanda Geller, and Irwin Garfinkel, "The Effect of Paternal Incarceration on Material Hardship," Working Paper 09-11-FF (Princeton: Center for Research on Child Wellbeing, November 2009).

34. Leonard M. Lopoo and Bruce Western, "Incarceration and the Formation and Stability of Marital Unions," *Journal of Marriage and Family* 67, no. 3 (2005): 721–34. See also Bruce Western and Sara McLanahan, "Fathers Behind Bars: The Impact of Incarceration on Family Formation," *Contemporary Perspectives in Family Research* 2 (2000): 309–24.

35. Lopoo and Western, "Incarceration and the Formation and Stability of Marital Unions" (see note 34).

36. Kathryn Edin, "Few Good Men: Why Low-Income Single Mothers Don't Get Married," *American Prospect* 11, no. 4 (2000): 26–31.

37. Comfort, *Doing Time Together* (see note 14); Braman, *Doing Time on the Outside* (see note 29).

38. Braman, *Doing Time on the Outside* (see note 29).

39. Comfort, *Doing Time Together* (see note 14).

40. Elijah Anderson, "Going Straight: The Story of a Young Inner-City Ex-Convict," *Punishment and Society* 3, no. 1 (2001): 135–52. See also Kathryn Edin, Timothy J. Nelson, and Rechelle Paranal, "Fatherhood and Incarceration as Potential Turning Points in the Criminal Careers of Unskilled Men," in *Imprisoning America: The Social Effects of Mass Incarceration,* edited by Mary Patillo, David Weiman, and Bruce Western (New York: Russell Sage, 2004), pp. 46–75.

41. Comfort, *Doing Time Together* (see note 14).

42. Anne M. Nurse, *Fatherhood Arrested: Parenting from within the Juvenile Justice System* (Vanderbilt University Press, 2002), pp. 52–54.

43. Haney, *Reforming Punishment* (see note 25).

44. Comfort, *Doing Time Together* (see note 14).

45. Hagan and Dinovitzer, "Collateral Consequences of Incarceration for Children, Communities, and Prisoners" (see note 14); Murray and Farrington, "Effects of Parental Imprisonment on Children" (see note 14).

46. Geller, Garfinkel, and Western, "Incarceration and Support for Children in Fragile Families" (see note 32).

47. Raymond R. Swisher and Maureen R. Waller, "Confining Fatherhood: Incarceration and Paternal Involvement among Nonresident White, African American, and Latino Fathers," *Journal of Family Issues* 29, no. 8 (2008): 1067–88; Maureen R. Waller and Raymond Swisher, "Fathers' Risk Factors in Fragile Families: Implications for 'Healthy' Relationships and Father Involvement," *Social Problems* 53, no. 3 (2006): 392–420; Rachael A. Woldoff and Heather M. Washington, "Arrested Contact: The Criminal Justice System, Race, and Father Engagement," *Prison Journal* 88, no. 2 (2008): 179–206.

48. Lopoo and Western, "Incarceration and the Formation and Stability of Marital Unions" (see note 34).

49. Christopher Wildeman, "Paternal Incarceration and Children's Physically Aggressive Behaviors: Evidence from the Fragile Families and Child Wellbeing Study," *Social Forces* (forthcoming); Murray and Farrington, "Effects of Parental Imprisonment on Children" (see note 14).

50. Joseph Murray and David Farrington, "Parental Imprisonment: Effects on Boys' Antisocial Behavior through the Life-Course," *Journal of Child Psychology and Psychiatry* 34, no. 12 (2005): 1269–78.

51. Michael E. Roettger and Raymond R. Swisher, "Examining Racial Variations in the Associations of Father's History of Incarceration with Son's Delinquency and Arrest in Contemporary U.S. Society," Working Paper 09-01 (National Center for Marriage Research, 2009).

52. Wildeman, "Paternal Incarceration and Children's Physically Aggressive Behaviors" (see note 49).

53. Amanda Geller and others, "Parental Incarceration and Child Wellbeing: Implications for Urban Families," *Social Science Quarterly* 90, no. 5 (2009): 1186–1202; Amanda Geller and others, "Beyond Absenteeism: Father Incarceration and Its Effects on Children's Development," Working Paper 09-20-FF (Princeton: Center for Research on Child Wellbeing, January 2010).

54. Sara Wakefield, "Parental Disruption of Another Sort? Bringing Parental Imprisonment into a Model of Children's Mental Health and Well-Being," paper presented at the Annual Workshop on Criminology and Population Dynamics, June 1–2, 2009, in Baltimore, Md.

55. Joseph Murray and David Farrington, "Parental Imprisonment: Long-Lasting Effects on Boys' Internalizing Problems through the Life Course," *Development and Psychopathology* 20, no. 1 (2008): 273–90.

56. Holly Foster and John Hagan, "Incarceration and Intergenerational Social Exclusion," *Social Problems* 54, no. 4 (2007): 399–433; Christopher Swann and Michelle Sheran Sylvester, "The Foster Care Crisis: What Caused Caseloads to Grow?" *Demography* 43, no. 2 (2006): 309–33; Christopher Wildeman, "Imprisonment and Infant Mortality," paper presented at the Annual Meeting of the Population Association of America, April 30–May 2, 2009, in Detroit, Mich.

57. Candace Kruttschnitt, "The Paradox of Women's Imprisonment," *Daedalus* (forthcoming).

58. Swann and Sylvester, "The Foster Care Crisis" (see note 56).

59. Murray and Farrington, "Effects of Parental Imprisonment on Children" (see note 14).

60. Wildeman, "Paternal Incarceration and Children's Physically Aggressive Behaviors" (see note 49).

61. Wildeman, "Imprisonment and Infant Mortality" (see note 56).

62. Angela Hawken and Mark Kleiman, "What a Novel Probation Program in Hawaii Might Teach Other States," *American Prospect* (April 10, 2007).

63. William Saylor and Gerald Gaes. "Training Inmates through Industrial Work Participation and Vocational and Apprenticeship Instruction," *Corrections Management Quarterly* 1, no. 2 (1997): 32–43.

64. Cindy Redcross and others, "Transitional Jobs for Ex-Prisoners: Implementation, Two-Year Impacts, and Costs of the Center for Employment Opportunities (CEO) Prisoner Reentry Program," MDRC Report (2009); Erin Jacobs and Bruce Western, *Report on the Evaluation of the ComALERT Prisoner Reentry Program,* report for the Kings County District Attorney, New York (2007).

65. Carol Shapiro and Meryl Schwartz, "Coming Home: Building on Family Connections," *Corrections Management Quarterly* 5, no. 3 (2001): 52–61.

Unmarried Parents in College

Sara Goldrick-Rab and Kia Sorensen

Summary

Noting that access to higher education has expanded dramatically in the past several decades, Sara Goldrick-Rab and Kia Sorensen focus on how unmarried parents fare once they enter college. Contrary to the expectation that access to college consistently promotes family stability and economic security, the authors argue that deficiencies in current policy lead college attendance to have adverse consequences for some families headed by unmarried parents.

Although rates of college attendance have increased substantially among unmarried parents, their college completion rates are low. One explanation is inadequate academic preparation. Another is financial constraints, which can force unmarried students to interrupt their studies or increase their work hours, both of which compromise the quality of their educational experiences and the outcomes for their children.

The authors point out that although many public programs offer support to unmarried parents attending college, the support is neither well coordinated nor easily accessed. Over the past three decades, loans have increasingly replaced grants as the most common form of federal and state financial aid. Confusion about what is available leads many low-income students to the two most "straightforward" sources of income—loans and work, both of which involve significant costs and can operate at cross-purposes with public forms of support. Too much work can lead to reductions in public benefits, and earnings do not always replace the lost income.

A growing body of experimental evidence shows that providing social, financial, and academic supports to vulnerable community college students can improve achievement and attainment. Contextualized learning programs, for example, have enabled participants not only to move on from basic skills to credit-bearing coursework, but also to complete credits, earn certificates, and make gains on basic skills tests. Another successful initiative provided low-performing students with special counseling services and a small stipend of $150 per semester when they used those services. And researchers are conducting experimental performance-based financial aid programs at community colleges to test their effectiveness. Goldrick-Rab and Sorensen conclude that more effective support could enable unmarried students to complete college degree and certificate programs.

www.futureofchildren.org

Sara Goldrick-Rab is an assistant professor of educational policy studies and sociology at the University of Wisconsin–Madison. Kia Sorensen is a doctoral candidate in sociology at the University of Wisconsin–Madison.

It is almost an article of faith in the United States that college degrees confer substantial benefits not only on individuals but on their families. Families headed by college-educated adults, for example, are more likely to be intact, stable, and economically secure than those headed by adults who have not attended college. Opportunities for higher education can be both a preventative measure to promote family stability—for example, by encouraging young people to have high hopes for the future and to avoid early family formation—and a transformative one—for example, by strengthening the assets of families once they have formed. The benefits of higher education also appear to be transmitted across generations, further increasing its returns.[1]

Most of the articles in this volume rely primarily on research that uses data from the Fragile Families and Child Wellbeing Study. Because most of the research they review uses these unique data, the authors of these articles can use the term "fragile families" in the strict sense—families in which the parents were unmarried when the child was born. Since relatively few participants in the Fragile Families study attended college, and data collection on college-going was not a focus of that study, in this article we rely on several other sources of national data. We use the term "unmarried parenting students" in this article to describe individuals who may be part of fragile families in the sense that they are not married while parenting during college (this group, for example, includes divorced, widowed, separated, never-married, and cohabiting students) and are economically vulnerable. But we cannot know from the data we use whether they were partnered at the time of the child's birth and thus were "fragile families" in the strictest sense.

The fragile families under scrutiny in this volume of *The Future of Children*—families headed by parents who are unmarried at the time of their child's birth—would seem to be perfect candidates for the family-strengthening benefits of higher education. But although opportunities for college-going in this country have expanded dramatically over the past several decades, the unmarried parents in these families are still among the Americans least likely to attend college.[2] And, ironically, although earned degrees confer large economic benefits, the downsides of attending college may be substantial for these families.

In this article our focus is the role of postsecondary education in the lives of unmarried parents in fragile families who are attending college. Research into this field is in its earliest stages. Even providing a statistical portrait of college enrollment among these parents is difficult. National statistics on undergraduates collected by the National Center for Education Statistics (NCES) likely underreport the presence of parents by limiting the definition of "parent" to students claiming financial responsibility for one or more children.[3] Students with children for whom they are not financially responsible are therefore not flagged as parents in NCES data.[4] This may be a growing problem, given strengthened social policies (for example, child support laws and statutory rape laws) that provide incentives for some parents to avoid or decline to claim financial responsibility. Moreover, NCES data do not make it possible to assess marital status at the time of childbirth, or to know whether parenting students reside with their children.

We begin by discussing rates of college participation and completion among unmarried parents in the United States and looking at the financial and academic conditions that shape their college experiences. Then we describe ways in which attending college may have both positive and negative effects on the children of unmarried parents. We pay particular attention to the institutional barriers facing unmarried parenting students and note areas where reforms could promote higher rates of success. Finally, drawing on a review of empirical research on potential interventions, we conclude with several policy recommendations.

College Access and Success among Unmarried Parents

During the past fifty years, the hope of attending college has taken root among young Americans across all racial, ethnic, and socioeconomic lines. Between 1972 and 2004, the share of African American high school seniors who expected to attend at least some college rose from 85 percent to 94 percent.[5] The share of high school seniors in the bottom quartile of the socioeconomic distribution expecting to attain more than a high school degree rose from 66 percent to 89 percent.[6] The share of unmarried parents experiencing at least some form of post-secondary education has also increased significantly over the past few decades, though the change has been more notable among unmarried mothers than fathers.

Rates of College Participation

Among all undergraduates, the share of unmarried parents nearly doubled over the past twenty years (from 7 percent to just over 13 percent).[7] Unmarried parents make up an especially substantial segment of undergraduates from racial and ethnic minority backgrounds. For example, more than one-third (36 percent) of African American female undergraduates nationwide are unmarried mothers, and 15 percent of African American male undergraduates are unmarried fathers. Unmarried parents make up more than one in five Native American undergraduates (21 percent) and 16 percent of all Latino undergraduates (compared with 10 percent of white and 9 percent of Asian undergraduates).[8]

More than two-thirds of the increase in college attendance among unmarried parents since 1990 is attributable to attendance among unmarried mothers. Although the representation of unmarried fathers has been growing, a greater proportion of the increase in unmarried parents is driven by the attendance of women. Overall, 8 percent of male undergraduates and 17 percent of female undergraduates are unmarried parents.[9] Of course, the appearance of these trends may be affected by the way parenting students are counted in federal data.

One reason for the apparent gender disparity among unmarried parents in attending college is that women are more likely than men to choose to begin or reenter college after having children.[10] School reentry is common among mothers (even among high school dropouts), and mothers' rates of college-going tick upward as children get older.[11] Data from the Fragile Families and Child Wellbeing Study indicate that many unmarried mothers wait until they are in their late twenties and their children enter school before entering or re-entering college.[12] In fact, 25 percent of women entering college after the age of thirty are not married at the time of entry.[13] In addition, parents who are not currently married appear *more* likely than currently married or cohabiting parents to enter college.[14]

Despite the fact that more unmarried parenting students are attending college, their attendance patterns, completion rates, and financial circumstances are quite different from those of nonparenting students and, in some cases, from married parenting students and other low-income students.

Rates of College Success

Parenting students who are not married while they are enrolled tend to complete four-year degrees at rates far lower than other college students, on average.[15] Among all students who started college in 1995–96, 29 percent attained a bachelor's degree by 2001, compared with just under 5 percent of unmarried parents. Among unmarried parents, 11.8 percent earned an associate's degree (roughly the same share as the rest of that cohort), and 30 percent completed a postsecondary certificate (compared with 12 percent of the cohort as a whole). Unmarried parents were much more likely to depart college early, without a timely return to school (46 percent compared with 35 percent).[16]

One reason for these lower rates of completion is that it can take longer for parenting students to finish degrees.[17] In fact, by neglecting these longer time periods to degree attainment, analysts sometimes tend to make ultimate rates of degree completion appear lower than they are. Although delays in completion (and the older age at which the degree is earned) affect labor market returns and employment opportunities, many unmarried mothers nevertheless acquire their postsecondary degrees—but, as Nan Astone and her colleagues put it, they do so "in a discontinuous fashion."[18] According to one study, "one-third (33.7 percent) of low-income single women with children and slightly more than one quarter (28.8 percent) of low-income married women with children take more than 10 years to complete a bachelor's degree, compared to 15.6 percent of all women, 16.5 percent of all low-income women, and 12.7 percent of all men."[19] Other researchers, examining educational attainment according to early life course patterns, find clear differences in college-going and attainment based on the speed and trajectory of family formation. As table 1 illustrates, 57 percent of individuals who move rapidly into adult roles such as marriage and childbearing attend some college but only 6 percent complete bachelor's degrees—and they are unlikely to continue pursuing their education at age twenty-four.[20] Individuals who do not become parents by age twenty-four and remain unmarried are far more likely to attend and complete college, and many are still continuing their education at age twenty-four.

According to some analysts, the main reason why women who enter college at later ages have lower rates of college completion than women who enter at younger ages is that they are more likely to enroll part time,[21] and part-time enrollment necessarily extends time to degree. Another study that tracked the college enrollment of low-income women (some of whom were mothers) from 1970 to 2000 found that degree attainment continued to tick upward after the usual six-year mark—rising, over that thirty-year period, to a 71 college completion rate.[22]

In addition to staying in college longer, unmarried parenting students are much more likely to have delayed college entry (85 percent did not enter right out of high school, compared with 32 percent of other students). And they tend to enroll without sufficient academic preparation. Eight percent begin college without a high school degree; 18 percent, with a General Educational Development (GED) credential (compared with 6 percent of all students).[23] Only 5 percent have taken at least one Advanced

Table 1. Early Life Course Patterns at Age Twenty-Four, by College Attainment

Percent

Pattern	No college	Some college	Currently enrolled in college	College degree or higher
Fast starters (tend to be married with children)	37	57	9	6
Educated partners (tend to be cohabiting or married without children)	9	54	27	37
Educated singles (no partner or children)	1	38	30	61
Working singles (no partners, no children, with long-term jobs)	34	59	16	7

Source: D. Wayne Osgood and others, "Six Paths to Adulthood: Fast Starters, Parents without Careers, Educated Partners, Educated Singles, Working Singles, and Slow Starters," in *On the Frontier of Adulthood: Theory, Research, and Public Policy*, edited by Richard A. Settersten and others (University of Chicago Press, 2005), figure 10.1.
Note: Percents do not add to 100 because those now in college overlap with the categories of "Some college" and "College degree."

Placement course before college (compared with 20 percent of other students), and nearly half (45 percent) score less than 700 on the ACT/SAT (compared with 18 percent of other students). As a result they are much more likely to require at least some form of developmental education at the start of their postsecondary experience.

Likely because of those barriers, unmarried parenting students are more than three times more likely than average to be enrolled in short-term vocational postsecondary programs, which are much less likely to conclude with a college degree.[24] Given their weak academic preparation and lack of financial resources, unmarried parents often choose a community college (49.1 percent of all enrollment of unmarried parenting students is in that sector), where they make up 16.4 percent of the student body.[25] They are underrepresented at four-year institutions (only 6.4 percent of undergraduates at public four-year colleges and 8 percent of those at private not-for-profit four-year colleges are single parents).[26] Carol MacGregor posits that unmarried mothers enroll disproportionately in community college because they "are more likely to have to make up for an educational deficit."[27] But the decision may also reflect financial constraints, because parenting while attending college, particularly without a partner, involves distinct economic disadvantages.

More than half (59 percent) of unmarried parents attending college earn less than $10,000 a year, with 38 percent earning less than $5,000 annually. They therefore overwhelmingly attend colleges and universities where tuition and fees are less than $2,000 a year. But as college costs rise, the impetus grows to try and "do it all"—that is, to raise children while both working full time and attending college full time. For example, national statistics indicate that in 2007–08 three-fourths of all unmarried parents who were enrolled in college full time were working at least fifteen hours a week; and 30 percent were working forty or more hours a week. By contrast, in 1989–90, less than half (48 percent) of unmarried parents enrolled full time in college worked at all.[28]

Many students are unaware that working while attending college can compromise other sources of income. For example, the federal calculations of eligibility for student financial aid are affected by an "income protection allowance" (IPA). The IPA sets an income threshold above which up to half of a student's earnings is included in his or her expected family contribution (EFC). By increasing a student's EFC, the IPA can serve to decrease (or even eliminate) eligibility for Pell Grants. In effect, students may be penalized for working to meet their unmet financial need—a penalty that, as we show below, can be substantial. For this reason, the IPA is commonly known as the "work penalty" (though an empirical relationship to college persistence or graduation has not been established). While the IPA has increased over time, particularly for independent students (which includes all students who claim dependents), it has not been eliminated and continues to affect need analysis calculations.[29] Some argue that student earnings should not affect Pell Grant eligibility for families earning less than $25,000.[30]

Thus, while unmarried parents are more likely than other students to apply for federal aid (40 percent of unmarried fathers and 76 percent of unmarried mothers apply), their expected family contributions are growing because of their greater proclivity to work, in turn reducing the amount of aid for which they qualify. Overall, 60 percent of unmarried parents (43 percent of unmarried fathers and 66 percent of unmarried mothers) have an EFC of $0. But the average EFC for an unmarried parenting student swelled from $800 in 1989–90 to $2,451 in 2007–08. From 1989–90 to 1999–2000, the proportion of unmarried parents receiving financial aid while enrolled full time declined from 94 percent to 79 percent.[31] The problem is that earnings from work rarely fully offset declines in financial aid, and earnings require time to generate. As a result, national data indicate that for 87 percent of unmarried parents attending college in 2007–08, there was a gap between their verified budgets (as reported on the federally mandated aid application) and their expected family contribution and all financial aid grants they received. For 25 percent of those students, the gap was $11,500 or more. For comparison purposes, the U.S. Department of Agriculture estimates the annual cost of raising a child under the age of five to be $11,000.[32]

One reason why unmarried parents face such large gaps between their verified budgets and their EFC and financial aid is that they are less likely to borrow money (at least from federal loan sources, as reported in national data). Given their higher costs of attendance, it is remarkable that cumulative debt levels are about the same for unmarried parents as for all other students.[33]

Another challenge affecting unmarried students stems from restrictions on the Pell Grant related to students' academic preparation and degree plans. Specifically, to receive a Pell Grant, a student must possess a high school diploma or GED or pass an approved "ability-to-benefit" test (a test of basic education). In addition, the student has to indicate an intention to earn a degree (rather than try out a few classes), enroll in at least one class for credit (developmental courses typically do not carry credits), and make satisfactory academic progress (typically a C average). The Pell can be received for up to thirty hours of noncredit developmental coursework, but at least one credit must be taken in a given semester. Given the academic backgrounds of many unmarried parenting students, these requirements likely affect their Pell receipt.

In summary, although a significant share of unmarried parents enroll in college, they often run into difficulties of various kinds and fail to complete degrees. Often they must delay their initial enrollment or interrupt their studies, both of which decisions decrease their chances to complete their degrees.[34] Mothers are more likely to enroll in community college, partly because they struggled academically in high school and partly because they can't afford a four-year college. And while they are attending school, they spend long hours at work, in some cases sacrificing their ability to take full advantage of available financial aid. Thus, although in one sense they are successful—having made it to college—they are also squeezed for time and money in ways that might compromise both the quality of their educational experiences and the outcomes for their children.

Effects of Postsecondary Education on Family Well-Being

As Sara McLanahan observes, children are increasingly experiencing divergent destinies shaped by their mothers' education. Children born to well-educated women are gaining from their mothers' substantial investments of both money and time in higher education, while those born to less-educated women are not. In particular, McLanahan notes that "although their parents are more educated than they were 40 years ago, children's claims on their parents' resources are weaker."[35] In other words, increasing access to postsecondary education has not led to uniformly positive, widespread benefits for future generations.

McLanahan describes several possible reasons for this failure, including flaws in the labor market and the influence of feminism and birth control policies. To that list, we would add inadequate postsecondary education policies. The relationship between college attainment and family outcomes is not straightforward, even though it is typically described that way. Although college-educated adults are, on average, better off on a wide variety of measures, college-going does not result in uniformly positive benefits for everyone—and under current policy conditions it cannot. In this section, we explain this line of reasoning and examine some relevant research evidence. In the next section, we describe how various policies and institutional practices hinder the ability of unmarried parents to access and succeed in postsecondary education.

A Conceptual Model

We begin with a conceptual framework (figure 1) showing the four primary pathways by which postsecondary education can affect family formation and stability. In assessing those effects, it is important to take account of three critical features of college-going. The first is how college participants are selected, since only those who attend can benefit.[36] While college attendance has become more common over time, it is by no means universal.

Second, the important nonpecuniary benefits of postsecondary education accrue through both intra-generational and inter-generational mechanisms.[37] That is to say, some of these benefits involve contemporary changes in the income and health of the college-goer, while others involve changes in the future life chances of successors (children). And the two are related—for example, if postsecondary education affects one's choice of marital partner (and we have reason to believe it does), the benefits accrue both immediately and in the future.

Third, there may be substantial heterogeneity in the effects of postsecondary education. The extent to which college access is limited or unequally distributed affects college outcomes—as participation becomes more universal and participants more heterogeneous, the more outcomes will vary. So it is possible that when college was the privileged domain of those fortunate enough to afford

Figure 1. Conceptual Model of How Postsecondary Education Affects Family Formation and Stability

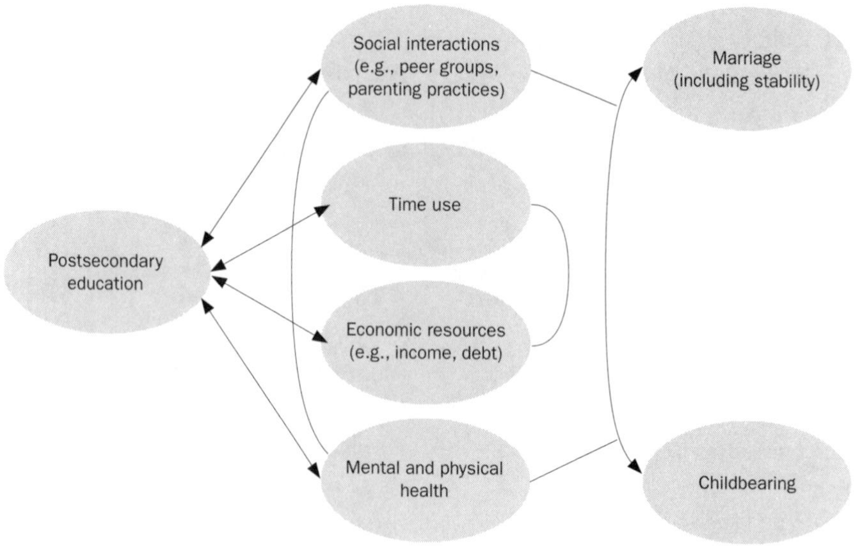

it, primarily white men, its benefits were more robustly positive. As more college-goers attend despite significant financial and academic constraints, the positive returns may wane.[38] Indeed, there is little reason to think that all pathways opened up by college-going are positive or consistent. For example, although on average women with higher levels of education have higher rates of marriage,[39] lower rates of divorce,[40] and lower levels of fertility,[41] not all college-educated women will experience such effects.[42] Similarly, although unmarried mothers are more likely than married mothers to enter college (probably in part because they stand to reap the greatest economic returns), the experience of pursuing college without appropriate financial and emotional supports may result in unanticipated penalties for this vulnerable group. As Carol MacGregor notes, "The potential loss of income and time demands of student-life might reduce time women are able to spend with children and lead to negative behavioral outcomes."[43] At a minimum, these hypotheses deserve further exploration.

Our conceptual model (see figure 1) posits that four characteristics of individuals (their social interactions, time use, economic resources, and mental and physical health) are affected by college attendance in ways that, in turn, affect their children and family well-being. Some of these hypothesized relationships are positive, promoting healthy outcomes, while others are negative. The benefits of college attendance among unmarried parents may be especially substantial, because college-educated parents serve as role models for their children and acquire skills that both improve their parenting and help increase their household income. But attending college may reduce the amount of time parents have to spend with their children and generate economic and emotional stressors that compromise the quality of parent-child interactions.

All of these relationships are, to some extent, supported by research—though the evidence is not conclusive. Although research indicates that women with more education (and higher educational aspirations) delay childbearing and also that many unmarried mothers start college after having a child in an effort to improve their lives, evidence on how postsecondary education affects family well-being more broadly conceived is scarce. Moreover, it is not clear how parenting while in college influences other child outcomes.[44] Investigating those pathways is therefore an essential next task for researchers.

Social Interactions

Attending college helps students form social networks, which are thought to result in a variety of benefits, including economic returns. But the social networks have other, nonmonetary, benefits as well. In particular, as a group of researchers recently noted, attending college can give students increased opportunities for selecting romantic partners.[45] Although the research in question was generally referring to students in elite universities, less prestigious settings—including community colleges—also bring together students in ways that help them form new relationships.[46] In other words, part of the benefit of attending college (any college) may accrue through effects on the "marriage market."

The "marriage market theory" likens the marriage search process to a job search. Based on the marriage market one faces, one assesses the quality of available potential mates and one's own ability to attract a mate, and then weighs this information to choose the best available potential partner. The Fragile Families data indicate that repartnering after a nonmarital birth is fairly common (for example, within five years of that birth, 20 percent of women are living with a new partner), though it is less common among women who obtain additional education following their child's birth. That said, when they do repartner, women who have gone back to school are significantly more likely to "trade up" and partner with better-educated men. In fact, women who get additional education following their child's birth increase their odds of repartnering with a college-educated man by 62 percent.[47]

One concern is that even though, on average, attending college appears to increase the appeal of individuals in a competitive marriage market, it may make it less likely that some will find a satisfactory spouse.[48] For example, as black women earn more college diplomas than black men, they are left with a sparse market of college-educated African American men from which to choose, if they wish to marry someone from the same racial background. Likely as a result, the correlation of educational attainment between marital partners is weaker among African Americans than it is among whites, with African Americans more likely than whites to marry across educational groups and black women more likely than white women to marry someone with less education.[49] This relationship may also be affected by the lower rates of college completion among African American men, since intermarriage between individuals with "some college" and college graduates is waning.[50]

Some evidence suggests that changes in the marriage market for African American women, resulting from their higher rates of college success, may harm their families' well-being. For example, research indicates that in unfavorable marriage markets individuals often have to lower their standards, a move associated with poorer quality of relationships between unmarried parents (based on measures of whether a parent is fair, loving, helpful, or critical) and lower probabilities of marriage.[51] Distinguishing between developmental care (involvement in children's intellectual, physical, and social development) and nondevelopmental care (all other forms of parenting), researchers argue that certain forms of marital educational homogamy are associated with greater time spent on developmental care. The relationship holds only among highly educated adults and is stronger for fathers, for whom "homogamy produces a 43 percent increase in … weekday developmental care."[52] Data from the Fragile Families study lead to similar conclusions, with authors finding that certain forms of educational homogamy have positive effects on socio-emotional indicators of children's development at age five, affecting school readiness.[53]

Attending college also affects family well-being by helping unmarried mothers form networks of similarly well-educated friends, including friends who shape their decisions about parenting practices and expectations of educational success for children.[54] For example, research indicates that middle-class mothers with more education are more committed to the concerted cultivation of their children. Annette Lareau's qualitative study of twelve families with third and fourth graders from upper-middle-class, working-class, and disadvantaged backgrounds describes the different parenting techniques of parents from different class backgrounds. Families with more education give their children little leisure time and instead stress lessons and activities to fully develop their cognitive and social potential. These parents also interact with their children in a deliberate manner, often talking to them as if they were adults, reasoning with them, and encouraging them to make eye contact. Such parenting leads children to gain a sense of confidence that has implications for how they then interact with other adults and institutions.[55]

Although attending college may promote unmarried mothers' social interactions with better-educated women, it does not have unambiguously positive social effects.

In contrast, families with less parental education use a parenting style that Lareau terms "natural growth." From this perspective, being a good parent means providing the essentials in life such as food, comfort, and shelter. These parents give their children more independent leisure time and spend more time interacting with extended family. They are also more likely to speak to their children using directives and to establish clear boundaries between adults and children. As a result, working-class children are said not to develop a sense of entitlement in their interactions with adults and institutions. In this way, differing parenting styles are thought to affect children's schooling outcomes, as educators reward the behaviors encouraged by middle-class parents, not those facilitated by working-class parenting.

Although attending college may promote unmarried mothers' social interactions with better-educated women, it does not have unambiguously positive social effects. It may, for example, impair relationships with family and friends who are not in college. For example, first-generation college students (who predominate among unmarried parenting undergraduates) describe serious tensions between themselves and their parents over their college attendance. One participant in a research study reported, "People in my family don't understand that [college], you see. They are all against me. Why do you think you have to be better than the rest of us? We're all happy. Why can't you just be happy with this? And I just—I'm not. I'm too smart for my job. I'm smarter than my bosses."[56] Unmarried parents also often struggle with social interactions at school. For example, Jillian Duquaine-Watson describes a particularly "chilly climate" on community college campuses. She reports that unmarried mothers lack friends on campus and are poorly treated by their professors.[57]

Time Use

Studies tend to show that parents with more education (regardless of marital status) commit more time to their children than do less-educated parents and exhibit less gender specialization between the spouses.[58] But although all parents who have completed college may tend to spend more time with their children, unmarried parents who are attending college find that the time they have to spend with their children is quite constrained. Because financial aid, as noted, is often insufficient to meet students' needs, many unmarried parents must work long hours. Although financial aid once made it possible for students to devote time exclusively to studying and parenting—with school essentially replacing work—students today very commonly study, parent, *and* work.[59] Analyses of data from the Community College Survey of Student Engagement indicate that unmarried parents attending two-year colleges spend a substantial amount of time both working and caring for their children. More than one-third report spending thirty or more hours each week working for pay, while another 17 percent devote twenty-one to thirty hours. In addition, nearly 60 percent of unmarried mothers and 30 percent of unmarried fathers say they allocate thirty or more hours each week to child care, while also attending school.[60] Several studies indicate that students who work more than twenty hours a week are significantly less likely to complete college than those who do not (though a causal relationship between the two has not been established).[61] Said one low-income mother, "It's just trying to find time to actually study. You sit down to study and you've got a kid that's constantly wanting, you know, and won't go to bed unless you go to bed."[62] Likely as a result, unmarried parents often begin a college semester enrolled full time and gradually drop courses as the semester progresses.[63]

Economic Resources

The links between college attainment and individuals' income and occupation are positive and well established.[64] But as the cost of college attendance rises, and need-based financial aid (particularly in the form of grants) diminishes, attending college compromises some students' economic resources. The many public programs that offer support to unmarried parents attending college—Pell Grants, federal subsidized loans, Temporary Assistance to Needy Families, the earned income tax credit, food stamps, subsidized housing, the nutrition program for Women, Infants, and Children (WIC), Medicaid, the Workforce Investment Act, and Head Start—are neither well coordinated nor easily accessed. Confusion about what is available leads many low-income students to the two most "straightforward" sources of income—loans and work. Both involve significant costs and can work at cross-purposes with public forms of support. For example, as noted, too much work can lead to reductions in benefits, and earnings do not always replace the lost income. As one single mother reported in a research study, "It's a struggle trying to figure out the right amount of work and still get the benefits I need to stay in school."[65] In addition, time spent working can compromise time spent studying, resulting in poor grades and, again, the loss of financial aid.

Beyond enabling (or even inducing) some poor financial decisions, college may also diminish the economic resources of students who do not complete a degree and of those who incur significant debt from student loans and other forms of credit used to finance attendance. Evidence on whether debt delays marriage and the arrival of a first child is inconclusive, but debt payments do seem to figure into families' calculations about their capacity to raise a child. According to one survey, 25 percent of low-income college graduates said that debt drove them to delay childbearing, and 20 percent said that debt caused them to delay marriage.[66] Studies indicate that financial stress has generally negative effects on family stability.[67]

Mental and Physical Health

On average, college-educated adults are said to live longer, healthier lives and to have better access to health care.[68] One recent study, for example, found that even among individuals with the same household income, college graduates report being somewhat happier than high school graduates.[69] But experiences may also vary widely—for example, while in college, many unmarried parents forgo health insurance. In one qualitative study of low-income mothers attending college, the author found that "balancing the right amount of work and aid often put the women in precarious situations, especially regarding health care coverage."[70]

Moreover, the severe time and economic constraints facing parents exacerbate their stress levels. Lorraine Johnson and her colleagues note that more mothers (married or unmarried) could complete degree programs if they could "work with community college staff and faculty members to resolve stress-related problems early in their academic careers."[71] Mothers attending college feel "conflict over the short-term sacrifices versus long-term gains for their families and stress from competing demands of familial and school roles."[72] In a qualitative study of mothers enrolled in two different colleges, one single mom reported feeling guilty that "on Tuesdays I'm here from 9:00 in the morning until 9:00 at night and my poor child is at school and then he's with me for a while and then he goes off with somebody else for my night class."[73]

Limits of Current Policies

The way the nation's postsecondary education system is structured complicates the efforts of unmarried parents to enroll and succeed in college in several ways. Financial aid policies that are intended to make college affordable include rules that make it difficult for parenting students to access the money they need to succeed in college. And policies that make individuals with drug convictions incurred while in school ineligible for financial aid make it much more difficult for unmarried fathers to participate—let alone succeed—in postsecondary education.

In years past, only a relatively select group of privileged individuals attended college—those who could afford to live at school, enroll in classes full time, and devote little or no time to work. Today, however, with enrollment growing extremely fast at nonresidential two-year colleges, more and more students mix class attendance with heavy work schedules, participating in student activities to only a limited extent. Researchers examining widely attended, less selective four-year state colleges find that such practices are increasingly common there as well.[74] In addition, many students are enrolled at multiple colleges—switching between them, combining attendance, and cycling in and out.[75] Many attend college near home while working, supporting their families, and also attending online.

Delaying entry to college is also increasingly common, with many students taking advantage of a perception (not necessarily an accurate one) that it is possible to enter at any point, step in and out, and gradually make progress toward a degree.[76] Increasing numbers of students now attend college despite having insufficient financial resources and serious deficiencies in academic preparation. They do so in the face of emotional, cultural, and interpersonal vulnerabilities that once might have inhibited them from attending at all. Even members of the most "at-risk" groups will intersect with the postsecondary system at some point in their lives—whether after forming families, during or after a period of incarceration, or as adults in need of retraining.[77]

As the composition of the undergraduate population has grown more diverse, financial support for college students has gradually eroded. In particular, over the past three decades, loans have increasingly replaced grants as the most common form of federal and state support for students seeking to finance college. The 1992 reauthorization of the Higher Education Act included amendments that increased the availability of student loans and made it easier to obtain them. It also created an unsubsidized Stafford non-need-based loan program. The result was a substantial shift in the composition of student aid packages from grants to loans. Student borrowing has since grown substantially, and debt burdens have become more unequal, with students from low-income households, black students, and Hispanic students significantly more likely to have debt exceeding 8 percent of their monthly income, even net of family income and other background factors, such as gender, occupation, and the type of college attended.[78]

Current financial aid rules reward students who attend college full time without working and penalize those who take fewer classes and integrate work for pay into their schedules.[79] The Pell Grant (to which all students are entitled if they meet income-based qualifications) is perhaps the most important element of federal policy affecting an unmarried mother's ability to enroll in higher education.[80] Both the amount of the grant and the process through which it is accessed limit its usefulness and reflect several flawed assumptions.[81] It penalizes students for attending college less than full time, is not available to anyone with a drug conviction incurred while in school, and requires that students make adequate academic progress. But students who most need the Pell Grant struggle to make ends meet (which requires them to work and reduce their course loads), are less well prepared academically for college, and are more likely in need of second attempts at a college degree.[82]

As noted, several policies may be especially discouraging to unmarried fathers' participation in college. For one, as explained earlier, the method the federal government uses to count parents in higher education (presumably to assess the need for services) likely contributes to a disproportionate undercount of dads. Men who are unwilling or unable to pay child support, or who fathered a child with a woman under the age of eighteen, have little incentive to claim financial responsibility for their children and thus be recorded as fathers.

Second, the reauthorization of the Higher Education Act in 2000, which contained the "aid elimination penalty," blocked access to financial aid for adults with drug convictions (disproportionately men). By one estimate, the penalty has caused more than 200,000 students to be ineligible for federal grants, loans, and work study. Although the penalty has since been revised (today only students who receive drug convictions while they are enrolled in college and do not pass two unannounced drug tests are ineligible for aid), some observers suggest that even in its current form it discourages college enrollment (because the financial aid application includes a question about drugs) and perpetuates dropout among vulnerable populations.[83] Darren Wheelock and Christopher Uggen write that "relative to whites, racial and ethnic minorities are significantly more likely to be convicted of disqualifying drug offenses and significantly more likely to require a Pell Grant to attend college … It is therefore plausible that tens of thousands have been denied college funding solely on the basis of their conviction status."[84]

Another federal policy that is problematic for unmarried fathers is that since 1994 it has not been possible to use Pell Grants to support college course-taking while in prison, a change that has made college much less affordable for that (disproportionately male) population. Ironically, the number of state prison systems offering postsecondary education is rising (from thirty in 2002 to forty-three in 2003–04). In Texas and North Carolina, more than 10 percent of all inmates participate in some form of college coursework.[85] There is also some evidence that college admissions officers are using criminal records to screen applicants, resulting in a significant barrier to college entry for a substantial number of African American men.[86]

Recommendations for Reform

Federal, state, and local policies shape decisions made by unmarried parents with regard to college-going and completion in important ways. Policy reforms could greatly enhance the extent to which the benefits of postsecondary education accrue to unmarried parents and also ensure that those benefits are distributed more equitably.

The federal government should alter the way that NCES collects data on parents, specifically asking all students if they have any children. To improve analyses of the extent to which childbearing and marital status affect the pursuit of higher education, it would also be helpful to record children's dates of birth and the couple's date of marriage (if any).

Evidence continues to accumulate on the efficacy of interventions aimed at increasing college attainment among disadvantaged adults such as the unmarried mothers and fathers in fragile families. In particular, several new programs at community colleges have been piloted and evaluated in recent years. Next, we review the findings of studies that could inform efforts to enhance college participation or completion, or both, among unmarried parents. We focus on the results of research conducted using rigorous methodologies that allow policy makers to feel reasonably confident that the effects are the direct result of the intervention.

Reforms Aimed at Enhancing Participation

As noted, many unmarried parents seeking to attend college face numerous barriers, including financial constraints and lack of academic preparation. A key question is which kinds of programs are most effective at overcoming those barriers.

Among financially independent adults with no previous college experience, simplifying the aid application process substantially increased the likelihood of attending college and receiving need-based grant aid.

One possible reform would be to simplify the notoriously complex application form, especially its demands for information from applicants.[87] For applicants with children, who must file as "independent" students for financial aid purposes, the process is especially complicated. A recent experimental evaluation of a program conducted with H&R Block has yielded promising findings. By randomly assigning more than 10,000 low- and moderate-income families to receive tax preparation services that included substantial help completing and submitting the financial aid application, researchers were able to identify the potential impact of a more systematic simplification process. Among financially independent adults with no previous college experience, simplifying the aid application process substantially increased the likelihood of attending college *and* receiving need-based grant aid.[88]

Dual enrollment programs are another promising approach to increasing rates of college attendance and completion, particularly among students whose parents did not attend college. These programs are designed to move students more seamlessly from high school to college by allowing them to earn college credit while still in high school, thereby potentially reducing the time (and associated costs) spent in college. Today nearly every state has some form of dual enrollment policy, either formalized at the state level or locally negotiated between colleges and high schools.[89] One rigorous evaluation of dual enrollment programs in Florida and New York City found that participants who enrolled in college after high school remained enrolled longer, had higher grade point averages, and earned more credits than comparable students who had not participated in dual enrollment programs.[90] Furthermore, students who took multiple college courses through dual enrollment saw larger returns to that investment, and low-income students appeared to benefit disproportionately. Another study using quasi-experimental methods and national data found, however, that although dual enrollment programs benefit students in terms of increasing rates of college degree completion, they do not help any one group more than another.[91]

Although one goal of dual enrollment is to ease the transition to college for struggling students, it turns out that dual enrollment is used much more often by relatively advantaged students. Low-income students appear to make less use of dual enrollment programs because of their restrictive admissions requirements, their distribution across states and localities, a lack of awareness among some groups of students, and perceived or real costs. But the most rigorous evidence to date indicates that low participation rates in dual enrollment among low-income students may be attributable to students' unwillingness to participate.[92]

The requirement by some colleges that students with inadequate high school preparation must take adult basic education classes before taking credit-bearing courses is also problematic. The practice of separating noncredit basic skills instruction from academic college coursework is common and affects many students, especially at the community colleges where unmarried parents are particularly likely to enroll. A promising alternative is contextualized learning programs. For example, the Integrated Basic Education and Skills Training program (I-BEST) in Washington State takes a new pedagogical approach to instruction that includes team-teaching and reduces barriers between credit and noncredit coursework. Findings from I-BEST, based on a quasi-experimental evaluation, indicate that participants are more likely than nonparticipants to move on from basic skills to credit-bearing coursework and successfully complete credits, earn certificates, and make gains on basic skills tests.[93]

Reforms Aimed at Supporting College Completion

One key to enhancing the college completion rates of unmarried parents is providing a strong safety net, including robust academic, financial, and emotional supports, for vulnerable students.[94] As intermediate goals, policy makers could focus on increasing rates of full-time attendance among unmarried parents and reducing the time they spend working while parenting and in school.

There is a growing body of experimental evidence on the effects of providing social supports to community college students. For example, as part of the MDRC Opening Doors initiative, low-income students who were just starting college and who had histories of academic difficulties were provided with additional counseling and given a small stipend of $150 per semester when they used those services in two Ohio community colleges. Counselors had smaller-than-usual caseloads to enable them to give more time to students, and students were given a designated contact in the financial aid office. Students receiving the intervention used counseling and financial aid services at greater rates than control group students who had access to standard campus services. Program effects were positive and statistically significant while services were being provided, though most of the initial effects diminished over time.[95]

Another program used an experimental design to evaluate the effects of providing student success courses (taught by a college counselor who provides basic information on study skills and the requirements of college) or supplemental support (through "success centers" offering supplementary individualized or group instruction in math, reading, and writing), or both, to community college students on academic probation. Unlike typical support service models, this program required participation. It appears to have increased the number of credits students earned, improved their grade point averages, and in turn reduced their rates of continued academic probation.[96]

MDRC is also examining the effectiveness of performance-based financial aid programs at community colleges in several states.[97] Building on the results of an earlier evaluation in Louisiana, the demonstrations are designed both to help low-income parents attend college by giving them enhanced financial aid to cover more of the costs of schooling and also to supply an incentive for academic progress. In that earlier evaluation, two New Orleans-area community colleges offered students a scholarship of $1,000 per semester for a maximum of two semesters, as long as they were enrolled at least on a half-time basis and maintained a grade point average of C or better. These scholarships did not affect any other financial aid for which the student qualified, and students were paid in installments so that guidance counselors could confirm that students maintained academic progress and at least part-time enrollment. In the study, low-income parents who were eligible to participate in the program were randomly assigned to two groups: a program group that was given the scholarship along with special counseling or a control group that received regular financial aid and the same counseling that was available to all students. An analysis of the transcripts of initial participants after three semesters revealed that Opening Doors students experienced higher rates of full-time enrollment, passed more courses, and earned more total credits than students in the control group.[98]

Another financial approach provides emergency funding directly to students when they need it. For low-income students who may already be struggling to meet their financial obligations, an unexpected expense such as an auto repair, a rent increase, or an eviction can sometimes be the catalyst for delaying or severing their chance at a diploma. Preliminary, nonexperimental evidence from two programs suggests that these emergency funds (ranging from $11 to more than $2,000) help keep students enrolled.[99]

Child care is another form of support that studies suggest unmarried parents need in college, though it has not yet been empirically linked to improved degree completion. Although surveys consistently indicate that a lack of high-quality, affordable, on-campus child care prevents full engagement in college life, only half of all colleges provide any form of care on campus, and most child care centers are over-enrolled. In fact, national data indicate a serious shortage of campus child care centers—with existing resources meeting only one-tenth of demand. The shortage is particularly severe when it comes to infant care—only about one-third of campus child care centers accept infants. And between 2002 and 2009, federal support for the Child Care Access Means Parents in School Program (the sole federal funder of such centers) fell 40 percent (to just $15 million)—or (at most) just $8 for each family headed by a parenting student, according to calculations by the Institute for Women's Policy Research.[100] While the federal government recently assessed the status quo as "adequate," future interventions testing the effects of expanded funding and support for additional centers should be considered and evaluated.[101]

Conclusion

Postsecondary education can confer many important benefits on those privileged to engage in it—benefits that extend both to participants and to their children. But participation could be far broader and more beneficial if vulnerable groups of students had more effective support in their efforts to complete degrees. One group especially in need of support is unmarried parenting students, a segment of the undergraduate population that is growing in numbers and yet is increasingly at risk of not completing college.

Each of the reforms described here has the potential to enhance degree completion rates among unmarried parents. For all of the reasons we have described, making postsecondary education a more successful experience for more parents ought to be an important part of any family-friendly agenda.

Endnotes

1. Philip Oreopoulos and Kjell Salvanes, "How Large Are Returns to Schooling? Hint: Money Isn't Everything," NBER Working Paper 15339 (Cambridge, Mass.: National Bureau of Economic Research, 2009); Lisa Barrow and Cecilia Rouse, "Does College Still Pay?" *Economists' Voice* 2, no. 4 (2005): 1–8; Barbara Wolfe and Robert Haveman, "Social and Nonmarket Benefits from Education in an Advanced Economy," in *Education in the 21st Century: Meeting the Challenges of a Changing World,* edited by Yolanda Kodrzycki (Boston: Federal Reserve Bank of Boston, 2003); Philip A. Trostel and Todd M. Gabe, "Fiscal and Economic Effects of College Attainment," Staff Paper 566 (University of Maine School of Economics, 2007) (www.umaine.edu/soe/files/2009/06/soe_566trostel.pdf [Aug. 5, 2009]); Paul Attewell and David E. Lavin, *Passing the Torch: Does Higher Education for the Disadvantaged Pay Off across the Generations?* (New York: Russell Sage Foundation, 2007); Janet Currie and Enrico Moretti, "Biology as Destiny? Short- and Long-Run Determinants of Intergenerational Transmission of Birth Weight," *Journal of Labor Economics* 25, no. 2 (2007): 231–63; Pedro Manuel Carneiro and others, "Maternal Education, Home Environments and the Development of Children and Adolescents," Discussion Paper 3072 (Bonn: Institute for the Study of Labor, 2007).

2. Jennie E. Brand and Yu Xie, "Who Benefits Most from College? Evidence for Negative Selection in Heterogeneous Economic Returns to Higher Education," *American Sociological Review* (forthcoming).

3. Unless otherwise noted, all statistics in this paper are based on the authors' calculations using the National Postsecondary Student Aid Study (Washington: National Center for Educational Statistics, 2009–10) (http://nces.ed.gov/datalab/quickstats/ [Aug. 5, 2009]).

4. It is also the case that students who claim financial responsibility for persons who are not children may be inaccurately labeled as parents. However, this is likely a less-common occurrence than the undercounting of parents who do not claim financial responsibility for their children.

5. Steven J. Ingels and others, "Trends among High School Seniors, 1972–2004. NCES 2008–320" (Washington: National Center for Education Statistics, 2008), p. 126 (http://nces.ed.gov/pubs2008/2008320.pdf [Aug. 10, 2009]).

6. Sara Goldrick-Rab and Josipa Roksa, "A Federal Agenda for Promoting Student Success and Degree Completion" (Washington: Center for American Progress, 2008) (www.americanprogress.org/issues/2008/08/degree_completion.html [Aug. 15, 2009]).

7. U.S. Department of Education, National Center for Education Statistics (NCES), National Postsecondary Student Aid Study: 1986–97 (NPSAS:87), 1989–90 (NPSAS:90), 1992–93 (NPSAS:93), 2008 (NPSAS:08), Data Analysis Systems (http://nces.ed.gov/pubs/web/97578f.asp).

8. As of 2007–08, undergraduates who were unmarried parents were disproportionately nonwhite (45 percent white, 30 percent African American, and 17 percent Latino).

9. Christina Chang Wei and others, "A Decade of Undergraduate Student Aid: 1989–90 to 1999–2000. NCES 2004–158" (Washington: National Center for Education Statistics) (http://nces.ed.gov/DAS/epubs/2004158/overview.asp [Aug. 3, 2009]). These are national statistics, and the gender breakdown is very similar to that calculated using the Community College Survey of Student Engagement, which finds that 78 percent of unmarried parents in college are women (calculations by the Institute for Women's Policy Research; see note 32).

10. Claudia Buchmann and others, "Gender Inequalities in Education," *Annual Review of Sociology* 34 (2008).

11. Nan M. Astone and others, "School Reentry in Early Adulthood: The Case of Inner City African Americans," *Sociology of Education* 13 (2000): 133–54; Frank F. Furstenberg Jr. and others, "Adolescent Mothers in Later Life," *Family Planning Perspectives* 19, no. 4 (1987): 142–51; Cheryl Elman and Angela O'Rand, "The Race Is to the Swift: Socioeconomic Origins, Adult Education, and Wage Attainment," *American Journal of Sociology* 110, no. 1 (2004): 123–60. On postsecondary education among high school dropouts, see Jacob A. Klerman and Lynn A. Karoly, "Young Men and the Transition to Stable Employment," *Monthly Labor Review* Aug. (1994): 31–48.

12. Carol Ann MacGregor, "Education Delayed: Family Structure and Postnatal Educational Attainment," Working Paper 09-07-FF (Princeton: Center for Research on Child Wellbeing, July 2009); Ellen M. Bradburn and others, "Women's Return to School Following the Transition to Motherhood," *Social Forces* 73, no. 4 (1995): 1517.

13. Susan P. Choy and Mark D. Premo, "Statistical Analysis Report: Profile of Older Undergraduates: 1989–90" (NCES 95–167, Washington, 1995) (http://nces.ed.gov/pubs95/95167.pdf [Aug. 10, 2009]).

14. Astone and others, "School Reentry in Early Adulthood" (see note 11); MacGregor, "Education Delayed" (see note 12).

15. Baccalaureate and Beyond Longitudinal Study, 2000–2001, National Center for Education Statistics, U.S. Department of Education. B&B uses the same definition of unmarried parents as the NPSAS. (http://nces.ed.gov/dasolv2/tables/mainPage.asp?mode=NEW&filenumber=20 [Aug. 5, 2009]).

16. Calculations using the 1995–1996 Beginning Postsecondary Study, Quick Stats, (Washington: National Center for Educational Statistics) (http://nces.ed.gov/datalab/quickstats/ [Aug. 5, 2009]).

17. Attewell and Lavin, *Passing the Torch* (see note 1).

18. Audrey Light and Wayne Strayer, "Who Receives the College Wage Premium? Assessing the Labor Market Returns to Degrees and College Transfer Patterns," *Journal of Human Resources* 39 (2004): 746–73; Elman and O'Rand "The Race Is to the Swift" (see note 11); Astone and others, "School Reentry in Early Adulthood" (see note 11).

19. Center for Women Policy Studies, "Profile of Low-Income Women Students in Postsecondary Educational Institutions" (Washington: Center for Women Policy Studies, 2010) (www.centerwomenpolicy.org/pdfs/PSEFactSheet.pdf [Feb. 10, 2010]).

20. The sample comes from the Michigan Study of Adult Life Transitions (MSALT) and consists of individuals residing in white middle- and working-class suburbs in the Detroit metropolitan area, where only 5 percent of the population are minorities (p. 322). Data collection began in 1984 when subjects were in sixth grade and the ninth wave of data was collected in 1999. The sample size is just over 1,400.

21. Jerry A. Jacobs and Rosalind B. King, "Age and College Completion: A Life-History Analysis of Women Aged 15–44," *Sociology of Education* 75, no. 3 (2002): 11–30.

22. Attewell and Lavin, *Passing the Torch* (see note 1).

23. Richard J. Murnane and others, "Does a G.E.D. Lead to More Training, Postsecondary Education, and Military Service for School Dropouts?" *Industrial and Labor Relations Review* 51, no. 1 (1997): 100–16.

G.E.D. holders have a higher probability of college enrollment than high school dropouts, but less than half obtain any college education by age 26.

24. Calculations from 1995–1996 BPS data, using Quick Stats (Washington: National Center for Education Statistics, 2009) (http://nces.ed.gov/datalab/quickstats/ [Aug. 5, 2009]).

25. From U.S. Department of Education, 1992–93 National Postsecondary Student Aid Study (NPSAS: 93), 2008 (NPSAS:08) (Washington: National Center for Educational Statistics, 2009) (http://nces.ed.gov/pubs/web/96237.asp#ugwithdepentdentsp [Aug. 5, 2009]).

26. U.S. Department of Education, National Center for Education Statistics, 2003–04 National Postsecondary Student Aid Study (NPSAS: 04) (Washington: National Center for Education Statistics, 2009) (http://nces.ed.gov/programs/coe/2008/analysis/sa_table.asp?tableID=1006 [Aug. 5, 2009]).

27. MacGregor, "Education Delayed" (see note 12), p. 15.

28. U.S. Department of Education, National Center for Education Statistics, 2008 National Postsecondary Student Aid Study (NPSAS: 08) (Washington: National Center for Education Statistics, 2009) (http://nces.ed.gov/datalab/quickstats/selections.aspx [Feb. 28, 2010]).

29. Before 2009, a single parent with one child was able to protect $10,520 in income. Because of recent reforms, beginning in 2009 that same family could protect $17,720 of its income. By 2012–13, it will be able to protect $22,630 in income. Subsequent increases for all groups will be pegged to increases in the Consumer Price Index.

30. For more, see "Apply to Succeed: Ensuring Community College Students Benefit from Need-Based Financial Aid" (Washington: Advisory Committee on Student Financial Assistance, 2008) (www2.ed.gov/about/bdscomm/list/acsfa/applytosucceed.pdf [Aug. 15, 2009]); Amy Ellen Duke and Julie Strawn, "Congress Expands Access to Postsecondary Education and Training for Low-Income Adults" (Washington: Center for Law and Social Policy, 2007); Sandy Baum, "Lowering Work and Loan Burden: The Current Status of Student Reliance on Grants, Loans, and Work," in *Reflections on College Access and Persistence* (Washington: Advisory Committee on Student Financial Assistance 2006), 62–75.

31. Wei and others, "A Decade of Undergraduate Student Aid" (see note 9). The data in the second half of the sentence are older than those used in the first half, but similar computations could not be performed with the more recent data.

32. Kevin Miller and others, "Improving Child Care Access to Promote Postsecondary Success among Low-Income Single Parents" (Washington: Institute for Women's Policy Research, 2010).

33. Comparison of student budgets minus all aid, and comparison of cumulative debt, using NPSAS 2008.

34. Clifford Adelman, "The Toolbox Revisited: Paths to Degree Completion from High School through 2006" (Washington: Department of Education, 2006) (www2.ed.gov/rschstat/research/pubs/toolboxrevisit/toolbox.pdf [Aug. 9, 2009]).

35. Sara McLanahan, "Diverging Destinies: How Children Are Faring under the Second Demographic Transition," *Demography* 41, no. 4 (2004): 607–27.

36. It is possible that postsecondary education generates "spillover" effects on nonparticipants, for example by shaping family members' ambitions for college. Here we think of these as indirect effects.

37. For more on nonpecuniary returns, see Oreopoulos and Salvanes, "How Large Are Returns to Schooling?" (see note 1).

38. This possibility is also acknowledged by Oreopoulos and Salvanes, "How Large Are Returns to Schooling?" (see note 1).

39. Joshua R. Goldstein and Catherine T. Kenney, "Marriage Delayed or Marriage Forgone? New Cohort Forecasts of First Marriage for U.S. Women," *American Sociological Review* 66 (2001): 506–19.

40. Steven P. Martin, "Growing Evidence of a Divorce Divide? Education and Marital Rates in the U.S. since the 1970s," Working Paper (New York: Russell Sage Foundation, 2004) (www.russellsage.org/publications/workingpapers/divorcedivide/document [Aug. 10, 2009]).

41. Jennie Brand and Dwight Davis, "The Impact of College Education on Fertility: Evidence for Heterogeneous Effects," *Demography* (forthcoming).

42. Ibid.

43. MacGregor, "Education Delayed" (see note 12), p. 20.

44. MacGregor, "Education Delayed" (see note 12).

45. Richard Arum and others, "The Romance of College Attendance: Higher Education Stratification and Mate Selection," *Research in Social Stratification and Mobility* 26, no. 2 (2008): 107–21.

46. Melinda Mechur Karp and others, "An Exploration of Tinto's Integration Framework for Community College Students," Working Paper (New York: Community College Research Center, 2008) (http://ccrc.tc.columbia.edu/Publication.asp?UID=615 [Jan. 2, 2010]).

47. Sharon Bzostek and others, "Mothers' Repartnering after a Nonmarital Birth," Working Paper 06-27-FF (Princeton: Center for Research on Child Wellbeing, May 2010) (http://crcw.princeton.edu/publications/publications.asp [Feb. 28, 2010]).

48. Pierre-Andre Chiappori and others, "Investment in Schooling and the Marriage Market," *American Economic Review* (forthcoming); Kristen Harknett, "Mate Availability and Unmarried Parent Relationships," *Demography* 45, no. 3 (2008): 555–71; Robert D. Mare, "Five Decades of Educational Assortative Mating," *American Sociological Review* 56 (1991): 15–32.

49. Robert D. Mare, "Educational Assortative Mating and the Family Background of the Next Generation," *Sociological Theory and Methods* 21, no. 2 (2006): 253–77.

50. Christine R. Schwartz and Robert D. Mare, "Trends in Educational Assortative Marriage," *Demography* 42, no. 4 (2005): 621–46; Michael J. Cuyjet, *African American Men in College* (Indianapolis: Jossey-Bass, 2006).

51. Harknett, "Mate Availability" (see note 48).

52. J. Bonke and G. Esping-Andersen, "Parental Investments in Children: How Educational Homogamy and Bargaining Affect Time Allocation," Working Paper (Copenhagen: Rockwool Foundation Research Unit, 2007) (www.atususers.umd.edu/wip2/papers_i2007/Bonke_Andersen.pdf [April 21, 2010]).

53. A. Beck and C. Gonzalez-Sancho, "Educational Assortative Mating and Children's School Readiness," Working Paper 09-05-FF (Princeton: Center for Research in Child Wellbeing, March 2009).

54. Oreopoulos and Salvanes, "How Large Are Returns to Schooling?" (see note 1); Attewell and Lavin, *Passing the Torch* (see note 1); Anne Martin and others, "The Joint Influence of Mother and Father Parenting on Child Cognitive Outcomes at Age 5," *Early Childhood Research Quarterly* 22, no. 4 (2007): 423–39.

55. Annette Lareau, *Unequal Childhoods: Class, Race, and Family Life* (University of California Press, 2003).

56. Kristin B. Wilson, "Institutional Influences Affecting the College-Going Decisions of Low Income Mothers Attending a Rural Midwestern Community College" (Ph.D. dissertation, University of Missouri–Columbia, 2008), p. 91.

57. Jillian M. Duquaine-Watson, "'Pretty Darned Cold': Single Mother Students and the Community College Climate in Post–Welfare Reform America," *Equity & Excellence in Education* 40, no. 3 (2007): 229–40.

58. L. C. Sayer and others, "Educational Differences in Parents' Time with Children: Cross-National Variations," *Journal of Marriage and Family* 66, no. 5 (2004).

59. Kathleen Shaw and others, *Putting Poor People to Work* (New York: Russell Sage Foundation, 2006); Wei and others, "A Decade of Undergraduate Student Aid" (see note 9). For example, single parents faced additional challenges when welfare regulations decreased that form of support for single parents in college —the proportion of single parents receiving welfare while enrolled in college full time declined from 34 percent in 1995–96 to 9 percent in 1999–2000.

60. Kevin Miller and others, "Improving Child Care Access to Promote Postsecondary Success among Low-Income Single Parents" (Washington: Institute for Women's Policy Research, forthcoming).

61. Brian Pusser and others, "Returning to Learning: Adults' Success in College Is Key to America's Future" (Indianapolis: Lumina Foundation for Education, 2007); Steven Brint and Allison Cantwell, "Student Time Use and Academic Outcomes" (unpublished paper, Department of Sociology, University of California–Riverside, 2008).

62. Wilson, "Institutional Influences Affecting the College-Going Decisions" (see note 56), p. 88.

63. Ibid.

64. Wolfe and Haveman, "Social and Nonmarket Benefits from Education" (see note 1).

65. Wilson, "Institutional Influences Affecting the College-Going Decisions" (see note 56), p. 83.

66. Sandy Baum and Marie O'Malley, *College on Credit: How Borrowers Perceive Their Education Debt: Results of the 2002 National Student Loan Survey* (Braintree, Mass.: Nellie Mae, 2003).

67. Pamela Smock and others, "Everything's There Except Money: How Money Shapes Decisions to Marry among Cohabitating Adults," *Journal of Marriage and the Family* 67 (2000): 680–96; R. Catalano, "The Health Effects of Economic Insecurity," *American Journal of Public Health* 81 (1991): 1148–52; Lillian B. Rubin, *Families on the Fault Line* (New York: HarperCollins, 1994); Vonnie C. McLoyd, "Minority Children: Introduction to the Special Issue," *Child Development* 61, no. 2 (1990): 263–66.

68. Michael Grossman, "Education and Nonmarket Outcomes," in *Handbook of the Economics of Education*, vol. I, edited by Eric Hanushek and Finis Welch (Amsterdam: Elsevier B.V., 2006), pp. 578–635.

69. Oreopoulos and Salvanes, "How Large Are Returns to Schooling?" (see note 1).

70. Wilson, "Institutional Influences Affecting the College-Going Decisions" (see note 56), p. 107.

71. Lorraine G. Johnson and others, "Managing Stress among Adult Women Students in Community Colleges," *Community College Journal of Research & Practice* 24, no. 4 (2000): 289–300.

72. Nancy L. Deutsch and B. Schmentz, "I Was Starting from Ground Zero: Constraints and Experiences of Adult Women Returning to College," Working Paper (Charlottesville: University of Virginia, 2009), p. 2.

73. Ibid., p. 21.

74. Rebekah Nathan, *My Freshman Year: What a Professor Learned by Becoming a Student* (Cornell University Press, 2005); Timothy T. Clydesdale, *The First Year Out: Understanding American Teens after High School* (University of Chicago Press, 2007).

75. Sara Goldrick-Rab, "Following Their Every Move: How Social Class Shapes Postsecondary Pathways," *Sociology of Education* 79, no. 1 (2006): 61–79; Sara Goldrick-Rab and Fabian Pfeffer, "Beyond Access: Explaining Socioeconomic Differences in College Transfer," *Sociology of Education* 82, no. 2 (2009): 101–25.

76. Goldrick-Rab and Roksa, "A Federal Agenda for Promoting Student Success and Degree Completion" (see note 6); Sara Goldrick-Rab and Seong Won Han, "The Class Gap in the Gap Year," *Review of Higher Education* (2010).

77. Goldrick-Rab and Roksa, "A Federal Agenda for Promoting Student Success and Degree Completion" (see note 6); Jenny Nagaoka and others, "Barriers to College Attainment: Lessons from Chicago" (Washington: Center for American Progress, 2009) (www.americanprogress.org/issues/2009/01/chicago_schools.html [Aug. 12, 2009]); Linda Harris and Evelyn Ganzglass, "Creating Postsecondary Pathways to Good Jobs for Young High School Dropouts: The Possibilities and the Challenges" (Washington: Center for American Progress, 2008) (www.americanprogress.org/issues/2008/10/post-secondary_pathways.html [Aug. 12, 2009]).

78. Derek V. Price, "Educational Debt Burden among Student Borrowers: An Analysis of the Baccalaureate & Beyond Panel, 1997 Follow-Up," *Research in Higher Education* 45, no. 7 (2004): 701–37.

79. Goldrick-Rab and Roksa, "A Federal Agenda for Promoting Student Success and Degree Completion" (see note 6); Sara Goldrick-Rab and others, "How Money Matters (or Doesn't) for College Success," *Higher Education: Handbook of Theory and Practice,* vol. 24 (Netherlands: Springer, 2009), pp. 1–45.

80. Neil S. Seftor and Sarah E. Turner, "Back to School: Federal Student Aid Policy and Adult College Enrollment," *Journal of Human Resources* 37, no. 2 (2002): 336–52; Seftor and Turner write, "The behavioral effects for the traditional college-aged students associated with changes in the availability of Pell funding are modest, but the responsiveness among older students is marked." Wilson, "Institutional Influences Affecting the College-Going Decisions" (see note 56).

81. David Deming and Susan Dynarski, "Into College, Out of Poverty? Policies to Increase the Postsecondary Attainment of the Poor," Working Paper 15387 (Cambridge, Mass.: National Bureau of Economic Research, 2009).

82. Goldrick-Rab and others, "How Money Matters (or Doesn't)" (see note 79).

83. Natasha H. Williams, "The Impact of Medicaid and Other Social Public Policy on African American Men, Their Children and Families" (Morehouse School of Medicine, Students for Sensible Drug Policy, 2006) (http://aspe.hhs.gov/medicaid/july06/RoxanneLeopperAttachment1.pdf [Aug. 10, 2009]); Students for Sensible Drug Policy, *Harmful Drug Law Hits Home: How Many College Students in Each State Lost Financial Aid Due to Drug Convictions?* (Washington, 2006) (http://ssdp.org/states/ssdp-state-report.pdf [Aug. 7, 2009]).

84. Darren Wheelock and Christopher Uggen, "Race, Poverty and Punishment: The Impact of Criminal Sanctions on Racial, Ethnic, and Socioeconomic Inequality," in *The Colors of Poverty: Why Racial and Ethnic Disparities Persist*, edited by David Harris and Ann Chih Lin (New York: Russell Sage, 2008), p. 23.

85. Jeanne B. Contado and Wendy Erisman, "Learning to Reduce Recidivism: A 50-State Analysis of Postsecondary Correctional Education Policy" (Washington: Institute for Higher Education Policy, 2005) (www.ihep.org/Publications/publications-detail.cfm?id=47 [Aug. 5, 2009]). Nearly all credentials earned while in prison are vocational and are not college degrees. Most instruction is offered by community colleges.

86. Marsha Weissman and others, "Closing the Doors to Higher Education: Another Collateral Consequence of a Criminal Conviction," Center for Community Alternatives (www.communityalternatives.org/pdf/HigherEd.pdf [Aug. 5, 2009]).

87. Susan Dynarski and Judith Scott-Clayton, "Complexity and Targeting in Federal Student Aid: A Quantitative Analysis," NBER Working Paper 13801 (Cambridge, Mass.: National Bureau of Economic Research, 2008).

88. Eric Bettinger and others, "The Role of Simplification and Information in College Decisions: Results from the H&R Block FAFSA Experiment," NBER Working Paper 15361 (Cambridge, Mass.: National Bureau of Economic Research, 2009).

89. Melinda Karp and others, "Dual Enrollment Students in Florida and New York City: Postsecondary Outcomes" (New York: Community College Research Center, 2008).

90. Ibid.

91. Brian An, "The Impact of Dual Enrollment on College Performance and Attainment" (Ph.D. dissertation, Department of Sociology, University of Wisconsin–Madison, 2009).

92. Ibid.

93. Davis Jenkins, Matthew Zeidenberg, and Gregory Kienzl, "Building Bridges to Postsecondary Training for Low-Skill Adults: Outcomes of Washington State's I-Best Program" (New York: Community College Research Center, 2009).

94. Goldrick-Rab and others, "How Money Matters (or Doesn't)" (see note 79); Regina Deil-Amen and Sara Goldrick-Rab, "Institutional Transfer and the Management of Risk in Higher Education" Working Paper (Madison, Wisc.: Wisconsin Center for the Advancement of Postsecondary Education, 2009).

95. Susan Scrivener and Michael Weiss, "More Guidance, Better Results?" (New York: MDRC, 2009) (www.mdrc.org/publications/524/full.pdf [Aug. 5, 2009]).

96. Susan Scrivener and others, "Getting Back on Track" (New York: MDRC, 2009) (www.mdrc.org/publications/514/full.pdf [Aug. 10, 2009]).

97. LaShawn Richburg-Hayes and others, "Paying for College Success" (New York: MDRC, 2009) (www.mdrc.org/publications/531/policybrief.pdf [Aug. 10, 2009]).
98. LaShawn Richburg-Hayes and others, "Rewarding Persistence" (New York: MDRC, 2009) (www.mdrc.org/publications/507/full.pdf [Aug. 10, 2009]).
99. Christian Geckeler and others, "Helping Community College Students Cope with Financial Emergencies" (New York: MDRC, 2008) (www.mdrc.org/publications/479/full.pdf [Aug. 10, 2009]).
100. Because single parents are undercounted, the amount per family is likely overstated. Kevin Miller, Barbara Gault, and Abby Thorman, "Improving Child Care Access to Promote Postsecondary Success among Low-Income Single Parents" (Washington: Institute for Women's Policy Research, forthcoming).
101. ExpectMore.Gov., "Detailed Information on the Child Care Access Means Parents in School Assessment," (www.whitehouse.gov/omb/expectmore/detail/10002082.2007.html [Last update 1/09/2009, Jan. 16, 2010]).

Marriage and Fatherhood Programs

By Philip A. Cowan, Carolyn Pape Cowan, and Virginia Knox

Summary

To improve the quality and stability of couple and father-child relationships in fragile families, researchers are beginning to consider how to tailor existing couple-relationship and father-involvement interventions, which are now targeted on married couples, to the specific needs of unwed couples in fragile families. The goal, explain Philip Cowan, Carolyn Pape Cowan, and Virginia Knox, is to provide a more supportive developmental context for mothers, fathers, and, especially, the children in fragile families.

The authors present a conceptual model to explain why couple-relationship and father-involvement interventions developed for middle- and low-income married couples might be expected to provide benefits for children of unmarried parents. Then they summarize the extensive research on existing couple-relationship and father-involvement interventions, noting that only a few of the programs for couples and a handful of fatherhood programs have been systematically evaluated. Of those that have been evaluated, few have included unmarried couples as participants, and none has investigated whether interventions may have different effects when unmarried fathers live with or apart from the child. Furthermore, although the funders and creators of most programs for couples or for fathers justify their offerings in terms of potential benefits for children, the authors note that the programs rarely assess child outcomes systematically.

Next, the authors consider whether interventions for working-class or middle-class fathers or couples that have shown benefits for family members and their relationships might be helpful to fragile families, in which the parents are not married at the time of their child's birth. Because evidence suggests that couple-oriented programs also have a positive effect on father involvement, the authors recommend integrating couple and fatherhood interventions to increase their power to reduce the risks and enhance the protective factors for children's development and well-being. The authors emphasize the need for more research on program development to understand the most effective ways to strengthen co-parenting by couples who are the biological parents of a child but who have relatively tenuous, or already dissolved, relationships with one another.

In closing, the authors summarize how far the family-strengthening field has come and offer suggestions for where it might go from here to be helpful to fragile families.

www.futureofchildren.org

Philip A. Cowan is a professor of psychology, emeritus, at the University of California–Berkeley. Carolyn Pape Cowan is an adjunct professor of psychology, emerita, at the University of California–Berkeley. Virginia Knox is the director of Family Well-Being and Children's Development at MDRC.

Although many fragile families demonstrate remarkable strengths, with some maintaining stability and promoting family members' well-being while struggling against almost overwhelming odds, these families face disproportionate levels of financial impoverishment, poor health, psychological distress, relationship conflict, and both residential and relationship instability, all of which are risk factors for the development and well-being of children and adolescents.[1] A 1998 Fragile Families study made two important discoveries with implications for increasing the stability of these families.[2] First, around the time of a child's birth, most unmarried fathers are romantically involved with the child's mother and intend to be actively involved with the child. Second, both couple and father-child relationships in these families tend to dissolve over time.[3]

Researchers responded to these findings with a call for preventive interventions to capitalize on the "magic moment" around childbirth to improve the quality and stability of couple relationships in fragile families and preserve the active engagement of fathers in the lives of their children.[4] But although many couple-relationship interventions and a few father-involvement programs exist as potential program models, no empirical evidence was available to indicate whether these programs, many of which were designed for married couples, would be effective for the unwed parents in fragile families. The obvious strategy, then, was to try to adapt the intervention programs that have been found effective for other families and tailor them to the specific needs of fragile families. In this article, we review evidence on whether existing programs designed to strengthen the relationship between parents and to encourage fathers to become involved in rearing their children might be helpful for at least some types of families with unmarried parents.

We begin by addressing the policy context of the growing interest in this topic. We then present a conceptual model to explain why couple-relationship and father-involvement interventions developed for middle- and low-income married couples might be expected to provide benefits for children of unmarried parents. Next, taking note that couple-relationship and father-involvement approaches to strengthening families are typically mounted by different organizations and offered to different families, we summarize the extensive research on these interventions in middle-income and low-income married couples and the emerging research on those interventions in fragile families. In closing, we summarize how far the family-strengthening field has come and offer suggestions for where it might go from here to be helpful to fragile families. We argue that there are good empirical reasons for integrating interventions for couple relationships and father involvement more fully, so that intervention curricula can take advantage of what is known about the connections between couple-relationship status and quality and the vicissitudes of father involvement.

The Policy Context

In the last half of the twentieth century, several marked changes in family structure led some social observers to conclude that families were in a state of decline.[5] Increases in the rates of divorce, nonmarital births, and single parenthood, and the resulting drop in the share of fathers available to children on a regular basis, led family service providers and politicians to advocate for programs to strengthen couple relationships and encourage fathers to become active and remain positively involved in rearing their children, including paying financial support. During the 1990s, federal welfare reform set strengthening two-parent families as a policy goal. Strategies to achieve that goal for lower-income families included removing marriage penalties from welfare regulations and increasing economic self-sufficiency and child support compliance among low-income, nonresident fathers, especially through the Welfare-to-Work program. Strengthening child support enforcement for nonresident fathers and improving their capacity to pay support also became part of a responsible-fatherhood agenda.

In 2001, the administration of President George W. Bush did not renew funding for the Welfare-to-Work program, which many states had used to subsidize responsible-fatherhood programs. That same year the federal Administration for Children and Families launched a Healthy Marriage Initiative and a Responsible Fatherhood Initiative. In 2005, the initiatives were given a boost when Congress approved the Deficit Reduction Act, which included $100 million a year to support programs to encourage and strengthen marriage, especially for low-income families, and $50 million a year for separate programs to promote responsible fatherhood.

In the spring of 2010, President Barack Obama proposed a $500 million Fatherhood, Marriage, and Family Innovation Fund, half of which would support comprehensive responsible-fatherhood programs, including those with marriage components. While such programs provide a wide variety of services, the proposal requires that successful state applicants for grants under this fund "would need to demonstrate strong linkages with states' Child Support Enforcement programs, and there will be a preference for applicants that will make resources available to community-based organization to help implement components of these initiatives."[6] This language suggests that the Obama administration would re-emphasize the traditional mission of responsible-fatherhood programs, namely, increasing economic self-sufficiency and child support compliance. Because the proposal also requires evaluation of these state-administered programs, it would also provide new, and sorely needed,[7] evidence about the effectiveness of such efforts. Although it is unclear how much emphasis the Obama administration would place on stronger family relationships and increased father involvement, our review of past and ongoing research suggests that such efforts have the potential to benefit children in low-income families. In our view, such efforts also merit continued development and support.

A Framework for Interventions

Proponents of strengthening couple relationships and increasing father involvement in fragile families offer three arguments based on empirical findings. First, demographic data showing that families are in a state of decline and that children are at increased risk for problematic outcomes can be used to justify a need for interventions to strengthen families to slow or stop further decline—within families and in society as a whole. Second, as noted, the Fragile Families finding that unmarried men are present when their children are born but tend to drift away later on suggests strongly that interventions before the drift occurs could have a salutary effect on all family members. Third, evidence from a family process perspective indicates that identifying risk and protective factors associated with couple functioning, father involvement, and children's well-being will help service providers design effective interventions to produce the desired outcomes.

Two of us have developed a multidomain family risk model that has been empirically validated in studies of middle-income and low-income married parents and in the design of successful couple and father-involvement interventions.[8] A similar risk model has been shown to be relevant to fragile families, especially when the unwed couples have a long-term commitment to each other before the mother becomes pregnant.[9] It may be less applicable to unmarried couples whose relationships are created by an unexpected and unwanted pregnancy, or to fragile families long after the parents have separated and the father is no longer involved in the mother's or child's life.

The multidomain risk model describes how events in five key family domains interact to affect individual family members, the quality of family relationships, and child and adolescent well-being. Various studies show that information gathered from five family domains predicts how successfully children or adolescents cope with academic, social, and emotional challenges. The first is the level of adaptation of each family member—that is, self-perceptions and indicators of mental health and psychological distress. The second is the quality of the relationship between the parents—for example, problem solving, emotional regulation, commitment, and satisfaction. The third is both couple and parent-child relationship patterns as transmitted across the generations. The fourth is the quality of the mother-child and father-child relationships. And the fifth is the balance between life stressors and social supports outside the immediate family. Models similar to our five-domain model have described links between family processes and children's development in both middle-income and low-income families.[10]

Parents in fragile families are attempting to cope with all of the stressors of any new parents who must find new strategies to balance the cumulative demands of a puzzling new infant, lack of sleep, work pressures or loss of work, new financial demands, less contact with friends, and complex interactions with family and kin.

The five-domain model can also be used to explain variations in the quantity and quality of fathers' involvement with their children.[11] Men who have many symptoms of psychological distress, who report negative relationships with their fathers while growing up, who have a stormy or distant relationship with their child, who report high life stress (such as poverty or job loss), and who are isolated from supportive social networks are less likely to spend quality time with their children. But the most salient predictor of father involvement—in both married and unmarried families—is the quality of the father's relationship with the mother.

Our working hypothesis, based on three sets of findings, is that this risk model also applies to fragile families. The first finding is that, despite differences in the stability of their unions, both married and unmarried couples face similar challenges as they make the transition to parenthood. An extensive body of research shows that even for middle-class couples who are married, that transition represents a period of disequilibrium that leads to distress for many couples.[12] Most new parents are vulnerable to growing marital dissatisfaction that unfolds over many years and is linked with long-term academic, social, and emotional difficulties for the children.[13] Until recently, empirical research that investigates relationship changes in unmarried low-income couples when they become parents has been in surprisingly short supply. It is reasonable to assume, however, that the arrival of a new baby will have similar or even greater negative effects on couples who have more tenuous relationships.

Second, studies of low-income married couples find that poverty exacerbates the strain for couples and parent-child relationships, and that such strain is linked, as it is in middle-income families, with negative outcomes for the children.[14] Third, emerging evidence from the Fragile Families study shows that, as for middle-income and low-income married couples,[15] the single best predictor of father involvement in fragile families is how the father and mother get along.[16] Marital conflict and distress between partners who are unmarried at the time their baby is born, and their increasing negative relationship quality over time, are both correlated with less collaborative co-parenting, less effective parenting, and a variety of negative outcomes for children by age five.[17]

We conclude that parents in fragile families are attempting to cope with all of the stressors of any new parents who must find new strategies to balance the cumulative demands of a puzzling new infant, lack of sleep, work pressures or loss of work, new financial demands, less contact with friends, and complex interactions with family and kin. Many but not all of these couples in fragile families lack a solid relationship foundation with a long-term future orientation that can help them withstand the temblor of parenthood and its aftershocks. The vulnerability of the relationship between the parents, along with the vulnerability of the father's relationship with the child, presents an optimal entry point for preventive interventions to strengthen families before stress turns into distress.

Marriage-Promotion, Marriage-Education, and Couple-Relationship Programs

In the past few years, providers of programs for couples have been changing their descriptors—from "marriage promotion" to "promotion of healthy marriage" to "marriage education" to "strengthening couple relationships." The data on the negative consequences for children of marriages filled with unresolved conflict, violence, or frosty silences have convinced many policy makers not to support getting married and staying married in all circumstances. The preferred descriptor of most programs for couples today appears to be "marriage education," which suggests that all couples can learn how to make their marriages or cohabiting relationships better. Our concern with this term is its implication that marriage educators know what a healthy marriage is and can transmit this knowledge to all couples in the same way that teachers convey reading and math skills. We think it preferable to talk about interventions to strengthen key family relationships—both couple and parent-child—backed by evidence that such an approach will be good for the parents and for their children.

Table 1. Characteristics of Selected Couples Intervention Programs

Program	Population served	Curriculum focus	Format	Frequency and duration	Background of group leaders	Assessments
Prevention and Relationship Enhancement (PREP) (Markman and Stanley)	Originally for middle-class premarital couples; now many new adaptations to diverse populations	Couple communication	Psychoeducation class/workshop; lecture; coached practice	Four 2- to 3-hour meetings or weekend workshops (8–12 hours)	Originally university faculty and graduate students; now professional and paraprofessional	Before, immediately after program, and at 1.5, 3, 4, and 5 years afterwards
Becoming a Family (Cowan & Cowan)	Middle-class couples having a first child	Couple communication, individual, parent-child, generational patterns, life stress and social support	Groups of 4–6 couples; open-ended discussion followed by specified agenda with exercises	Twenty-four 2-hour sessions extending from 3 months prepartum to 3 months postpartum (total of 48 hours)	University faculty and graduate students	Prepartum, 6 months postpartum, then 18, 36, and 66 months
Bringing Baby Home (Gottman, Gottman, and Shapiro)	Middle-class couples having a child	Couple communication, individual, co-parenting, parenting	Classes with coached practice	Weekend workshop (16 hours)	Licensed health and mental health professionals	Pretest, immediate posttest, 1 year postpartum
Family Foundations (Feinberg)	Middle-class couples having a child	Couple communication, co-parenting, parenting	Groups of 6–10 couples, psychoeducation	Four 2-hour sessions prepartum, 4 sessions postpartum (total of 16 hours)	Childbirth educators, nurses, family workers	Pretest, 6 months postpartum, 1 year postpartum
Becoming Parents (Jordan)	Middle-class couples having a first child	Couple communication, co-parenting, parenting, life stress and social support	Groups of 4–15 couples; based on PREP with specific material focused on transition	Six 3.5-hour sessions prepartum; two 3-hour postpartum (total of 27 hours)	Nurses	Pretest, 6 months postpartum, 1 year, 2 years, 3 years
Schoolchildren and Their Families (Cowan & Cowan)	Middle-class couples with a first child entering kindergarten	Couple communication, co-parenting, parent-child generational patterns, life stress and social support	Groups of 4–6 couples, open-ended discussion followed by specified agenda with exercises	Sixteen 2-hour sessions (total of 32 hours)	Licensed mental health professionals	Pretest, 1 year, 2 years, 4 years, 10 years
Relationship Enhancement (RE) (Guerney)	Middle-class couples at all life stages	Couple communication	Psychoeducation class/workshop; home study	Classes or weekend workshop (16–24 hours)	Originally licensed mental health professionals; now professionals and paraprofessionals	Multiple studies
Practical Application of Intimate Relationship Skills (PAIRS) (Gordon)	Middle-class couples at all life stages	Couple communication, individual generational patterns	Psychoeducation class/workshop	Semester class, or weekend workshop (16–32 hours)	Originally licensed mental health professionals; now professionals and paraprofessionals	No random-assignment study to date
Collaborative Divorce Project (Pruett)	Middle-class couples in the process of divorce	Couple communication, parenting, custody and legal issues	Group meetings, classes, couple mediation sessions	Required meetings plus additional service (16+ hours)	Psychologists, counselors, lawyers	Pretest, posttests 15–18 months later
*Supporting Healthy Marriage (Knox, MDRC)	Low-income married couples with a child under age 18	Couple communication, generational patterns, life stress and social support	Groups of 6–20 couples	Nine to 15 sessions plus supplementary activities (total of 24+ hours)	Licensed mental health professionals; nurses, paraprofessionals	Pretest, 1 year, 3 years
**Young Parenthood Program (Florsheim)	Low-income teen parents having a first child	Couple communication, co-parenting	Work with one couple at a time	Counseling, 10 to 12 one-hour sessions (total of 10–12 hours)	Licensed therapist	Pretest, 2.5 months postpartum, 18 months postpartum
**Building Strong Families (Dion & Hershey, Mathematica)	Low-income unmarried couples having a child	Couple communication, co-parenting, parenting, generational patterns, life stress and social support	Groups of 4–6 couples	Varying number of weekly sessions, supplementary activities (total of 30–42+ hours)	Master's degree plus experience	Pretest, 1 year later, 3.5 years later, 5 years later

*Primarily low-income families
**Primarily low-income with a substantial proportion of fragile families

Faith-based and non-faith-based classes and groups for couples began to emerge during the 1960s. By 1978, more than fifty different programs were available in hundreds of communities, with meeting sizes ranging from 10 to 1,000 couples.[18] Two and a half decades later, in a *Future of Children* volume, Robin Dion noted that marriage-education programs were using more than 100 different curricula.[19] At this writing, the numbers are impossible to estimate, given federal, state, and private sponsorship of programs in communities across the United States. Most of these programs, however, lack evidence of effectiveness beyond the number of participants served and testimony from the consumers.

Table 1 provides a brief outline of the characteristics of a selected list of couple-strengthening programs, all of which have strong research designs and either final or ongoing evaluations of effectiveness. Table 2 shows the family domains that have been evaluated in each program. The tables cover nine long-standing programs for middle-income married couples and three new programs for low-income couples, two of which serve fragile families.

Programs for Middle-Class Married Couples

One of the key ways in which intervention programs for couples differ is the family life stage at which they recruit participants. Premarital couples were initially the main target of the Prevention and Relationship Enhancement Program (PREP).[20] Several programs offered groups for couples making the transition to parenthood—Becoming a Family, Bringing Baby Home, Family Foundations, and Becoming Parents.[21] The Schoolchildren and Their Families project focused on couples at another family milestone—beginning before their first child makes the transition to elementary school with follow-ups extending through the children's transition to high school.[22] Two programs initially tested on middle-class couples at any life stage were the Relationship Enhancement program and the Practical Application of Intimate Relationship Skills program (PAIRS).[23] Finally, one program, the Collaborative Divorce Project, attempted to help couples in the process of divorce resolve high-level conflicts in the interest of making life better for their children.[24]

As table 1 shows, programs also vary in terms of curriculum content, with some restricting discussion to couples issues (communication, problem solving, emotional regulation, task sharing, commitment), while others address issues of individual well-being and mental health, effective parenting practices, patterns to be repeated or rejected from the family of origin, and pressures associated with having or losing jobs, dealing with social institutions, and coping with difficulties in relations with kin and friends. The programs also vary considerably in format. The Young Parenthood Program involves a series of meetings between a therapist or counselor and an individual couple (teenage African American parents-to-be).[25] The Collaborative Divorce Project uses a variety of large-group, small-group, and couple counseling formats. All other programs conduct their intervention in couples groups, capitalizing on the power of participants' discovering that they are "all in the same boat."

Programs also vary by the composition of the group. Groups range in size from four to five couples with two group leaders, to large classrooms of attendees. Group meetings in some programs resemble a teacher-centered classroom in which leaders teach skills (PREP workshops, Bringing Baby Home workshops,

Table 2. Couples Intervention Programs: Significant Outcomes Published to 2009

Program	Self-reported marital quality	Observed marital quality	Individual adjustment	Parent-child relationship quality	Life stress/ social support	Children's outcomes
PREP	YES					
Becoming a Family	YES		NO	NO	NO	NO
Bringing Baby Home	YES	YES	YES	YES		YES
Family Foundations	YES	YES				
Becoming Parents	—	—	—	—		
Schoolchildren and Their Families	YES	YES	YES	YES	NO	YES
Relationship Enhancement (RE)	YES					
PAIRS	YES					
Collaborative Divorce	YES		YES	YES		YES
Young Parenthood Program	YES	YES	YES			
Building Strong Families	—	—	—	—	—	—
Supporting Healthy Marriage	—	—	—	—	—	—

Blank cells = domain not measured.
— = data not yet available.

PAIRS). Other programs (Becoming a Family, Schoolchildren and Their Families, Loving Couples Loving Children) have little in the way of leader-centered lectures. Instead, they present issues and exercises to be engaged in by the group, include an open-ended "check-in" during which participants bring their own issues to work on, and focus on group process and interaction as a way to provide safe support and to stimulate change. Finally, programs for couples vary in duration and intensity, ranging from one meeting (an all-day workshop) to sixteen weekly groups or classes, and from eight to forty-eight hours.

Box 1 offers a composite example of how the middle-class groups operate based on our own experience and on written materials from some of the interventions described in table 1. The box focuses on couple-relationship and communication issues, both of which are addressed in every intervention listed in the table. In programs that address other domains, the couples might return the following week to discuss ways of fostering their goals as individuals, for example, or of reducing personal stress. Discussions of age-appropriate parenting and discipline are also included in some of the other programs listed in table 1. A few programs, including PAIRS, Becoming a Family, Schoolchildren and Their Families, Building Strong Families, and Supporting Healthy Marriage, address intergenerational issues. During discussions of couple and parenting issues, participants are encouraged to talk about what they are trying to do in their current family relationships about repeating or changing practices in their family of origin; some hope to repeat favorite family traditions, but many want to create very different relationships as couples or as parents.

Interventions for middle-class couples have paid little attention to the world outside the family. Only in the groups for low-income couples (see below) have some interventions begun to address how partners cope with

Box 1. Sample Workshop on Couple-Relationship Issues

It is 7 p.m. on a Thursday. A male and female group leader finish rearranging chairs in a community center meeting room. Eight couples straggle in, each bringing infants swaddled in blankets and placing them and their paraphernalia in car seats around the outside of the circle. (Groups for low-income couples might begin a little earlier, with food and child care for the older children). The couples form little knots of conversation; though none knew each other before the groups started, some are becoming friends. The leaders must become assertive before the couples finally take their seats.

The leaders invite the parents to check in about events during the past week. One couple talks about their arguments about how to deal with their baby crying in the middle of the night. She wants to pick her daughter up immediately; he fears "spoiling" her. Other couples in the group share similar differences. The leaders help the couples see that there is no single correct solution, but acknowledge that parents do have to find ways of resolving this issue—and probably not at 4 a.m. over the crib of a screaming baby.

The leaders ask how each couple dealt with last week's "homework"—to spend half an hour together without talking about their new baby. Much laughter follows. Couples report strategies ranging from starting at baby's nap time, to recruiting a babysitter or relative for half an hour so that they could walk outside to talk. Another suggests that group members could babysit for each other. One couple admits not being ready yet to trust anyone to look after their infant son. Others urge the couple to try it. The leaders ask the couples how they hear this advice in light of their own concerns.

The next, more structured, part of this evening focuses on couple communication. The leaders present a mini-lecture illustrating common speaker and listener skills, and then ask couples to practice while the leaders circulate. The couples then engage in an exercise that provokes more laughter but also some teachable moments. Each partner independently writes the answer to a set of questions about the other, such as: What is your partner's favorite movie? Who is your partner's least favorite relative? What is your partner's greatest stress right now? These light and yet serious questions lead partners to discover that they don't know some basic things about each other and that it may be worthwhile to ask rather than guess about the answers.

The leaders wrap up by stressing important points raised in the meeting and then suggest a new "homework" assignment—to commit to doing one thing over the next week to nurture their relationship. The couples share their ideas and chat with each other as they pack up.

stressors (unemployment, housing crises, immigration issues, illness, poverty) and potential sources of support (extended family, friends and colleagues, government and private agencies) that can mitigate the negative effects of stress-inducing external circumstances.

Couples Program Outcomes

All the interventions except PAIRS have been evaluated using a research design that assigns participants at random to intervention and control groups. Despite differences in curriculum, format, duration, and intensity, each couple-relationship program listed in tables 1 and 2 has shown some positive effects on the participants, at least in the domains of the curriculum addressed in the meetings or classes.

All nine studies with published data noted a positive effect on marital satisfaction or quality as reported by the participants for periods ranging from a few months (PAIRS, RE) through one year (Bringing Baby Home), eighteen months (Young Parenthood Program), five years (PREP, Becoming a Family), and ten years (Schoolchildren and Their Families). In four of the studies listed in table 2, raters (who were not aware whether participants had been assigned to intervention or control groups) observed significantly less conflict and more cooperation between partners in the intervention group than those in the control group after the intervention ended. Four of the five programs assessing parents' individual adjustment found significant effects of the intervention, usually on mothers' or fathers' symptoms of depression.

Unwed couples in fragile families can benefit from father-involvement interventions, especially those that pay attention to the relationship between the father and mother of the child.

Three of four programs that assessed parent-child relationships reported significantly improved interaction. A new study of Bringing Baby Home using ongoing groups, rather than weekend workshops, reports "dramatically increased effects on parenting, and less negative ratings of child behavior, and better language development in toddlers from the twenty-four-session Cowan-type couples support group added to the workshop."[26] The Collaborative Divorce Project reported that compared with nonintervention controls, intensive group and couple-by-couple work with divorcing parents made significant differences in both parent-child relationships and children's problematic behaviors.

The Schoolchildren and Their Families study indicates that the content of the curriculum makes a difference to the outcomes. In that study, couples were randomly assigned to groups in which leaders emphasized either parenting issues or couples issues during the unstructured check-in segments of the sixteen-week sessions. In the groups that spent more time discussing parenting issues, parenting was more effective both one and two years after the intervention concluded, but couple relationships failed to improve. By contrast, couples in the groups that spent more time on couples issues not only fought less, but were significantly more effective at parenting. Children whose parents attended the parenting-emphasis groups showed fewer internalizing behavior problems both as they described themselves and as their kindergarten and first-grade teachers described them. Children whose parents attended groups emphasizing couple relationships had fewer externalizing problems and higher academic achievement than children in the control group. The effects of groups with both a parenting and couple-relationship emphasis in sixteen-week groups showed statistically significant gains in couple relationship quality and child outcomes ten years later as the children made the transition to high school.[27]

In addition to looking at the field of marriage education program by program, study by study, researchers have recently attempted to provide quantitative analysis of the field as a whole. Meta-analyses aggregate data from many studies and examine mean differences between intervention and control samples or, as in the majority of cases with no randomized control condition, differences in participants before and after the intervention. Two of the most recent and comprehensive analyses of marital-education programs, with data primarily from middle-income married couples, have been reported by Alan Hawkins and his colleagues and by Victoria Blanchard and her colleagues.[28] The Hawkins analysis examined 124 published and unpublished reports and found moderate-sized positive effects on participants' communication skills and relationship quality (mostly self-reports but some observations) both immediately after the conclusion of the intervention and in later follow-ups. The Blanchard report examined 97 of the same set of reports in a more detailed way. It found effects that were 50 percent larger six to seven months after the intervention than immediately after the intervention. These conclusions require some caveats. It is not clear how many of the studies included parents with children, and many of the studies used a relatively weak design without random assignment to control conditions. Furthermore, the studies were mostly of middle-class samples, and, as far as we can tell, did not include studies of interventions with fragile family couples because no such studies were available at the time the analyses were performed.

The few studies that have examined effects on aspects of family quality other than communication show that in middle-income samples, couple-relationship interventions improve mothers' and fathers' symptoms of depression and parenting style. From studies that describe correlations between risks and outcomes, one would expect to find that programs that have positive effects on individual and marital functioning would have positive effects on the children as well, but so far only Bringing Baby Home, the Collaborative Divorce Project, and Schoolchildren and Their Families have provided empirical support for this expectation.

Programs for Low-Income Couples

Evaluation results are not yet available from the largest-scale study of relationship skills programs for low-income couples. That study, Supporting Healthy Marriage (SHM),[29] is funded by the federal Administration for Children and Families and administered by MDRC in collaboration with Abt Associates, Child Trends, Optimal Solutions Group, and Public Strategies Inc. Supporting Healthy Marriage has enrolled 6,300 low-income married couples in eight sites across the United States in a randomized clinical trial that compares the effects of four different intervention programs with a no-treatment control. The SHM sites are using versions of PREP, PAIRS, and Loving Couples Loving Children (adapted by John and Julie Gottman from Bringing Baby Home), all outlined in table 1 but modified for use with low-income families. Program adaptations for low-income couples have left the essential features of each program intact while varying the learning modalities and adding new content aimed at the particular stresses and circumstances of low-income couples with children. SHM has added a case manager for each family to help address a broad range of noncouple issues, such as housing, job seeking and job loss, and health and mental health, that could impede participation or undermine relationships and to coach couples on the relationship skills they are learning in the group workshops. The intensity of some of the earlier couples programs has been increased from the weekend workshop level to twenty-four to thirty-two hours over nine to fifteen weeks. Programs for low-income families rely much less on written material and more on exercises to stimulate discussion and insight. They also contain culturally relevant examples and video demonstrations for Latino and African American couples.

Programs for Fragile Families

We are aware of only two couple-focused programs for fragile families that include research evaluations—one is a pilot study and one has just released an initial impact analysis. The first, the Young Parenthood Program, is targeted at unmarried African American teen couples, each of whom visits a therapist over a period of ten to twelve weeks.[30] Preliminary findings are that working with a therapist during the transition to parenthood significantly reduced intimate partner violence and increased both the quality of the couple relationship and the father's competence in collaborating with the mother on issues of co-parenting. The second program, Building Strong Families (BSF), is the only large-scale couples intervention specifically designed for fragile families.[31] Conducted by Mathematica Policy Research, Inc., BSF enrolled more than 4,000 low-income unmarried couples about to make the transition to parenthood (though not necessarily a first baby). BSF interventions were distributed over eight sites, with a range of program models that overlap with those of the SHM project—Loving Couples Loving Children, Love's Cradle (adapted by Mary Ortwein and Bernard Guerney from his Relationship Enhancement approach),[32] and Becoming Parents for low-income, low-literacy couples (adapted by Pamela Jordan from her own earlier Becoming Parents Program, which was based closely on the PREP intervention model).[33] Preliminary descriptions of the successes and obstacles to program implementation can be found on the website: www.buildingstrongfamilies.info. The BSF intervention groups are very similar, and in one site identical, to those mounted by SHM. Again, the process of the groups resembles a less open-ended version of the intervention described for middle-class couples in box 1. Some BSF sites integrated the relationship skills groups into an existing home-visiting program for new parents so that BSF participants were co-enrolled in both programs simultaneously.

A preliminary impacts report for the BSF evaluation was released in May 2010, with assessments fifteen months after couples entered the study. Overall, although the interventions resulted in more services being delivered to intervention participants than to controls, the interventions had no overall effect on couple status (getting married, staying together), couple relationship quality (ability to manage conflict, happiness, use of constructive and destructive conflict behaviors as rated by the partners), co-parenting quality, or father involvement. The subgroup and site-specific results, however, suggest that the effects of this type of program are likely to depend on how it is implemented or on the specific population being served, or both. One of the eight sites, Oklahoma, showed significant positive effects on most of these outcomes, and in all eight sites the intervention did help African American couples (not white or Hispanic couples). The Oklahoma program had higher attendance rates than most of the remaining BSF programs. Couples at that site reported attending group relationship workshops for eighteen more hours than control-group couples did, whereas couples at the remaining BSF sites reported spending only twelve hours more than control-group couples. The difference may not be attributable simply to the couples' absorbing the curriculum but to the fact that they were more strongly connected to the program and to each other. In contrast, the BSF site in Baltimore, which had a pattern of negative effects, served a population of couples who, on average, had more tenuous relationships with one another at the outset of the program and who attended relationship skills groups for only six more hours than the control-group parents.

Before we accept the conclusion that the BSF interventions do not work for fragile families, we point to three caveats. First, the next assessment at thirty months will be important, especially since we know that sometimes interventions take time to integrate into family life. Second, the data analysts used an "intention to treat" strategy, in which all participants entering the intervention condition are included in the analysis even if they never attend the program. (The strategy is standard practice in intervention studies.) But of the more than 2,200 intervention participants, 45 percent did not have even one spouse attend one group meeting. It seems that it would be very difficult for the 55 percent of those who did attend to show a positive intervention effect, when combined with the non-attenders. Third, as in traditional large-scale public health interventions, the study planners did not obtain pre-intervention measures of everything they looked at as outcomes. But without such measures, it is impossible to determine how couples' ability to benefit from the intervention depends on their characteristics at enrollment—in particular, the quality of their relationship.

The planners' reasoning was that because a randomized design ensured the comparability of experimental and control participants at the beginning of the study, only post-intervention measures were needed to assess intervention impact. But without pre-intervention measures, it is impossible to determine whether couples who were able to learn what was taught improved most as a function of their intervention participation. Clearly researchers need to find out more about the characteristics of the participants who did benefit from the intervention, the characteristics of the Oklahoma program and its participants that made it successful, and the characteristics of the Baltimore program and its participants that raised extra challenges.

In sum, substantial evidence attests to the effectiveness of couple intervention programs for middle-income couples, at least in terms of couple relationship satisfaction, and, in several studies, of observed behavior between the partners. Although the small pilot study[34] and the larger BSF study suggest that African American couples benefit from an intervention offered to couples, initial results from the larger BSF study of groups for couples are not what the designers hoped. More analyses and longer-term follow-ups are necessary to elucidate these early results. The Supporting Father Involvement program, conducted within the framework of father involvement and described below, does provide evidence that a couples group intervention may have positive outcomes for low-income unmarried couples and their children.[35]

Father-Involvement Programs

A father's involvement in his children's lives depends on a number of circumstances, the most obvious of which is legal status. In relation to the child's mother, a father may be married, separated, divorced, or never married (with paternity established or not), and each category makes a difference to both opportunities and motivation to be involved with his child.[36] In relation to the child, a father can be a biological parent, step-parent, adoptive parent, or de facto father with no legal status. His involvement with the child may also vary depending on whether he is living with the child's mother, in a romantic relationship with the mother, or living with the child. Research on father involvement suggests that demographic characteristics like race and ethnicity, socioeconomic status, and sex of the child also make a difference.[37] Researchers and service providers as yet have no systematic information about father-involvement interventions for men in each of these categories, so there is little to guide them except some common-sense hypotheses about the extent to which interventions designed to enhance father involvement need to be tailored differently to fit men in each of these family circumstances. Our own hypothesis is that traditional interventions for fathers who are actively trying to communicate and cooperate with the child's mother are worth trying, but that a different approach would have to be created for men who have, for example, been violent with the mother or estranged from her for a long while. Tables 3 and 4 list and describe the characteristics and outcomes of father-involvement programs that have been evaluated.

Interventions for Fathers in Low-Income Fragile Families

Unlike interventions for couples, which were designed for middle-class couples, interventions to encourage father involvement were initially intended for unmarried noncustodial fathers, a large share of whom were African American or Hispanic. Father-involvement programs in low-income families, however, have evolved significantly. The original programs were directed at men long separated from their children and were largely focused on increasing child support through job skills training. The next phase of programs, which were more successful at affecting multiple realms of fathers' involvement, provided ongoing intensive groups for fathers and focused on family relationships. A more recent program has targeted couples and has encompassed all five domains of family life in which risk and protective factors affect the quality of their interactions with their children; this program has shown promising effects.

As table 3 shows, the Young Unwed Fathers Project provided job training for young fathers separated from their families and attempted to persuade men to acknowledge paternity as a way to heighten their motivation for making child support payments.[38] The Partners for Fragile Families project recruited men who were no longer in a relationship with the mothers but were still in contact with them.[39] Using group meetings and individual mentoring, both projects tried to help men make connections with social support institutions that would buttress their fatherhood roles. Neither program produced measurable gains in fathers' direct involvement with their children, although Partners for Fragile Families did produce some increases in child support payments.

The Parents' Fair Share intervention was the first study of father involvement to use a random-assignment design to assign participants to intervention and control conditions.[40] It included case managers, peer-support sessions using a structured curriculum led by trained facilitators, employment training in the form of job-search assistance, and an administrative intervention that temporarily lowered child support orders. It also offered fathers the option of participating in mediation services with the child's mother. The program documented some successes: fathers in the program increased the amount of child support they paid, whereas fathers in the control group did not. Other modest benefits were shown by the least advantaged, least involved men: participants in the program group showed increased earnings and increased hands-on involvement with their children. Program evaluators also drew two important qualitative conclusions. First, despite negative stereotypes about low-income noncustodial fathers physically separated from their children for long periods, roughly one-third of the control fathers who had been separated from their children for more than three years saw them at least once a week and contributed

Table 3. Characteristics of Selected Father-Involvement Intervention Programs

Program	Population served	Focus of program model	Format	Frequency and duration	Background of group leaders	Assessments
*Young Unwed Fathers Project	Low-income noncustodial fathers under age 25	Job training, acknowledging paternity, child support payment	Individual and group meetings	Over 18 months	Not reported.	Mainly qualitative reports
*Parents' Fair Share	Low-income noncustodial fathers	Employment, peer support, father-involvement child support	Individual and group meetings	Variable	Trained leaders	Extensive survey data
*Partners for Fragile Families	Low-income noncustodial fathers age 16 to 25 still in contact with the biological mother	Establishing connections with men and agencies	Individual and group meetings, agency collaboration	Variable	Trained facilitators, job training staff	Mainly qualitative interviews, demographic data
*Prebirth Co-Parenting Program (Fagan)	Headstart African American and Hispanic fathers	Parenting, co-parenting	Groups of fathers	Five 90-minute sessions (total of 7.5 hours)	Social worker, nurse	Prepartum, 3 months postpartum
*Fathers and Sons Intervention Program (Caldwell)	African American fathers and their 8- to 12-year-old sons	Parenting, social networks	Groups of fathers and sons, psychoeducation	Fifteen 2-hour or 3-hour meetings plus 13 hours homework (total of 45 hours)	"Community facilitators"	Pretest, immediate posttest
*Supporting Father Involvement (SFI) (Cowan, Cowan, Pruett, & Pruett)	Low-income Mexican American and European American families	Individual, couple, parent-child, generational patterns, life stress and social support	Groups of 4–10 couples, open-ended discussion followed by specified agenda with exercises, games, etc., case manager	Sixteen 2-hour sessions (total of 32 hours)	License-eligible and licensed mental health professionals	Pretest, 2 months posttest, 13 months posttest
Marriage Moments (Hawkins)	Middle-class couples having a child	Couple, parenting	Videos and workbooks added to a home-visiting program	Self-administered	Trained home visitor	Pretest at 3 months postpartum, posttests at 4 and 9 months postpartum
Parenting Together (Doherty)	Middle-class couples having a child	Parenting, couple, individual	Couples groups, psychoeducation	Home visit plus 4 couples group meetings prepartum and 4 meetings postpartum (total of 10 hours)	Faculty and graduate students	Pretest, 5 months posttest
Dads for Life (Braver)	Middle-class fathers within 4–7 months of divorce		Groups of fathers, psychoeducation	Eight 2-hour sessions (total of 16 hours)	Faculty and graduate students	Pretest, posttests 3 months, 7 months, and 15 months later

*Primarily low-income with a substantial proportion of fragile families.

financially to their support, although not always as much as required by the support order. Second, including the custodial mothers in a father-involvement intervention is essential, a point to which we return.

More recent attempts to foster unmarried men's involvement with their children have used ongoing groups to focus on family relationships. The Prebirth Co-Parenting program[41] randomly assigned men to a five-session group program modeled on the Minnesota Early Learning Design (MELD) approach[42] or to a control group consisting of a five-session prenatal class emphasizing birth preparation. The MELD program emphasized the development of supportive co-parenting and the importance of fathers

Table 4. Father-Involvement Programs: Significant Outcomes Published to 2009

Program	Child support	Father involvement	Parent-child relationship quality	Individual adjustment	Couple relationship quality	Child outcome
Young Unwed Fathers Project	YES					
Parents' Fair Share	YES	Only for a subgroup			Negative change (increased conflict)	YES
Partners for Fragile Families	YES					
Prebirth Co-Parenting Program		YES			YES	
Fathers and Sons Intervention Program		YES	YES			NO
Supporting Father Involvement (SFI)	YES (according to mothers)	YES	YES	YES (short term)	YES (for couples groups)	YES
Marriage Moments		YES			NO	
Parenting Together		YES	YES	YES		
Dads for Life		YES	YES		YES	

Blank cells = domain not measured.

becoming involved with their infants. All the couples were unmarried, and about half the fathers were cohabiting with the mothers. Compared with the fathers in the control prenatal classes, the young fathers in the Prebirth Co-Parenting intervention showed stronger co-parenting behavior with the mother and greater involvement with their infants, according to assessments by both fathers and mothers.

The Fathers and Sons Intervention was developed from principles based on a review of research on risk factors in the target population—African American biological, nonresident fathers and their eight- to twelve-year-old sons.[43] Participants in the intervention groups were compared before and immediately after the intervention with fathers and sons in a nonrandom comparison group from a nearby community. The intervention groups showed positive effects on a number of identified risk and protective factors—parental monitoring, communication about sex, fathers' intentions to communicate, race-related socialization practices, and fathers' satisfaction with their parenting skills.[44] The findings were among the strongest we have seen for nonresident fathers. Significantly, the intervention was one of the longest-lasting (forty-five hours) in our survey of intervention programs.

Married and Divorced Fathers in Middle-Income Families

Father-involvement interventions for middle- and high-income families, created in university settings rather than social agency settings, emerged later than those for low-income families, and many fewer are described in the research literature. Not surprisingly, the interventions for middle-class fathers were focused not on enhancing men's social capital, but rather on dealing directly with family relationships. We exclude "parenting programs" from this review because most have not been evaluated and because even when they encourage fathers to participate, they are for the most part attended only by mothers. For example, a recent issue of the *Future of Children* describes many interventions for parents who maltreat their children, but none of the interventions directly addresses either couple relationships or father involvement.[45]

Dads for Life was directed primarily to middle-income divorced men.[46] The eight-session curriculum, administered by clinically trained leaders and attended by fathers, was focused heavily on a cognitive-behavioral approach to managing men's anger and helping them to reduce conflict with their children and ex-wives. The program had positive effects on the quality of divorced fathers' relationships with their children and ex-wives—outcomes that could perhaps have had benefits for the children, but the study did not assess such benefits.

Although the intended goal of all the interventions was to increase father involvement, two programs included both parents. The Marriage Moments program tested the effect of adding videos and workbooks to a post-birth home-visiting program in hopes of increasing both marital quality and men's involvement in the care of their infants.[47] Mothers reported increases in men's involvement, but the program did not produce the desired increase in the couple's satisfaction with their own relationship. The authors suggested that a group format rather than a couple-by-couple at-home format might have had stronger effects on both the couple and father-child relationships.

The Parenting Together program used couples groups with a focus on involving fathers more positively and directly in their children's lives.[48] Couples were randomly offered participation in a second-trimester home visit and four group meetings before and four after the birth of a first child, or a no-treatment condition. At five months postpartum, participation in couples groups produced a positive effect on fathers' self-worth and on emotional support, intrusiveness, and dyadic synchrony with their infants (Parenting Together was one of the few studies to use observations of parent-child interaction). Fathers in the couples groups were more directly involved with their infants after they came home from work than fathers in the control condition.

A New Couples Group Approach to Father Involvement

A new study attempts to pull together the intervention strands we have been describing, with a combination of couple-relationship and father-involvement interventions for both married and unmarried couples. The Supporting Father Involvement (SFI) project recruited 300 primarily low-income couples with babies or young children from four California counties.[49] Approximately two-thirds of the couples were married and one-third were unmarried (fragile families).

Based on two earlier interventions for middle-income couples (Becoming a Family, Schoolchildren and Their Families), the study had two unique design features. First, it compared the effect of a fathers group that met weekly for sixteen weeks and was led by clinically trained co-leaders, with a sixteen-week couples group with the same curriculum and leaders. Both interventions were compared with a control condition consisting of a single informational meeting in which the staff leaders discussed the importance of fathers to their children's development. One-third of the families were white and two-thirds were Latino (primarily Mexican American). A second design feature was that, unlike interventions for middle-income families, each family in both the intervention groups and in the control group was also offered a case manager to follow up and refer the family for additional services as needed.

The positive impact of the Supporting Father Involvement intervention could be seen in several family domains. Although mothers and fathers in the control group evaluated the single meeting very positively, the data showed no positive effects at follow-up. In fact, for most, family life was getting worse over an eighteen-month assessment period. Relationship satisfaction and father involvement declined, and parents described more problem behaviors on the part of their children over time. By contrast, men in the sixteen-week fathers groups became significantly more involved in care of their youngest child. In addition, neither the fathers nor the mothers described a significant increase in their children's problematic behavior over the eighteen months of the study. Even so, as with the parents in the control condition, the relationship satisfaction of parents in the fathers groups declined significantly over time. By contrast, parents in the sixteen-week couples groups also reported increased father involvement and no increase in the problematic behaviors in their children, but they also reported additional benefits: in contrast to both control and fathers group participants, their relationship quality and satisfaction as a couple remained stable over eighteen months, and their parenting stress declined.

In sum, in the SFI study, both fathers and couples group intervention formats improved fathers' involvement with their children, but the couples groups had added benefits for maintaining couple-relationship quality and reducing parenting stress. All of these changes, as noted, represent effects on family risk factors that are associated with negative outcomes for children. In the context of fragile families, the study produced two

Box 2. Participant Interview and Leader Assessment toward the End of a Sixteen-Week Couple-Relationship Group

Interview

Mother: We were in a couples group with a prime focus on parenting. The group keeps my interest because of the hands-on experiences that help us think about how to interact with each other and our child.

Father: In our group there's room for our own ideas and to think about what works best between us and with our child. Other couples bring their own personalities and styles—and the group leaders keep a sense of humor with it all—and we learn from that too.

Mother: These conversations helped me realize when to step in with issues with our daughter and when to listen and just be there. I've also noticed that, though he's always been a good father to her, now I see him wait sometimes to think before he steps in with her. It's made a real difference.

Leader's Assessment

One couple came to us with lots of issues, including his alcohol use, his anger, their inability to secure jobs, financial problems, communication issues within their marriage, and conflict with their daughter. Initially it appeared that the father had so much anger that it would be hard to control it in a group setting, but what we quickly learned was that he needed space to let out some of this frustration to deal with the everyday problems they were facing. The mom was very soft-spoken, but I felt that she understood her husband and knew what he needed and that her hope was that this group would provide that help. Fortunately it did. By the end of the group their marriage was stronger, and they were working as a team to deal with some of their daugher's issues. They were actively seeking employment throughout the group process. Before group ended she did find a job, and he was genuinely happy and supportive. It is clear from follow-up interviews with them that they have used some of the tools from the group and that they have a lot more hope and positive energy.

notable additional findings: the intervention effects were not significantly different for couples who were married or unmarried when they entered the study, and the effects did not differ by race or ethnicity. That is, a format that involves either couples or fathers working with clinically trained co-leaders can benefit both white and nonwhite fragile families with positive effects on mothers, fathers, and their children. Some qualitative comments from the participants and group leaders (see box 2) convey a little of what happened in the groups to produce the positive outcomes described by the quantitative data. A second trial of the SFI intervention for African Americans, primarily fragile families, is in progress now. Preliminary data reveal similar positive effects.

We are not suggesting that psychological interventions for fathers and couples are sufficient to produce widespread changes in father involvement. Barriers to father involvement are pervasive and often are not under the control of the participants or the intervenors. Elsewhere, the developers of the SFI intervention describe how men are struggling against culturally supported gender role stereotypes, government child support programs, workplace policies, the lack of father-friendliness in family service agencies, and the continuing tendency of social science researchers to include only mothers in family studies.[50] Without significant change in these social institutions, family-based interventions to support father involvement will find it difficult to move forward.

Conclusions

There is little doubt that groups that meet regularly over a period of time or classes for middle-class couples can help prevent the slide in marital quality that typically accompanies the early family-making years. The jury is still out on whether similar interventions will be successful for low-income married couples or for fragile families and their children, although the results of the Supporting Father Involvement intervention show that both low-income married couples and fragile families can benefit from couples groups. Reasons why this program and one of the eight sites of the Building Strong Families program showed positive outcomes for couples and father involvement require further explanation. It is certainly important to know more about how to support couples who sign up for the intervention and actually participate consistently in the program.

Recent research has shown that low-income married couples and unwed couples in fragile families can benefit from father-involvement interventions, especially those that pay attention to the relationship between the father and mother of the child. Researchers and service providers would do well, however, to consider whether the unmarried couple is living together or not, is romantically involved or not, or has separated physically and emotionally. Given the findings of existing father-involvement interventions with families described as fragile when the baby is born, our own tentative hypothesis at this point is that altering patterns of involvement for longtime separated, nonresident unmarried fathers will be extremely difficult and that it will be much more feasible to alter these patterns while the fathers are still in the home and in ongoing relationships with the mothers. This observation is consistent with the argument advanced by the Fragile Families project that the transition to parenthood (or a few years beyond, according to the Supporting Father Involvement findings) might be optimal times to help these families become less fragile.

We stress the fact that Supporting Father Involvement recruited participants who entered the program committed to co-parenting at least one young child together; both were the biological parents of the child, and 95 percent of the parents were living together at the study's start. There is no evidence that this intervention could be helpful for fragile families when couples are not committed to pursuing a relationship. We need to look elsewhere for programs to increase positive father involvement in fragile families with couple and parent-child relationships that have ended.

Investing in Interventions for Couples and Fathers

A number of unanswered questions about couple and fatherhood interventions concern issues of effectiveness and cost. Each of the projects we have reviewed has tested the effect of its intervention against some version of a no-treatment or low-dose control condition. Little information is available, as yet, about whether variations in curriculum content, leader training, format (didactic versus interactive), and dosage (optimal length of the intervention) might affect participants. Nor do researchers yet know whether specific intervention variations might have stronger effects for different subgroups of participants (for example, married or unmarried couples with different levels of psychological or economic distress). And, finally, the couples in studies so far have been white, African American, and Hispanic. It remains to be seen whether other ethnic or cultural groups with different norms concerning gender roles in the family and different attitudes about participating in family services can benefit from existing intervention programs or whether substantial modifications might be needed.

Most of these questions are directly relevant to issues of cost, which are critically important at a time when government funding of social programs is in crisis, but so far no per-family cost estimates have been published. Almost all the intervention programs described here (both those that have been completed and those that are in progress) have used well-trained intervenors who provide a complex set of services delivered over a long period of time. Establishing, for example, that certain interventions now requiring thirty-two hours of participation could be effective with sixteen hours instead, or with leaders requiring less training, would go a long way toward reducing costs. Reducing costs from what? Again, except for the Building Strong Families program, no data on costs have yet been published. Beyond demonstrating the effectiveness of interventions compared with controls, researchers must produce detailed information on costs and benefits. Such data will be essential to decisions about widespread adoption of couple relationship and fatherhood programs by both government and private family service delivery systems.

Integrating Couple-Relationship and Father-Involvement Perspectives

The couple-relationship and fatherhood-intervention fields emerged independently, with the curricula of the former focused primarily on couple communication and the latter focused on the father's role as a provider. The comparison of couple-focused and parenting-focused couples groups in the Schoolchildren and Their Families project suggests that a curriculum emphasis on issues between the parents in a couples group affects both couple and parent-child relationships, while a parenting focus fails to improve couple relationships. Furthermore, in comparison with a fathers' group for low-income parents in the Supporting Father Involvement project, couples' groups with the same staff and curriculum had similar effects on father involvement and children's problem behavior, but, in addition, reduced parenting stress and maintained the partners' satisfaction with their relationship as a couple. As noted, these findings hold for cohabiting fragile families participating in the Supporting Father Involvement study and buttress the argument that if the well-being of children is a primary concern, more attention to all of the relationships in the family might offer the most benefits for the adults and the children.

We are not recommending that fathers-only interventions be eliminated from efforts to foster the involvement of fathers in the lives of their children. We know that the longer a father has lived apart from his children and the longer his relationship with the mother has been severed, the less likely the two partners are to work together to establish a more amicable, effective co-parenting partnership and, thus, the more likely it is that targeting solely fathers in groups will be helpful. Our hope for the future is not to have all fathers attempting to work out new co-parenting relationships with the mothers of their children, but rather to make certain that intervention programs consider the state of the couple relationship in all varieties of fragile families, because regardless of whether parents are living together or apart, the quality of that relationship affects all members of the family.

Endnotes

1. E. Mark Cummings, Patrick Davies, and Susan B. Campbell, *Developmental Psychopathology and Family Process: Theory, Research, and Clinical Implications* (New York: Guilford Press, 2000).

2. Sara S. McLanahan and others, *Unwed Fathers and Fragile Families* (Princeton: Center for Research on Child Wellbeing, 1998).

3. Marcia J. Carlson and others, "Coparenting and Nonresident Fathers' Involvement with Young Children after a Nonmarital Birth," *Demography* 45(2): 461–88.

4. Sara McLanahan and Marcia J. Carlson, "Welfare Reform, Fertility, and Father Involvement. Children and Welfare Reform," *Future of Children* 12, no. 1 (2001): 147–66.

5. David Blankenhorn, *Fatherless America: Confronting Our Most Urgent Social Problem* (New York: Basic Books, 1995); David Popenoe, "American Family Decline, 1960–1990," *Journal of Marriage and the Family* 55 (1993): 527–41.

6. U.S. Department of Treasury. General Explanations of the Administration's Fiscal Year 2011 Revenue Proposals, 2010, available from www.ustreas.gov., p. 305.

7. For a review of limited evidence on the effectiveness of responsible fatherhood programs that attempt to increase economic self-sufficiency and child support compliance, see Virginia Knox, P. A. Cowan, and others, "Policies That Strengthen Fatherhood and Family Relationships: What Do We Know and What Do We Need to Know?" *Annals of the American Academy of Political and Social Science*, forthcoming.

8. Philip A. Cowan and Carolyn Pape Cowan, "Developmental Psychopathology from Family Systems and Family Risk Factors Perspectives: Implications for Family Research, Practice, and Policy," in *Developmental Psychopathology*, vol. 1: *Theory and Method* (2nd ed.), edited by Dante Cicchetti and Donald J. Cohen (Hoboken, N.J.: John Wiley and Sons, 2006), pp. 530–87; Philip A. Cowan and others, *The Family Context of Parenting in Children's Adaptation to Elementary School* (Mahwah, N.J.: Lawrence Erlbaum Associates. 2005).

9. Rand D. Conger and others, "Economic Stress, Coercive Family Process, and Developmental Problems of Adolescents," Special Issue: Children and Poverty, *Child Development* 65, no. 2 (1994): 541–61; G. H. Brody and D. L. Flor, "Coparenting, Family Interactions, and Competence among African American Youths," in *Understanding How Family-Level Dynamics Affect Children's Development: Studies of Two-Parent Families*, New Directions for Child Development, edited by J. P. McHale and P. A. Cowan (San Francisco: Jossey-Bass, 1996), pp. 77–91; R. S. Mistry and others, "Economic Well-Being and Children's Social Adjustment: The Role of Family Process in an Ethnically Diverse Low-Income Sample," *Child Development* 73, no. 3 (2002): 935–51; E. Mark Cummings, M. C. Goeke-Morey, and J. Raymond, "Fathers in Family Context: Effects of Marital Quality and Marital Conflict," in *The Role of the Father in Child Development*, 4th edition, edited by Michael E. Lamb (Hoboken, N.J.: John Wiley & Sons Inc., 2004), pp. 196–221.

10. Rand D. Conger and others, eds. *Families in Troubled Times: Adapting to Change in Rural America, Social Institutions and Social Change* (New York: Aldine de Gruyter, 1994); Gordon T. Harold, J. J. Aitken, and K. H. Shelton, "Inter-Parental Conflict and Children's Academic Attainment: A Longitudinal Analysis," *Journal of Child Psychology and Psychiatry* 48, no. 12 (2007): 1223–32.

11. Philip A. Cowan and others, "Supporting Fathers' Engagement with Their Kids," in *Raising Children: Emerging Needs, Modern Risks, and Social Responses,* edited by J. D. Berrick and N. Gilbert (Oxford University Press, 2008), pp. 44–80.

12. Carolyn P. Cowan and P. A. Cowan, "Interventions to Ease the Transition to Parenthood: Why They Are Needed and What They Can Do," *Family Relations: Journal of Applied Family & Child Studies* 44, no. 4 (1995): 412–23; A. F. Shapiro, John M. Gottman, and Sybil Carrere, "The Baby and the Marriage: Identifying Factors That Buffer against Decline in Marital Satisfaction after the First Baby Arrives," *Journal of Family Psychology* 14, no. 1 (2000): 59–70.

13. Gilad Hirschberger and others, "Married with Children: Attachment, Marital Satisfaction, and Divorce in the First Fifteen Years of Parenthood," *Personal Relationships* 16 (2009): 401–20.

14. Conger and others, "Economic Stress, Coercive Family Process, and Developmental Problems of Adolescents" (see note 9); Brody and Flor, "Coparenting, Family Interactions, and Competence among African American Youths" (see note 9); Mistry and others, "Economic Well-Being and Children's Social Adjustment" (see note 9).

15. Cummings, Goeke-Morey, and Raymond, "Fathers in Family Context: Effects of Marital Quality and Marital Conflict" (see note 9).

16. Marcia Carlson and Sara McLanahan, "Strengthening Unmarried Families: Could Enhancing Couple Relationships Also Improve Parenting?" *Social Service Review* 80, no. 2 (2006): 297–321.

17. Ibid.; Sara McLanahan, *Children in Fragile Families* (Princeton, N.J.: Princeton University, 2009).

18. David Mace and Vera Mace, "The History and Present Status of the Marriage and Family Enrichment Movement," *Journal of Psychotherapy and the Family* 2, no. 1 (1986). Although the emphasis of this article is on couple-relationship intervention programs with direct contact between provider and participant, other efforts to affect marriage and the quality of couple relationships include changing regulations regarding marriage licenses, self-help books, and information websites, such as the Administration for Children and Families (www.acf.hhs.gov/healthymarriage), the National Healthy Marriage Resource Center (www.healthymarriageinfo.org), Smartmarriages (www.smartmarriages.com,), and One Plus One (www.oneplusone.org.uk). Howard J. Markman, Scott Stanley, and S. L. Blumberg, *Fighting for Your Marriage: Positive Steps toward Preventing Divorce and Preserving a Lasting Love,* new and revised (New York: Wiley, 2001).

19. M. Robin Dion, "Healthy Marriage Programs: Learning What Works," *Future of Children* 15, no. 2 (2005): 139–56.

20. Markman, Stanley, and Blumberg, *Fighting For Your Marriage* (see note 18).

21. Carolyn P. Cowan and others, "Transitions to Parenthood: His, Hers, and Theirs," *Journal of Family Issues* 6 (1985): 451–81; Carolyn P. Cowan and P. A. Cowan, *When Partners Become Parents: The Big Life Change for Couples* (Mahwah, N.J.: Lawrence Erlbaum Associates, 2000); A. F. Shapiro and J. Gottman, "Effects on Marriage of a Psycho-Communicative-Educational Intervention with Couples Undergoing the Transition to Parenthood: Evaluation at 1-Year Post Intervention," *Journal of Family Communication* 5, no. 1 (2005): 1–24; Mark E. Feinberg, M. L. Kan, and M. C. Goslin, "Enhancing Coparenting, Parenting, and Child Self-Regulation: Effects of Family Foundations 1 Year after Birth," *Prevention Science* 10, no. 3

(2009): 276–85; Pamela L. Jordan, S. Stanley, and H. J. Markman, *Becoming Parents: How to Strengthen Your Marriage as Your Family Grows* (New York: Wiley, 2001), pp. xxi.

22. Cowan and others, *The Family Context of Parenting in Children's Adaptation to Elementary School* (see note 8).

23. Bernard G. Guerney, *Relationship Enhancement: Skill-Training Programs for Therapy, Problem Prevention, and Enrichment,* 1st ed., Jossey-Bass Behavioral Science Series (San Francisco: Jossey-Bass Publishers, 1977); Rita DeMaria, M. T. Hannah, and L. H. Gordon, *Building Intimate Relationships: Bridging Treatment, Education, and Enrichment through the PAIRS Program* (New York: Brunner-Routledge, 2003).

24. Marsha K. Pruett and R. K. Barker, "Effectively Intervening with Divorcing Parents and Children: What Works and How It Works," in *Strengthening Couple Relationships for Optimal Child Development,* edited by M. Schulz, M. Pruett, P. Kerig, and R. Parke (Washington: American Psychological Association, 2009).

25. Paul Florsheim and others, *The Young Parenthood Program: Preventing Intimate Partner Violence among Adolescent Mothers and Their Partners* (Denver: Society for Research in Child Development, 2009).

26. John Gottman, Julie Gottman, and A. Shapiro, "A New Couples Approach to Interventions for the Transition to Parenthood," in *Strengthening Couple Relationships for Optimal Child Development: Lessons from Research and Intervention,* edited by M. Schulz and others (Washington: American Psychological Association, 2009), p. 174.

27. Philip A. Cowan and others, "Group Interventions for Parents of Preschoolers: 10-Year Impact on Family Functioning and Teen's Adaptation," in P. Cowan (Chair), *From Preschool to High School: Individual and Family Risk and Protective Factors Predicting Teens' Academic and Social Adaptation* (San Francisco: Society for Research in Adolescence, April, 2006).

28. Alan J. Hawkins and others, "Does Marriage and Relationship Education Work? A Meta-Analytic Study," *Journal of Consulting and Clinical Psychology* 76, no. 5 (2008): 723–34; V. L. Blanchard and others, "Investigating the Effects of Marriage and Relationship Education on Couples' Communication Skills: A Meta-Analytic Study," *Journal of Family Psychology* 23, no. 2 (2009): 203–14.

29. Virginia Knox and D. Fein, "Supporting Healthy Marriage: Designing Marriage Education Demonstration and Evaluation for Low-Income Married Couples," in *Marriage and Family: Complexities and Perspectives,* edited by H. E. Peters and C. M. K. Dush (Columbia University Press, forthcoming). The website for the study is www.supportinghealthymarriage.org.

30. Florsheim and others, *The Young Parenthood Program* (see note 25).

31. M. R. Dion and others, *Implementing Healthy Marriage Programs for Unmarried Couples with Children: Early Lessons from the Building Strong Families Project* (Washington: Mathematica, 2006). The website is www.buildingstrongfamilies.info.

32. Guerney, *Relationship Enhancement* (see note 23).

33. Jordan, Stanley, and Markman, *Becoming Parents* (see note 21).

34. Florsheim and others, *The Young Parenthood Program* (see note 25).

35. P. A. Cowan and others, "Promoting Fathers' Engagement with Children: Preventive Interventions for Low-Income Families," *Journal of Marriage and the Family* 71 (2009): 663–79.

36. C. S. Tamis-LeMonda and N. Cabrera, eds. *Handbook of Father Involvement: Multidisciplinary Perspectives* (Mahwah, N.J.: Lawrence Erlbaum Associates, Publishers, 2002).

37. Philip A. Cowan and others., "Supporting Fathers' Engagement with Their Kids," in *Raising Children: Emerging Needs, Modern Risks, and Social Responses,* edited by J. D. Berrick and N. Gilbert (Oxford University Press, 2008). pp. 44–80; Ross D. Parke and Raymond Buriel, "Socialization in the Family: Ethnic and Ecological Perspectives," in *Social, Emotional, and Personality Development,* edited by Nancy Eisenberg (John Wiley & Sons, Inc. 1998), pp. 463–552. As in the field of couple interventions, there have been many fatherhood interventions at a distance, ranging from social movements (for example, Promise Keepers), to informational organizations (for example, the National Fatherhood Initiative [www.fatherhood.org], the National Center for Fathering [www.fathers.com], the National Center on Fathers and Families [www.ncoff.gse.upenn.edu], and the National Latino Fatherhood and Family Institute [www.nlffi.org]). More recently an informational website was mounted by the National Responsible Fatherhood Clearinghouse (www.fatherhood.gov), sponsored by the Federal Administration for Children and Families.

38. M. Achatz and C. A. MacAllum, *Young Unwed Fathers: Report from the Field* (Philadelphia: Public/Private Ventures, 1994).

39. K. Martinson and others, *The Implementation of the Partners for Fragile Families Demonstration Projects,* prepared for U.S. Department of Health and Human Services under Contract no. 100-001-0027 (Washington: Urban Institute, 2007).

40. Virginia Knox and C. Redcross, *Parenting and Providing: The Impact of Parents' Fair Share on Paternal Involvement* (New York: Manpower Research Development Corporation, 2000).

41. Jay F. Fagan, "Randomized Study of a Prebirth Coparenting Intervention with Adolescent and Young Fathers," *Family Relations* 57, no. 3 (2008): 309–23.

42. A. Ellwood, "Prove to Me That MELD Makes a Difference," in *Evaluating Family Programs,* edited by H. B. Weiss and F. H. Jacobs (Hawthorne, N.Y.: Aldine de Gruyter, 1988), pp. 303–13.

43. C. H. Caldwell and others, "Enhancing Adolescent Health Behaviors through Strengthening Non-Resident Father-Son Relationships: A Model for Intervention with African-American Families," *Health Education Research* 19, no. 6 (2004): 644–56; C. Caldwell and others, "Enhancing Parenting Skills among Nonresident African American Fathers," *American Journal of Community Psychology,* forthcoming.

44. Caldwell and others, "Enhancing Parenting Skills" (see note 43).

45. Richard P. Barth, "Preventing Child Abuse and Neglect with Parent Training," *Future of Children* 19, no. 2 (2009): 95–118.

46. J. T. Cookston and others, "Effects of the Dads for Life Intervention in Interparental Conflict and Coparenting in the Two Years after Divorce," *Family Process* 46, no. 1 (2007): 123–37.

47. Alan J. Hawkins and others, "Increasing Fathers' Involvement in Child Care with Couple-Focused Intervention during the Transition to Parenthood," *Family Relations* 57, no. 1 (2008): 49–59.

48. William J. Doherty, M. F. Erickson, and R. LaRossa, "An Intervention to Increase Father Involvement and Skills with Infants during the Transition to Parenthood," *Journal of Family Psychology,* Special Issue: *Relational Disorders and Relational Processes in Mental Health* 20, no. 3 (2006): 438–47.

49. Ibid.

50. Philip A. Cowan and others, "Six Barriers to Father Involvement and Suggestions for Overcoming Them" (National Council of Family Relations Report, 2009), p. 54.